Artists in Dylan Thomas's Prose Works
Adam Naming and Aesop Fabling

Artists in Dylan Thomas's Prose Works is an exploration of the rich but relatively neglected prose works of Dylan Thomas. Ann Mayer examines the changing conceptions of language and the creation of meaning evident in Thomas's numerous self-referential acts of writing and telling.

Through an analysis of the artist figures in Thomas's early experimental prose, *Portrait of the Artist as a Young Dog, Adventures in the Skin Trade,* and *Under Milk Wood,* Mayer shows how Thomas continually explored and reevaluated his vocation, the nature of his chosen medium, and the world itself. She links Thomas's prose works to his poetry through the blending of lyric and narrative strategies and examines Thomas's self-conscious concerns for his relationship to his modernist contemporaries.

Mayer goes beyond the traditionally New Critical approaches that dominate Thomas scholarship, using contemporary critical theory to offer new insights into the complexity and ambiguity of a major twentieth-century writer.

ANN ELIZABETH MAYER is assistant professor of English, University of Western Ontario.

Artists in Dylan Thomas's Prose Works

Adam Naming and Aesop Fabling

ANN ELIZABETH MAYER

McGill-Queen's University Press
Montreal & Kingston • London • Buffalo

© McGill-Queen's University Press 1995
ISBN 0-7735-1306-X

Legal deposit third quarter 1995
Bibliothèque nationale du Québec

Printed in Canada on acid-free paper

This book has been published with the help of a grant from the Canadian Federation for the Humanities, using funds provided by the Social Sciences and Humanities Research Council of Canada.

McGill-Queen's University Press is grateful to the Canada Council for support of its publishing program.

Canadian Cataloguing in Publication Data

Mayer, Ann Elizabeth, 1960–
Artists in Dylan Thomas's prose works: Adam naming and Aesop fabling
Includes bibliographical references and index.
ISBN 0-7735-1306-X
1. Thomas, Dylan, 1914–1953 – Prose. 2. Thomas, Dylan, 1914–1953 – Criticism and interpretation. I. Title.
PR6039.H52Z77 1995   828'.91208   C95-900479-3

This book was typeset by Typo Litho Composition Inc. in 11/13.5 Sabon.

Contents

Acknowledgments vii

List of Abbreviations ix

Introduction 3

1 The Written World 13

2 Solipsistic Adam 54

3 Portraits of the Artist 85

4 *Under Milk Wood* 136

Notes 171

Bibliography 181

Index 189

Acknowledgments

I would like to express my sincere appreciation to Don McKay, whose guidance and inspiration during the preparation of the book and afterwards have been invaluable. I am also grateful to Stan Dragland and Patrick Deane for their continued advice and support. Thanks also go to Sheila Rabillard, Don Gutteridge, and Tom Dilworth for their comments and suggestions, and to Marnie Parsons, David Bentley, and Sheila Deane for their valuable advice. As well, I am indebted to Walford Davies of the University College of Wales, Aberystwyth, John Ackerman, Ralph Maud, and the entire class of the inaugural year of the Dylan Thomas School, Summer 1988, for stimulating discussions and memorable visits to Thomas's haunts.

Grateful acknowledgment is made to J.M. Dent and Sons Ltd., New Directions Publishing Corporation, and the Trustees for the Copyrights of late Dylan Thomas for permission to quote from the works of Thomas: *Collected Poems 1934–1953* (1993), edited by Walford Davies and Ralph Maud; *Dylan Thomas: The Collected Stories* (1986); *The Collected Letters of Dylan Thomas*, edited by Paul Ferris (1987); *Under Milk Wood* (1954).

Abbreviations

CL   *Collected Letters*
CP   *Collected Poems*
CS   *Collected Stories*
QEOM "Quite Early One Morning"
UMW   *Under Milk Wood*

Artists in Dylan Thomas's Prose Works

Introduction

The initial impetus for this study was twofold: to explore the rich but relatively neglected prose works of Dylan Thomas, and to examine the numerous self-referential and metafictional instances within them. Many of the prose works contain representational forms such as dreams, fantasies, maps, books, and stories. Also predominant are a variety of artist figures, through whom Thomas explores the nature of creation and the medium with which he creates, through self-conscious acts of writing and telling.

In the existing critical studies of Dylan Thomas's work, the comparatively large body of short stories by the author has been largely passed over, considered "side issues" to his chief concern with poetry, or a "minor genre" within his writing. The later prose, especially, has been considered an "inferior side branch" of his work. However, Thomas himself considered his prose to be equal in importance to his poetry for much of his career. In a letter to John Lehmann in 1941, Thomas describes himself as a "26 year old poet and short story writer" (CL 479). While the first two published volumes which established Thomas's success were indeed poetry – *Eighteen Poems* (1934) and *Twenty-five Poems* (1936) – he wrote many short stories during this period, and his next three volumes consisted of poetry and stories together or stories alone: *The Map of Love* (1939), subtitled "Verse and Prose," contained sixteen poems and six stories; *The World I Breathe* (1940), published in America, contained a collection of poems from the first three books, and three stories in addition to those in *The Map of Love*; *Portrait of the Artist as a Young Dog* (1940) is a collection of ten stories. Letters to his publisher show Thomas's concern with the shape and content of *The Map of Love* and *The World I Breathe*, volumes that he intended to be unified with related poems and stories that reflected each other. Thomas's semi-autobiographical *Portrait of the Artist as a Young Dog*, the unfinished novel *Adventures in the Skin Trade* (1941), and the "play for voices," *Under Milk Wood* (1953) – which Thomas called "prose with blood pressure" (Ferris 292) – as well as the many earlier, experimental collected and uncollected short stories, may in many ways be seen as extensions of the concerns which arise from his poetry. A study of the stories is valuable not only to elucidate these relatively neglected works, then, but also in order to cast light upon themes and techniques in the poetry. The stories bear a more intimate and organic connection to the poems than most critics have allowed.

The current popularity of the recently published stories belies earlier criticisms, such as those of Kingsley Amis, who claimed that they are constructed upon "characters and situations ... which people in full possession of their faculties would not find interesting or important" (*Spectator* 1955, 227). Critics are only now beginning to appreciate what Derek Stanford calls a "poet's prose," valuable not only for providing further insights into the poetry, but as artistic creations of merit. These neglected pieces are worth studying because they are interesting in themselves, and because they illuminate Thomas's theories of the creative process. In so doing, they offer new insights into some of the aesthetic problems which attend his work. Thomas makes his closest approach to commenting on his own work in his letters, but even there he avoids direct explanations. In the same spirit his stories, essays, and other prose works do not provide accounts of the creative process relating to the poetry in the same direct way that Eliot's or Rilke's essays do. Thomas does not so much theorize the creative process as mythologize it. Numerous moments of self-reflexivity show his interest in linguistic and metafictional possibilities, which, when analysed, go a long way toward explaining some of the parodoxes and cruxes in various critical debates. Conscious of himself as a "devious craftsman" and manipulator, Thomas often revels in anarchy, dissolving binary oppositions, deconstructing his own creations, and upsetting rational conceptions of order, making the reader rethink the assumptions and categories with which s/he attempts to define Thomas's work.

The relation of the stories to the poems has been noted briefly by a few critics, primarily with regard to similarities in tone and theme. Elder Olson mentions the similar personal concerns of what he calls Thomas's "dark early period." John Ackerman sees the early stories, like the early poems, "owing much to a fertile imagination and an adolescent's obsessional introspective concerns with religion, sex, and death" (1986, 86), and notes that the early stories anticipate the later poetry in a search for "temps perdu" (87); however, Ackerman does not include in his discussions the writerly concerns that are common to both genres. Annis Pratt, in the most extensive exploration to date, examines the combination of personal and mythological symbols consistent with both genres, noting such similarities as the conflicting and merging images and transformations that are apparent in the struggle between the conscious and unconscious worlds.

The early prose, what Thomas called "this bastard thing, prose-poetry" (*New York Times Book Review* 17 February 1952, 17), is characteristically dense, sensuous, and almost surreal.[1] Like the early poems, it stresses the "Word" as something organic and creative, and embodies Thomas's conception of a "creative-destructive" life force. Some of the interpretive importance of the stories for the poems will be discussed in chapter 2.

Thomas's narrative prose changes dramatically from the style of *The Map of Love* and similar early stories to that in *Portrait*, becoming less densely symbolic and obscure, more relaxed in its use of syntax and image. The change in style, as well as a shift toward realism and concerns with the outer world rather than the earlier inner, even solipsistic, world, parallels a similar shift in the poetry. The dark, egocentric stories of the first period with their images of destruction give way to stories about other people; the *Portrait* stories look back and comment upon the writer of the earlier stories much the way such poems of the same period as "Once it was the colour of saying" and "After the Funeral" look back on a previous poetic style which valued the word over the things and people it was meant to represent. Both the poetry and the prose of this middle period turn away from language as a sole concern, and explore instead the possibilities of the structures created by language – poems and stories can function as commemoration, as consolation, and, through the creation of narrative in everyday experience, as a natural part of human existence. Although narrative as an aesthetic ingredient is crucial to the early work, *straightforward* narrative becomes more prominent in both genres of the later period, stylistically as well as thematically. The movement toward the last phase, with its progressing affirmation and faith, is again evident in both the poetry and the prose. The world of "Fern Hill," clearly the same place as the farm in "The Peaches," points the way toward the loving, nostalgic portrayal of innocence in *Under Milk Wood*. Thomas's work in radio and film during this time gave him a greater sense of the possibilities of combining drama with narrative, and a wider awareness of the possibilities of the spoken word. In both the poetry and the prose, the inclusion of other voices occurs with the turn toward the external world, apparent in the increased dialogue and the profusion of story-tellers; this culminates in the polyphonic "play for voices." Indeed, the prose may be seen to undergo as many transformations as the poetry, belying Treece's assertion that "for all essential purposes what the prose-writer Dylan Thomas had been in 1940 was what he was in 1952"; the prose is not, as Treece says, merely the "same sort of thing over again" (127). The progression in his prose reveals much about Thomas's changing conceptions of art.[2]

Discussion of the prose is not only sparse, it is also limited in scope. Since most critics consider the stories a "poetic by-product" (Stanford 156), they follow the same theoretical lines with which they approach the poetry. The bulk of Dylan Thomas criticism, written in the thirty years following his death, has taken a traditional approach to interpretation heavily influenced by New

Criticism. Thomas's use of myth, organic imagery, and highly crafted poetic forms has led even the most recent Thomas scholars to offer readings which emphasize the organic unity of structure and meaning. The notorious complexity and ambiguity in the stories and poems have been widely regarded as a challenge to reconcile the shifting and conflicting images. Such attempts at resolution have produced readings which are often valuable, yet which often contradict each other.

Similar New Critical readings of the prose are for the most part helpful but incomplete. Many who mention the prose comment on the change in style from the early difficult experimental stories to the "simply realistic" later ones without exploring the implications of such a change. Some studies, such as those of Treece, Tindall, Walford Davies ("Imitation"), and Peach, involve surveys of literary influence of various degrees of depth and credibility. Jacob Korg's 1948 study lays out the basic themes upon which later critics have expanded: elements of Welsh folklore, recurring patterns of sexual initiation, and a dualistic nature warring against itself. Annis Pratt's *Dylan Thomas' Early Prose: A Study in Creative Mythology* (1970), the first book-length study of the prose, examines the mythological, theological, occult, surrealistic, and literary influences; however, she limits herself to a consideration of the early prose and its effects upon the early and later poetry. Since Pratt is a critic concerned with archetypal structures, it is not surprising that she dismisses the later stories as "an inferior side branch of his total work. Whereas the early prose, finished by 1939, can be taken as a part of the symbolic universe of both the early and later poetry, the later prose ... represents a departure into a mode of writing that, had he lived, he might well have developed into a richer branch of his opus. ... As it stands, however, it represents a number of interesting attempts at what must be taken as a minor genre within his writing" (xi–xii).

Another body of the prose criticism examines the stories with regard to their biographical and sociological value. Apart from David Holbrook's conclusion in *Dylan Thomas and the Code of Night* that the stories are pathological products of a severely disturbed mind, these studies are straightforward discussions of the theme of sexual development (Richard A. Davies's work on *Portrait*, for example), of Thomas's Welshness, or of his social and geographical accuracy in depictions of Swansea, Laugharne, and Fern Hill. While John Ackerman's analyses of the "Welsh Dylan" stress the sense of nostalgia, mutability, community, faith, and love that he senses in both the poetry and the prose, Linden Peach, in the second book-length study of the prose, *Dylan Thomas's Prose Works* (1988), rather unconvincingly places Thomas in the tradition of Welsh writers Caradoc Evans and R.S. Thomas. Peach seems to argue that the prose works are valuable primarily because they reveal the "hypocrisy" and "repression" that Thomas supposedly witnessed in Welsh society, claiming that Thomas at times displays a "snarling hatred of the Welsh people" (6).

While these studies attempt to show that the prose is biographically and sociologically important, none really explore the implications of the autobiographical focus. Thomas's works abound in reflections of himself. These reflections are sometimes overt, like the boy "Dylan" and the "young Mr Thomas" in *Portrait*; sometimes in disguise, as "Marlais" in the early story "The Orchards"; or they may be displaced into artist figures like the madman/writer in "The Mouse and the Woman," or the poet-priest Reverend Eli Jenkins in *Under Milk Wood*. Artist figures of all sorts are important in Thomas's prose, and what they reveal about artistic creation, especially in moments of self-reflexivity, helps to explain some of the problems that the other approaches coast over.

In the tales story-tellers abound, and fabulation is a healthy component of everyday living. From the early inward-looking tales, to the metafictional portraits of the middle period, to the communal imaginative creations of the last work, Thomas moves through various levels of fabulation. The early prose works are often concerned with a purely linguistic existence in which the external world is not merely held at bay by fiction, but is often absent altogether. This, in some measure, anticipates the postmodernists' linguistic play where the world and reality have become problematical categories. Even the later, externally oriented, stories functioning on fictive rather than linguistic levels of self-reference often resemble the metafiction of later twentieth-century writers. The shift to the external world is not simply a move toward realism but involves a complication of the relationship between fiction and the world, and often involves an extension of the fictive into the real. The experimental fables of the early period, themselves metafictional (being fiction about fiction, not reality, and including an account of their own making), give way to fictions about reality, with the characters being fabulists; these in turn give way to *Under Milk Wood*, "A Winter's Tale," and other modern fables that, without naturalistically reflecting surface reality, approach actual human life through what Robert Scholes calls "ethically controlled fantasy" (3). Like the fairy-tale, Thomas's later fabulation is not "a turning away from reality, but an attempt to find more subtle correspondences between the reality which is fiction and the fiction which is reality" (Scholes 7).

This study explores Thomas's prose works in roughly chronological order, tracing the phases of Thomas's concerns with language and its relation to the world. Chapters 1 and 2 examine the experimental tales, predominantly those about writing, of Thomas's early period. Compelled by the phrase "in the beginning was the Word," Thomas attempts to move toward an edenic language characterized by a "virgin word" as yet without association. Exploring the artist's relation to his art, Thomas offers depictions of a number of artistic "roles." These early stories have as their central characters artists who are solipsistic Adams, creating their own worlds through language in utterances that may be characterized as "inner speech." Grappling with the problems of living and writing, these characters sometimes attempt to hold reality away with their fictions; at other times the stories in which they appear contain little or no solid external reality against which to measure their experience. Like some characters in the fictions of Jorge Luis Borges and John Barth, Thomas's early heroes are living in a highly verbal universe.

Chapter 3 examines the more realistic stories in the *Portrait of the Artist as a Young Dog* and the unfinished novel *Adventures in the Skin Trade*. In these stories the emphasis changes from an exploration of language to an exploration of story, and from creation on paper to creation in life. In this fictionalized autobiography, the stress is less on the problems arising from artistic creation, evident in the early stories, than on the ways that artistic creation can be useful. The autobiography, or shaped life, functions as an intermediary between worlds, between temporal life and the timelessness of art. The title of *Portrait* necessarily demands an examination of the relationship of Thomas's work to Joyce's *Portrait of the Artist as a Young Man;* this study goes beyond the issue of influence briefly cited by other critics, like Holbrook and Peach, who dismiss the similarities as a mark of Thomas's "derivativeness" and "inferiority." Actually, it may be shown that Thomas's allusion is a deliberate and serious attempt to place himself among and against, not only Joyce (whom he admired), but indeed many of his modernist contemporaries. Just as Joyce's relation to Stephen Dedalus is a complex one, so too is Thomas's relation to his fictionalized earlier self. Thomas's self-portrait, in dialogue with Joyce's, serves as an exploration of the role of the artist in relation to both art and society. By placing himself explicitly in relation to Joyce in the *Portrait*, Thomas comments on his relation to certain modernist tendencies, in terms of both similarities and differences, not just with regard to Joyce but with regard to modernism in general. Language, Thomas felt, could be made new not by imposing upon it superficial trends whose purpose is merely to be different, but by a stripping away of all imposed forms and ideas, by a rebirth of the old language. He questioned Auden's call for "new styles of architecture, a change of heart" when he asked, "does one not need a new consciousness of the old universal architecture and a tearing away from the old heart of the things that have clogged it?" (CL 93).

Although Thomas posed this question near the beginning of his poetic career, it is a concern that he never abandoned. Indeed, it may be argued that such a "new consciousness" of old forms is what he moves toward in *Under Milk Wood* and later poems. *Under Milk Wood* might at first seem out of place in a study of prose works, but it is in several ways integral to a study of Thomas's artist figures (and, with a writer who from the beginning has been breaking down generic distinctions, the category of "prose" becomes somehow arbitrary). *Under Milk Wood* returns to many of Thomas's earlier concerns, but in a genre that foregrounds its aurality and temporality. Blending lyric and narrative strategies, Thomas abandons his earlier solipsism for democratized art. Chapter 4 examines the "play for voices" and other last works in the light of a revival of older literary forms, a return to the roots of lyric in chant and song, and a re-emergence of narrative in fable. Thomas even moves toward a fictional depiction of the edenic existence he earlier postulated regarding language, for *Under Milk Wood* is a personal myth of innocence set in a "heaven on earth" where language functions as a representation of the world – and where the voices of the inhabitants of Llareggub are the voices of the place itself. *Under Milk Wood* and other radio works, like the later narrative poems, all stress the values of community over those of the individual, and the early solipsistic articulations give way to polyphonic voices. Although artist figures such as Eli Jenkins and Captain Cat are still present, they are not the sole spokespersons, for all the citizens of Llareggub function as tellers of their communally created story. *Under Milk Wood* is a result of Thomas's growing awareness that language and literary forms may be many-voiced.

Thomas's lifelong concern with the primacy of words, and his self-conscious role as an artist, have been surprisingly overlooked in his work. Although critical opinion has attempted to place Thomas as a "Modern" or "Romantic" poet, his career is ultimately anomalous. If one attempts to chart Thomas's career on a literary-historical graph, one finds his movement to be backward; through his depiction of artist figures in the prose works one sees him occupying various positions, beginning ahead of his time in a type of postmodernism, returning through modernism, to romanticism and, ultimately to folk lyric, and the sources of lyric in incantation and song. From the early neophyte Adam finding his linguistic bearings, to the young Aesop of the later period telling worlds into creation through communal acts, the artist himself informs us about all facets of his art: his chosen medium, his methods of fashioning, his literary inheritance, his relation to the world and his audience, and his awareness that we are all ultimately artist figures co-creating worlds.

1 The Written World

Thomas employs a wide variety of strategies in his early experimental fiction – fragmentation, repetition, dense poetic structures, metafiction, fable, myth, dream, implicit and explicit allusion – which combine to form a body of tales both diverse and complex. What these stories share is a concern with the nature of art and the creative process; it is through a study of these self-conscious tales, and more specifically through an analysis of the numerous artist figures within them, that one can reconstruct a Thomasian poetic which illuminates much in both the prose and the poetry. The early stories expose many concerns which Thomas maintains, or returns to, at later points in his career, such as the relations of language and art to experience, the artistic temperament, and the artist's relation both to his literary inheritance and to the world and people around him. Although the early stories are not as self-critical as the later, more openly autobiographical fictions, they are highly self-conscious, and Thomas appears in several stories in thin disguise, such as "Marlais" (Thomas's middle name) in "The Orchards." Separating himself from the fiction, Thomas often focuses on the artist who is a type, whether poet, hero, madman, or god. In many of the early works (both prose and poetry) art becomes a re-enactment of Genesis, in which the creator is also Creator; in other works the artist figure is a descendant of Romantic questors such as Shelley's *Alastor* poet or Browning's Childe Roland, pursuing grail-like visions. In each of these early works, the artist figure above all strives, for better or worse, to acquire a "virgin word" or Logos, what would be called a "transcendental signifier" in the terminology of deconstruction. Regardless of the artist's success or failure, these early stories generally are characterized by a dissociation of art from life. The fictional world that results from this split also reveals strong connections between language and landscape, which reflect Thomas's interest in the beginning of the world as Logos. His figures inhabit a written world in which all is image rather than reality, including the artist himself, who is his own creation.

The artist functions on a number of levels, not only as creator and creature, but as reader and translator of already existing creations. Some artist figures, such as the gardener in "The Tree" and Sam Rib in "The Map of Love," are, as elders of a community, the possessors of stories to be handed down to others. Like priests, they possess secret knowledge represented by the stories they tell, yet they also possess the power to alter these stories in their repetition, dissolving their literary inheritance in order to recreate new forms out of the raw materials. Other characters, like the young boy in "The Tree" or Beth Rib and Reuben in "The Map of Love," function as readers, interpreters of the worlds and stories passed down to them; like their elders, they too possess the ability to transform the written world through their acts of translation. The world which these characters inhabit is a constantly shifting one in which image slides imperceptibly into image, story into story and dream into dream. It is a curious space bearing the paradoxical characteristic of being simultaneously written and not-yet-written. The figure who ultimately emerges for Thomas is a kind of Adam who falls into language from a pre-linguistic state. Taking possession of the world around him by naming it, this Adam is so compelled by his new-found gift that he is tied to a purely linguistic world. His interest is in language and the structures of language, rather than in the external things that language refers to. This naming, linguistic function is central to many of the early stories and poems.

In the early tales the reader is always moving, in the representational forms of fantasies, dreams, maps, and stories, at the level of an interpreted universe. These are primarily metafictional stories in which fictionality and fabulation themselves are central themes and in which characters move through various levels of fiction rather than reality, with little or no reference to a phenomenal world. Living purely inside language, the artist, a solipsistic Adam, tells stories about himself.

The early stories' metafictional relations between author and character, tale and reader, are important to the interpretation of the early poems, which also function primarily at the level of image, without reference to any phenomenal world. Unlike such contemporaries in the 1930s as Auden or Spender, Thomas makes little or no reference to the world around him in his early work. His poems are purely about himself and his poems, his stories about himself and his stories. The creation of a metaphoric written world is one of several strategies that affiliate Thomas with many writers later in this century: his use of metafiction, combined with a strong use of folktale, parable, archetype, and a playful sense of subversion, aligns Thomas as closely with such postmodernists as Borges and Calvino as with modernists like Beckett or Joyce. Thomas's destructive-creative universe is at odds with any ultimate unity that might be reconstructed from fragments, as in Eliot or Pound; further, because there is no external reality against which to measure his heroes' fictional experiences, the stories can remain ambiguous and fragments can remain fragments with no straining after closure.

A number of the early stories illustrate, in the working out of their plots, the many problems of interpretation that arise for the reader. We might select the story called "The Tree" as an example of the way they investigate hermeneutic possibilities. In "The Tree" the central artist figure is a gardener, a story-teller who "knew every story from the beginning of the world" and who tells some of these stories to a child: " 'In the beginning,' he would say, 'there was a tree. ... In the beginning was the village of Bethlehem.' " Yet these are only stories, whose meaning becomes distorted through repetition and lack of specificity. The boy takes literally the metaphysician's view that Christ's cross and Adam's tree stood in one place.[1] His tree is both archetypal and literal. He conflates the biblical tree of knowledge with a tree in his garden, and the biblical Bethlehem with the nearby Welsh village also called Bethlehem. The boy sees only the similarities and not the differences between the things locked into language, and the story ends with the consequences of his misreading: the boy crucifies an idiot in a macabre repetition of the Christ story. "The Tree" reworks a phrase that is a preoccupation in many of Thomas's early poems, stories and letters, "in the beginning was the Word" – a phrase central to Thomas's conception of a written world. Here, however, it is significant that the gardener initiates his story with the words "in the beginning was a tree"; in his rendition, the physical world precedes its naming, as it does for Adam. The opening of his story functions much the way the phrase "once upon a time" does in a fairy-tale, distancing the event in time and hence from reality. However, he does not give the boy any clue that the biblical story should be distanced from actuality, the way fairy-tales are safely sheltering, and the boy, taking literally what we presume to be figurative – namely, the tree – refuses symbolism and abstract meaning. The story takes on local rather than universal meaning for the boy. Like Thomas in his poems, the gardener expresses himself through images; just as we, as readers of the poems, are often forced to read literally what are in fact metaphors, so the boy reads the gardener's story.

This adaptation of the tale is ambivalent, for it could potentially be a beneficial act. By resurrecting myths Thomas creates new forms out of them, and a similar capacity is available for the boy, who may in the future become an artist/story-teller like the gardener. The use of "dead and set fast symbologies of the past," as Joseph Campbell suggests, "will enable the individual to anticipate and activate in himself the centres of his own creative imagination" (*The Masks of God* 677). For the early Thomas this creative imagination is often destructive and morbid, as tales such as "The Tree" suggest. In his later career, Thomas abandons such self-consciously life-denying tales for a more comic and joyful vision, even parodying his own youthful morbidity. In *Under Milk Wood* Eden is recreated not as a scene of potential tragedy but as a personal symbol of a somewhat eccentric heaven on Earth for the inhabitants of a Welsh seaside village. In the early stories, however, allusions are to Eden's loss. The crucifixion in the garden suggests that the boy is falling, if not yet fallen. The world in these tales is a complex mix of innocence and sin, darkness and light. Because characters and events are presented ambiguously, their interpretation depends largely on the perspective and state of mind of the characters within the stories. As with "The Tree," biblical stories are given local parallels, and, put in a new context, their implications can change depending on how the story is read by those within it – for example, the repetition may offer a promise of fruition or be merely a sinister parody of the original. Because the boy is young and has no experience with the difference between fiction and reality, he is dealing with a new-found power; his equation of the words of the story with the physical reality around him makes his act of reading the gardener's story also one of writing. There is no difference between the concept that "in the beginning was the tree" and "in the beginning was the word," for, to the boy, the story (the "word") is actual, and the nature of those things made of language a reflection of the consciousness of the creator/reader. The world, as always an articulation of the word, is dependent for its meaning on the readership of its inhabitants.

THE JARVIS VALLEY TALES

"The Tree"(December 1933) is the first of a number of stories which take place in or near the mythical "Jarvis Hills." At least a year before the composition of "The Tree," Thomas had been contemplating writing a novel (CL 10) which would have revolved around the fictional Jarvis Valley and its inhabitants. In a letter to Pamela Hansford Johnson, Thomas reports on its early stages: "My novel, tentatively, very tentatively, titled 'A Doom on the Sun' is progressing, three chapters of it already completed. So far it is rather terrible, a kind of warped fable in which Lust, Greed, Cruelty, Spite etc., appear all the time as old gentlemen in the background of the story. I wrote a little of it early this morning – a charming incident in which Mr Stipe, Mr Stul,

Mr Thade and Mr Strich watch a dog dying of poison" (*CL* 134). The three chapters are most probably "The Tree," "The Enemies," and "The Visitor," all completed in the Red Notebook at the time of the composition of this letter. An entry in the Notebook titled "A Doom on the Sun" dated May 1934 would eventually become the story "The Holy Six," a continuation of "The Enemies." Some of the above-mentioned characters with anagrammatic names appear in "The Holy Six." A week later Thomas finds his task becoming somewhat daunting, saying "My novel of the Jarvis valley is slower than ever. I have already scrapped two chapters of it. It is as ambitious as the Divine Comedy, with a chorus of deadly sins, anagrammatized as old gentlemen, with the incarnated figures of Love and Death, an Ulyssean page of thought for the minds of the two anagrammatical spinsters, Miss P. and Miss R. Sion-Rees, an Immaculate Conception, a baldheaded girl, a celestial tramp, a mock Christ, & the Holy Ghost" (*CL* 136). While the novel never materialized, the Jarvis Valley and many of these characters appear in a loosely connected group of short stories including "The Tree," "The Enemies," "The Holy Six," "The Visitor," "The Map of Love," and "A Prospect of the Sea." After much delay in publication, owing to problems with "obscenity," some of these "difficult and violent tales" (*CL* 227) appeared together in the volume *A Map of Love*, and all would eventually be collected in *The World I Breathe*.

Thomas created in the Jarvis Hills a characteristically Welsh environment based loosely on his memories of childhood summers in West Wales, embellished with a mythical and often sinister and occult spirit. He imbues the hills with an identity and a history. As in his poems, the landscape of the Jarvis Valley is alive, and its life is very much connected to that of its inhabitants. The earth is typically described in anatomical terms; in "The Enemies," the Jarvis Hills are specifically female: "Outside the window was the brown body of the earth, the green skin of the grass, and the breasts of the Jarvis hills; there was a wind that chilled the animal earth, and a sun that had drunk up the dews on the fields; there was creation sweating out of the pores of the trees; and the grains of sand on far-away seashores would be multiplying as the sea rolled over them" (19). The Jarvis Hills are named after "great-uncle Jarvis," a prolific madman: "here was the first field wherein mad Jarvis, a hundred years before, had sown his seed in the belly of a bald-headed girl who had wandered out of a distant county and lain with him in the pains of love" ("The Map of Love" CS 110). Each hill is associated with a different lover of mad Jarvis, and each has a voice which sounds to the valley's inhabitants. The valley is not only female, but rather both female and male, for the spirit of Jarvis also rings through it. In both "The Tree" and "The Map of Love," the hills are personified: when the boy in "The Tree" views the hills from the tower and asks "Who are they?", the gardener answers that "they are the Jarvis Hills ... which have been from the beginning" (10). Also in "The Map of Love" the pronoun "who" rather than "what" is applied to the hills; identity and place are inseparable: when the children ask the voice they hear "where are you?", it answers "I am Jarvis," and when they ask "who are you?" it replies "here, my dears, here in the hedge with a wise woman" (112).

In "The Holy Six" the hills have many voices whose characters depend on the personalities of those who hear them: "The roots beneath their feet cried in the voices of the upspringing trees. It was to each member of the expedition a strange and a different voice that sounded along the branches. They reached the top of the hills, and the Jarvis valley lay before them. Miss Myfanwy smelt the clover in the grass, but Mr Lucytre [Cruelty] smelt only the dead birds. There were six vowels in the language of the branches. Ole Vole [Love] heard the leaves. Their sentimental voice, as they clung together, spoke of the season of the storks and the children under the bushes" (97). The landscape takes on the character or emotions of the figures in it. Creation and destruction are both equally present in the valley, powered by the same force that "through the green fuse drives the flower." For those characters associated with corruption and evil, the landscape and its voices mirror them. Mr Owen of "The Enemies," having claimed a plot of land in the middle of the valley as his own, works in a garden more suggestive of death than of fruition: "Up came the roots, and a crooked worm, disturbed by the probing fingers, wriggled blind in the sun. Of a sudden the valley filled all its hollows with the wind, with the voice of the roots, with the breathing of the nether sky. Not only a mandrake screams; torn roots have their cries; each weed Mr Owen pulled out of the ground screamed like a baby" (17)

Yet for the innocent idiot in "The Tree," the valley is described as "immaculate"; in "The Map of Love" the children search for a sheltering "island," "surrounded by loving hills." For the boy in "A Prospect of the Sea," the valley is alternately "wonderful," "nice," "innocent," and Edenic, or a place of death and corruption, depending on the hopes or fears brought forth by his imagination. Pulled in opposite directions by the moon and the sun, by the cries of an owl and a seagull, by the stories of the past and the promise of the future, he hears more than one voice impelling him: " 'Once upon a time,' said the water voice. 'Do not adventure any more,' said the echo" (93). The Jarvis Hills represent sin, superstition, madness, and death; they also represent fruition, organic life, and growth. For some of their inhabitants, they are a source of both life and death. The idiot in "The Tree" is tied to them as if by an umbilical cord: "The life of the Jarvis valley, steaming up from the body of the grass and the trees and the long hand of the stream, lent him a new blood. Night had emptied the idiot's veins, and dawn in the valley filled them again" (9). But as well as being a source of life for the idiot, the hills are also the vehicle of his death, for the voices of the hills, so much a part of himself, are what impel him to go to the garden and his imminent crucifixion: "He could not tell why he had come; they had told him to come and had guided him, but he did not know who they were" (10).

A similar combination is seen in "The Visitor," written from the point of view of Peter, the poet. In this story, life and death are constantly implied in one another. From his sick-bed Peter travels in a vision over the Jarvis Hills; at an indeterminate moment he becomes a ghost – for at the end of the story he is supposedly dead, although he is conscious of his friends covering his face with a sheet. Like Peter himself, the landscape over which he travels is a valley of alternating death and life, and is ultimately characterized by a force common to both, and yet more fundamental than either: "And the blood that had flowed flowed over the ground, strengthening the blades of the grass, fulfilling the wind-planted seeds in its course, into the mouth of the spring. ... There was life in the naked valley, life in his nakedness. He saw the streams and the beating water, how the flowers shot out of the dead, and the blades and roots were doubled in their power under the stride of the spilt blood. And the streams stopped. Dust of the dead blew over the spring, and the mouth was choked ... Life in this nakedness, mocked Callaghan at his side, and Peter knew that he was pointing, with the ghost of a finger, down on to the dead streams. But as he spoke ... a life burst out of the pebbles like the thousand lives" (29–30).[2] Often the hills either represent or are contrasted to a post-lapsarian Eden. In "The Tree" the "immaculate hills" are to the "east" of the boy's home. On Christmas Day when the idiot enters the garden, it is to witness the "desolation of the flower-beds and the weeds that grew in profusion on the edges of the paths" (10). Similarly "The Enemies" opens with an image of Mr Owen "picking the weeds from the edges of his garden path" (16). In "The Map of Love," Beth Rib – an allusion to the creation myth – and Reuben are ashamed to love and to become a "single strength": "first fear shot them back. Wet as they were, they pulled their clothes on them" (111). They eventually follow the advice of "Jarvis" and consummate their love, accepting their fallen state.

In "A Prospect of the Sea," the boy falls asleep and dreams of "green Eden": "the garden was undrowned, to this minute and forever, under Asia in the earth that rolled on to its music in the beginning evening. When God was sleeping, he had climbed a ladder, and the room three jumps above the final rung was roofed and floored with the live pages of the book of days;[3] the pages were gardens, the built words were trees, and Eden grew above him into Eden, and Eden grew down to Eden through the lower earth, an endless corridor of boughs and birds and leaves" (91). But the boy has already been kissed by his "princess"/ "broom-rider"/"country girl" and entered the world of experience. No longer the innocent Adam who "could think of no words" to describe the world around him, he "said hard words to the world" (91). He wakes from his dream of Eden to witness a vision of Noah preparing for the flood.[4]

While in "The Tree" and "The Enemies" we see a sinister foundering of life, in "The Map of Love" and "A Prospect of the Sea" there is the hope of new life, and a healthy respect for natural, sexual love. All the stories represent the contrast between innocence and experience, as in a Blakean world. However, in Thomas's stories, the nature of the contrast is determined by the characters' reading, or misreading, of what the written world offers. "The Map of Love" begins with Sam Rib showing the children, Beth Rib and Reuben, his map, which is a visual representation of their own story. The winds drawn on the map blend "like a girl and a boy": "the cherubs blew harder; wind of the two tossing weathers and the sprays of the cohering sea drove on and on; on the single strand of two coupled countries, the weathers stood. Two naked towers on the two-loves-in-a-grain of the million sands, they mixed, so the map arrows said, into a single strength. But the arrows of ink shot them back; two weakened towers, wet with love, they trembled at the terror of their first mixing, and two pale shadows blew over the land" (110). The map, like the legend of Adam and Eve implicit in the story, is an artistic rendering of something in the world that the children inhabit – qualified by the fact that there is no real world in these tales. Paralleling the geography of the Jarvis Valley over which the children journey, the map embodies a story which the children will repeat. When they face their fear and "blend" like the winds, they do so by "mapped waters," or waters already travelled and rendered into artistic form. Sam is a double creator, being both the "father" of Beth Rib ("Sam Rib had made her") and the artist who created the map. It is Sam Rib who decrees, Godlike, that mating is natural: "Here the grass mates, the green mates, the grains ... and the dividing waters mate and are mated. The sun with the grass and the green, sand with water, and water with the green grass, these mate and are mated for the bearing and fostering of the globe" (111). Unlike the tone of "The Enemies" or "The Holy Six," the tone of "The Map of Love" suggests that the valley holds a positive force, and it is not simply a derogatory joke that the hills are named after a famous fornicator. Each rendering of the story of the fall, repeated by Jarvis and his ancestors, is a promising one: the "compassionate" voices of the hills declare Beth and Reuben "the children of love," and Sam Rib's creative purpose is to melt them, like the winds, into a "single strength." The final image is one of newness. They symbolically re-enact the story of their ancestors by obeying the "oracle" in the valley voices, swimming "up river" to the island. But the symbolic consummation by the island "white in a new moon" suggests innocence and an acceptance of possibility and future growth inherent in the newly fallen world.

The boy in "The Tree" has similarly to understand and repeat a story which has already been mapped. Like Beth Rib and Reuben, he is in an active relationship with the world around him, which he idealizes and subjectively alters: "The house changed to his moods, and a lawn was the sea or the shore or the sky or whatever he wished it" (5). The gardener, who is, like Sam Rib, the possessor of the stories, is to the child an "apostle" who passes the stories on to him. Yet unlike Beth Rib and Reuben, the boy in "The Tree" does not yet possess the literacy to comprehend fully the words that he must assimilate; he is a novice not yet ready to be introduced to the tales of the tribe by his elder. As a Christmas present, the gardener offers the boy the key to a tower, but the boy does not understand its significance, and is disappointed: "Before it was dark, he and the child climbed the stairs to the tower, the key turned in the lock, and the door, like the lid of a secret box, opened and let them in. The room was empty. 'Where are the secrets?' asked the child. ... 'It is enough that I have given you the key,' said the gardener, who believed the key of the universe to be hidden in his pocket along with the feathers of birds and the seeds of flowers. The child began to cry because there were no secrets" (9). It is perhaps only to the child that there appears to be no "secrets" in the tower; for the gardener, the key to the universe may well be in the apparently empty room, for the tower offers a view of the valley. But for the child who is too young to understand its significance, it is not enough that the gardener gave him the key. The child, like a reader who needs to be given a "key" to "unlocking" the secrets of a poem or story, expects a simplistic revelation of secrets. Thus, disappointed, he understands the significance of neither the tower nor the stories that the gardener offers him. The boy must experience the reading of the tower and biblical stories for himself, so the gardener does not clarify the meaning of the empty room. Similarly, the gardener does not clarify the distinction between "the tree" and "a tree" for the boy; although the boy's limited wisdom and literacy lead to tragedy for the idiot rather than promise, as in "The Map of Love," the boy repeats a story that was there, like the hills, "from the beginning."

"The Enemies" and "The Holy Six" offer an even more complicated reading in which there exist both a conventional symbolic meaning and a revised one. In the first story, one religious order is undermined by another. The Reverend Mr Davies, the representative of accepted religion, is "like an old god beset by his enemies," that is, the Owens, who have "faith in the powers of darkness" and indulge in such "unholy" pastimes as crystal-ball gazing. Conventionally it should be clear that the Owens are to be feared and Mr Davies to be pitied. Yet Thomas, like Blake, takes the traditional dichotomy of the forces of darkness and light and complicates it. Mr Davies is an "old god" rendered obsolete; the powers of darkness are also the powers of fruition, and thus have more to offer than the forces of light. The "sinister" forces are alive and creative, while the "holy" force is death-like. Mr Owen, one of the enemies of the "old god" Mr Davies, is also in a perverse way made godlike, like Sam Rib, with the power to decree increase: " 'multiply, multiply', he had said to the worms disturbed in their channelling, and had cut the brown worms in half so that the halves might breed and spread their life over the garden and go out, contaminating, into the fields and the bellies of the cattle" (18). The worms are both positive and negative, for they "contaminate" and fertilize. Significantly the worms themselves multiply by being cut in two, and in a similar way they break down matter to encourage new growth, doubly expressing the destructive-creative world of Thomas's early work. Both Mr and Mrs Owen are associated not only with the powers of destruction but also with the powers of creation. Mr Davies, in contrast, fearful of Mrs Owen's pregnant body and the animal earth which Mr Owen tills, is too old to create, and the "hill caves were full of shapes and voices that mocked him because he was old" (20). His fear of creation is what makes him an obsolete god: " 'He is frightened of the dark,' thought Mrs Owen, 'the lovely dark.' With a smile, Mr Owen thought, 'He is frightened of the worm in the earth, of the copulation in the tree, of the living grease in the soil.' They looked at the old man, and saw that he was more ghostly than ever. The window behind him cast a ragged circle of light round his head"(20). He is delivered from the "dark mind and the gross dark body" as he becomes a ghost. But although the circle of light suggests a halo, his attainment of holiness is at the expense of life, and, at best, the halo is "ragged."

The ambiguity of these symbols results in part from the focalization of the story, which presents the tale neither solely from Mr Davies', the Owens', nor an omniscient point of view. We see a variety of pictures which become superimposed. We see from a distance Mr Owen in his garden, and Mr Davies lost in the Jarvis Hills; we see through Mrs Owen's eyes an image of Mr Davies in the crystal ball. We also see through the eyes of Mr Davies, as he views a picture which somehow is different from a reality he later encounters: "He saw a young man with a beard bent industriously over the garden soil; he saw that the house was a pretty picture, with the face of a pale young woman pressed up against the window" (18). As the image in the crystal ball and the one we see of Mr Davies on the hill come together, the perspectives merge, and the reader is left to weigh the ambiguity, just as in previous stories the characters were left to interpret impressions for themselves.

Our interpretation of the Owens is further complicated in "The Holy Six," where they encounter characters who are the embodiment of the deadly sins lust, greed, envy, fear, cruelty, and spite. Thomas called "The Holy Six" a "fable," which might be taken to imply that it is not only fabulous but also a story containing a moral; indeed, it does resemble a morality play with its cast of emblematic characters. But Thomas subverts the genre by removing the fable's conventional moral imperatives. Mrs Owen becomes associated with the virgin Mary, her pregnancy being caused by the previously mentioned "immaculate conception" (around her the "immaculate circle broadened, taking a generation's shape"). She is, however, at the same time still a "witch" with the powers of prophecy. Her crystal ball enables her to read the story of the future in a subtly logogenetic world. She is now, when contrasted to the Holy Six, associated with the powers of light: "Light was in the room, the world of light, and the holy Jewish word. On clock and black fire, light brought the inner world to pass, and the shape in his image that changed with the silent changes of the shape of light twisted his last man's-word. The word grew like light" (99). Yet to the ironically named Holy Six, themselves life-deniers, Mrs Owen is a sinister force, and they read her character into her handwriting: "She put malignity in the curves and tails of the characters, a cloven foot, a fork, a snake's sting coming out from the words in a separate life as the words lay back giddy from her revolving pen along the lines" (98). To the Holy Six, sex is perversion and women are images of death.

The anagrammatic names are transparent keys to the characters' personalities, and their perceptions of Mrs Owen, coloured by their spite, cruelty, and so forth, determine their own fates. Accompanied by the ghostly Mr Davies, who now acts as a guide through the world of the dead, the Holy Six are inexplicably reduced, one by one, as each slips, in death, into an individual vision characteristic of his name. The expansion of a word into a larger vision is seen for example in Mr Stipe's spiteful actions: "He crept with ghost Davies through a narrow world; in his hair were the droppings of birds from the boughs of the mean trees; leading the ghost through dark dingles, he sprung the spiked bush back, and pissed against the wind. He hissed at the thirsty dead who bit their lips and gave them a dry cherry; he whistled through his fingers, and up rose Lazarus like a weazel. And when the virgin came on a white ass by his grave, he raised a ragged hand and tickled the ass's belly till it brayed and threw Mary among the corpse-eaters and the quarrelling crows" (101). Davies is now a convert to the Jarvis Valley's ethos, and the Holy Six, having undergone their visions and been "baptized" by Reverend Davies, are transformed, as Davies was; their baptism strips the Word – their names – of meaning, and after a rebirth, they are at the end of the story left to "honour" the forces which they had originally opposed. Forming a circle around the Owens and their unborn child, they seem to acknowledge that the forces of creation and decreation remain inseparable.

While the Jarvis Hills in such stories as "The Enemies" and "The Holy Six" represent physical creation, in "A Prospect of the Sea" they also become a source of imaginative, and by extension, artistic, creation. Of all the Jarvis Valley stories, "Prospect" perhaps most resonates with Thomas's own circumstances. As in "The Tree" and "The Map of Love," the central character is a youth; in this case he is transparently like Thomas himself. Reminiscent of the later Thomas who identifies himself with the shepherd in the note to the *Collected Poems 1934–1952* [5] (and also like Thomas's father), the boy in "Prospect" both believes and doesn't believe in the existence of God: "he did not believe in God, but God had made this summer full of blue winds and heat and pigeons in the house wood" (87). The mythical soul of the hills provides scope for the imagination of a potential writer. As in "Fern Hill," the boy's imagination transforms the landscape, for not only does he imagine that the cornfield is the sea – it actually becomes the sea. The boy is transported back to an innocent time in which he becomes analogous to Adam naming the world. The Jarvis Hills have been decreated, reduced at first to the "hills with no name," and the boy had "no words to say how wonderful the summer was." This world is pre-linguistic, and pre-narrative, for as he first imagines a tale of a mermaid princess, his subsequent contemplation of the edenic landscape erases it from his consciousness: "under the innocent green of the trees ... the story of the princess died" (88). At first "there were no words for the sky and the sun and the summer country; the birds were nice, and the corn was nice" (88), but he soon develops the ability to find "harder" words than "nice," and he takes possession of the world around him. He also displays an ability to go beyond mere naming and to create stories.

Early in the tale, before his visions return him to a pre-linguistic state, he "made up a story" in which there is a "drowned princess from a Christmas book." He "creates" a story from fragments of existing stories he has read. This might at first suggest either a potential artist without much imagination, or, worse, a plagiarist (something the early Thomas was indeed accused of being); however, it also suggests a future writer rewriting existing myths to make them personally relevant. In this metafictional passage, the artist figure first dissolves the hard shapes of his literary inheritance in order to "create" it (or recreate it) afresh. Employing archetypes from fairy-tales ("in seven-league boots he was springing over the fields"), he is aware that all stories are in fact part of one large, continuous story that is infinitely repeatable with variations: "he forgot how the story ended, if ever there were an end to a story that had no beginning" (87). The story with no end is characteristic of many of Thomas's tales, which themselves embody the timelessness and lack of closure that results from continual rewriting, or perpetual creation and decreation. Significantly, Thomas once called his collected poetry parts of one long poem which he continuously rewrote, being "not individual poems but pieces of poetry moving towards a poem" (CL 591).

Also standard in much of Thomas's work is the boy's habit of self-reflectiveness. The boy stands outside of himself and tells stories as if about a separate character: "This is a story, he said to himself, about a boy on a holiday kissed by a broom-rider." His story is apparently broken by an intrusive reality much different from his desired vision; however, for the young Thomas living inside language, the first fiction gives way to another fiction, as "the story, like all stories, was killed as she kissed him; now he was a boy in a girl's arms, and the hill stood above a true river, and the peaks and their trees towards England were as Jarvis had known them when he walked there with his lovers and horses for half a century, a century ago" (90). Although these events are more true to the world around him than his storybook vision, the boy is still somewhat detached from himself, a writer who is both author and character.

As in "The Map of Love," where the map is transformed into a real landscape, artistic visions apparently are transformed into reality for the boy, as his storybook princess appears before him as a live girl: "The boy, still standing timidly in the first shade, saw the broken, holiday princess die for the second time, and a country girl take her place on the live hill" (89). But the country girl possesses many characteristics different from those of the princess, and her reality becomes so frightening for the boy that he reverts to his earlier fantasy. Rather than emerging from fantasy into reality, the boy merely moves from myth to romance, for the country girl is as much a fantasy as the storybook princess; this time, however, his imagination brings out fears instead of wishes, and he sees the girl as a witch: "The stain on her lips was blood, not berries; and her nails were not broken but sharpened sideways, ten black scissor-blades ready to snip off his tongue." It becomes clear that the adventure which the boy is frightened away from is sexual, as it is for many of Thomas's heroes, and his coupling with the girl from a "once upon a time" story is brought up short by his present fear of going on, and the voice that warns him to "not adventure anymore." His fear of sex (which is perhaps by extension a subconscious fear of creation), as well as the images employed to illustrate it (blood, scissors), is itself derived from folk-tales and superstitions;[6] he imagines, for example, that what he is facing is "death ... consumption and whooping cough and the stones inside you ... and the way your face stays if you make too many faces in the looking-glass" (89). Mirrors occur often in the short stories, often as images of solipsistic fiction. The superstitious fear that his face will freeze from too much self-absorption may be an early warning to himself against creation derived from excessive self-reflexivity. In this case, his forbidden repetition of the "once upon a time" adventure is stopped by other opposing stories.

The boy moves between the fictional worlds of story and dream. But the curse of having to live inside fictions is turned to his advantage. When the boy "awakes" from one dream, it is into another dream in which he no longer is restricted to the one meaningless and bland word "nice," but instead stands like Adam surveying a landscape over which he has achieved linguistic dominion. He then uses his new-found power with language to extricate himself from a predicament and to turn his defeat into triumph. Initially the boy seems to be pulled in opposite directions, one voice taunting him with the past and with already created stories ("once upon a time"), and another ("do not adventure any more") telling him that he should not progress. Able neither to retrieve the past nor to go on, he is momentarily at an impasse. The voice that tells the potential artist "you shall never go back" warns him that he can never again be the pre-linguistic Adam; nor, as the stories have already been written, can he create something entirely new. But the second, contradictory voice is the "echo" of the first, and therefore the opposing forces have the same source. Thus the boy solves his dilemma by embracing both voices; as an artist, he can appropriate the already existing stories, and by rewriting them create his own mythology. The final image is paradoxically one of going forward. He more openly borrows an Old Testament story, only slightly altering it to his own purposes. Long outside the garden of Eden, the boy witnesses Noah preparing for the flood: "On a hill to the horizon stood an old man building a boat, and the light that slanted from the sea cast the holy mountain of a shadow over the three-storied decks and the Eastern timber. And through the sky, out of the beds and gardens, down the white precipice built of feathers, the loud combs and mounds, from the caves in the hill, the cloudy shapes of birds and beasts and insects drifted into the hewn door. A dove with a green petal followed in the raven's flight. Cool rain began to fall" (93–4). Typical of the synchronic vision in so much of Thomas's work, the beginning of the flood and its ensuing destruction are coterminous with its end and the renewal of life, for the Dove enters the ark with the leaf of promise already in its beak. The symbol of life carried on from the past is representative of all life in Thomas's work, a life which is a story with no beginning or end, or which is *all* beginnings and endings. As old stories supply the seeds for new ones, the continuation of life and artistic creation are indistinguishable. A similar flood occurs at the end of "Prologue to an Adventure," in which the hero is similarly warned not to go on; but again the flood issues in the adventure proper, and, as the adventure here is also one of sex and creation, the flood is emphasized not as a portent of destruction but as a prelude to new life. In the "Prologue"[7] to the *Collected Poems*, written many years later, Thomas describes himself as Noah, and his poems as the very arks which sustain life.[8] The "Prologue" was considered (by Thomas, and now by others) to be a poem at least equal in importance to the rest in the volume. As such appropriations of the deluge myth suggest, the concept of a prologue, something containing the seeds of the future, is just as important as the ensuing adventure. This may explain why most of Thomas's prose works involve fledgling artists, weakly disguising Thomas himself at an earlier stage of his career rather than at the stage at which he was really writing. By focusing on various stages of the process of the development of the artist, he defers the possibility that he has arrived at the end of his development. In the circuitous story with no beginning or end, it is appropriate to go back to any previous point and follow that as far as the form of his work allows – but not, of course, to its "obvious conclusion," for there is none.

This overriding method might itself have necessitated the abandonment of the proposed novel, whose form would have required a plot and a sustained focus artificial to the organic cyclical pattern. Instead, it probably seemed more natural for Thomas to create a series of fragmentary glimpses, loosely linked by the pervading spirit of the Jarvis Valley. These stories become a cycle of myths forming a personal mythology for Thomas. As with most mythologies, its scope is universal, containing the heavenly and the satanic, the realistic and the visionary, the natural and the supernatural. Thomas specifically alludes to the mythological status of the Jarvis Valley stories in "The Orchards," where he places the tales of the Owens, Mr Davies, and the Holy Six not only in a mythological past of their own but also in real Welsh myth, joining the ranks of the myth cycles in the *Mabinogion*. In "The Orchards" the central character, a young writer, dreams a story much the way the boy in "A Prospect of the Sea" does, but, we are told, "this was a story more terrible than the stories of the reverend madmen in the Black Book of Llareggub."[9] Thomas's own stories of the Jarvis Valley, collected into the fictional "Black Book," become a part of the mythic inheritance of his central character. But, as this character is clearly autobiographical, Thomas is in fact creating his own literary ancestry out of his own works. Extrapolating, this would make Thomas in some sense his own creation.

The sinister-sounding Black Book of Llareggub refers not only to Thomas's own, real works, but also to the real works of others, for it is a dark imitation of the "Black Book of Carmarthen" (National Library of Wales), a cycle of tales originating from the area in Wales from which Thomas's family came. Thomas therefore is creating his own mythology first by borrowing from other stories, as in the biblical allusions of the Jarvis Valley tales, altering them to suit his needs, and then applying his inventions of the more universal stories to local legend. The final product, his own myth, he then adds to his legitimate, collective literary inheritance. The complex layering of myth upon myth culminates in the story "The Orchards," which is more explicitly about writing and artistic creation than the previously discussed Jarvis Valley stories. It, and the stories within it, are said to be "more terrible" than the others, perhaps because of the inextricability of life and fiction in them. Here, more fully than in any other Jarvis Valley story, the character is living inside a written world, and the lesson that he learns from the Jarvis Valley is that "the word is too much with us."

THE FALL INTO LANGUAGE

Many of Thomas's stories from his early period go beyond the distortions portrayed in such stories as "The Tree" and, foregrounding the idea that "in the beginning was the Word," focus on aspects of the Word as primal energy. Through a decreative strategy, Thomas turns used words back to uncreated matter which is then potential for recreation. The term "decreation" is borrowed from Simone Weil, who defines it as the act of making something created pass into the uncreated; this differs from "destruction," which makes something created pass into nothingness (Weil 350ff). For Weil, decreation allows for the liberation of energy with a so-called death, so that new forms may be developed out of that energy. This is similar to the natural law of energy in "The force that through the green fuse drives the flower."[10]

Words become flesh in stories such as "The Mouse and the Woman," in which a madman in an asylum creates an Eve-like woman with paper and pen. His madness disengages his ability to distinguish between fiction and reality, and the blurring of borders is experienced by the reader as well as the character within the story. Likewise in "The Orchards," the character Marlais is seen in the act of writing, a struggle which blurs the borders between his dreams, his writing, and the "real" world around him. Like the madman, Marlais envisions elusive female figures that become painfully real to him. In such characters, to use Shakespeare's words, "the lunatic, the lover, and the poet" are very much "compact" and their creations out of words become tangible realities.

"The Mouse and the Woman" is one of several self-referential works containing references to language, myth, writing, and artistic creation. It is especially interesting as a representative work which consistently pairs references to language and recurring allusions to Eden, Adam and Eve, and the Fall. It may help to explain problems of interpretation for the reader of Thomas's poems, who is often baffled by their difficulty, especially with the early poems. The density of these poems, combined with the evasive strategy of Thomas's imagery, is destabilizing for the reader. Even more confusing is the combination of Thomas's gestures toward myth-making, the structures implied by myth, and his concurrent impulse to break down sense. Thomas's self-reflexive early poems reveal a violent dialectic in the ritualistic enacting of a conflict that he had with his own medium: for Thomas, language's ability both to reveal and conceal meaning, its paradoxical capacity to limit interpretation and offer endless possibilities for interpretation, is central to his poetics. This conflict is worked out in metaphoric terms in "The Mouse and the Woman," an account of the creative process which helps to illuminate several of the early poems.

Thomas's early poems use the myth of the fall as a metaphor for the creation of meaning. The post-lapsarian world is physically and linguistically one of separation, multiplicity, and death. The alphabet in "When once the twilight locks no longer," for example, is a "Christ-cross-row of death,"[11] and in "From love's first fever to her plague," "the root of tongues ends in a spentout cancer." To some degree, the fall is a fortunate one, for as poems such as "The force that through the green fuse drives the flower" suggest, death is intimately connected to birth, or rebirth. But while the generative possibilities of a linguistically fallen world are seen as positive, the death inherent in a word's being locked into meaning is not. Thus, the fall into language is accompanied by an equally strong impetus to return to an edenic state, in which the virgin word is as yet without association. In "Notes on the Art of Poetry," Thomas describes his first awareness of language, and his enjoyment of the materiality of words – their shape and sound – saying: "that was the time of innocence; words burst upon me, unencumbered by trivial or portentous associations; words were their spring-like selves, fresh with Eden's dew, as they flew out of the air. They made their own original associations as they sprang and shone" (548). For anyone other than a child in the early stages of language acquisition, an edenic state of language is an impossibility, partly because, as Bakhtin notes, all speech is a response to words that have been uttered before; we can never confront a linguistically virgin world. In a less nostalgic mood, Thomas complained: "We look upon a thing a thousand times, perhaps we shall have to look upon it a million times before we can see it for the first time. Centuries of problematical progress have blinded us to the literal world; each bright and naked object is shrouded around with a thick, pea-soup mist of associations; no single word in all our poetical vocabulary is a virgin word, ready for our first love, willing to be what we make it" (CL 93). In singling out "poetical vocabulary," Thomas points to an even more fundamental reason why purely edenic language is not possible: this edenic state would require an essential language in which there is no split between sign and referent; such a state would preclude the Saussurian gap in which the play of meaning resonates – and this play is, for Thomas, the essence of poetry. Again, in "Notes on the Art of Poetry," Thomas says that "the best craftsmanship always leaves holes and gaps in the works of the poem so that something that is not in the poem can creep, crawl, flash, or thunder in" (554). Therefore, Thomas moves "in the direction of the beginning," towards Eden,[12] but it is "in the direction of" only, for he never actually arrives. It might be suggested that arrival would be the death of poetry. At the same time, he moves symbolically outward into the world of signification. The resultant dual movement to both create and decreate meaning is played out in most of the early writing.

"The Mouse and the Woman" is a metafictional story which dramatizes the artist's conflicting impulses regarding language. Its original title was "Uncommon Genesis," identifying it as one of Thomas's many tales of creation. It tells the story of the creation of a woman; more generally, it is about the creation of stories. The creator within the short story is a madman in an asylum, consistent with Thomas's conception of the artist as one with unusual vision.[13] Similar in style and content to much of Thomas's early experimental prose, it uses myth – specifically the story of Adam and Eve – combined with dream, hallucination, and the fictional worlds of artistic creation, all worlds of the madman's making in which he almost exclusively lives, divorced from the phenomenal world around him.

The madman/artist creates a woman by writing her into existence, and Thomas renders this creation in a birth image that is typically at once anatomical and biblical: "She had moved in his belly when he was a boy, and stirred in his boy's loins. He at last gave birth to her who had been with him from the beginning. ... It is not a little thing, he thought, this writing that lies before me. It is the telling of a creation. It is the story of birth. Out of him had come another. A being had been born, not out of the womb, but out of the soul and the spinning head. ... He had given a woman being. His flesh would be upon her, and the life that he had given her would make her walk, talk, and sing. And he knew, too, that it was upon the block of paper she was made absolute" (75). An idea seeking a form, the woman is brought forth from his subconscious and enters his waking reality; however, as soon as she is made "absolute" her creation becomes problematic, for she then becomes locked into one identity, no longer subject to the transformations that characterize a living world or a living language. "Caught between believing in her and denying her," the madman almost immediately begins to hear alternating voices telling him that she is "dead, alive, drowned, raised up" (74); eventually, as "the music of creation" is heard, he writes something upon the paper, following which, we are told, "the woman died." This passage is ambiguous, for he *may* have written the words "the woman died"; therefore we do not know at what level of fiction we are operating. At this moment of writing, creation is coexistent with destruction. The woman's "creative murder" is analogous to Thomas's conception of art as process rather than stasis, where decreation is desired, and a continual breaking down necessary in order to rebuild out of the raw materials. In an often quoted letter to Vernon Watkins, Thomas attempts to criticize his friend's poetry for lacking the decreative dynamic of his own works: "I can see the sensitive picking of words, but none of the strong, inevitable pulling that makes a poem an *event*, a happening, an *action* perhaps, not a still-life or an experience *put down*, placed, regulated … I don't ask you for vulgarity, though I miss it; I think I ask you for a little creative destruction, destructive creation: 'I build a flying tower, and I pull it down'" (*CL* 278). The woman's creative murder is "decreation" rather than "destruction." She does not pass into nothingness, but undergoes a transformation which returns her to the realm of idea. While effecting an avoidance of closure in the art, the madman renders her potential for further recreations. This is prefigured in the madman's mind before the murder, when the woman vanishes – but, we are told, "she returned 10 times, in 10 different shapes." The "murder" that the reader witnesses, then, is only one of an infinite number of transformations. The woman functions the way language potentially might for Thomas: she is reduced to raw material in order to be created anew with fresh meaning.

Since the woman in the story functions at the level of language, the world that the woman and madman inhabit is representative of the text. The madman's world is inside his head, and is a fiction, whether dreamt or written. It is overtly described in self-reflexive terms as something to be "deciphered"; it is a written world full of "translating symbols": "Look at the million stars, he said. They make some pattern on the sky. It is a pattern of letters spelling a word. One night I shall look up and read the word." Curiously, this decoding is something that the artist/madman fears, and when the moment eventually occurs it is apocalyptic. As it was for the creation and destruction of the woman, the creation of meaning in the written world is concomitant with an equally strong impulse to break down the symbolic order. Continual decipherment, or the creation of meaning, both aggravates the artist's madness and sustains him. The story's structure is circular, ending with an image of the asylum which echoes the story's beginning. The circularity ensures that the poet's ambivalence toward the fall into language remains intact.

The fall of man in Eden is also linked to a linguistic fall in numerous poems from Thomas's early period that are self-conscious commentaries on writing and on the creation of the very myths they utilize as a shaping force. Even in relatively late poems, where Thomas looks back on his early work, he admits, as in "Ceremony after a fire raid," that "I know the legend / of Adam and Eve is never for a second / silent in my service" (*CP* 107). An investigation of this motif in the poems is valuable, therefore, to an understanding of both the poetry and the prose.

The poem "In the beginning" (*CP* 22) focuses on the idea of the Logos, which occurs frequently in the early poetry and prose. Explicitly linking the creation of the world with the Word, Thomas rewrites Genesis borrowing from the Gospel of St John:

> In the beginning was the word, the word
> That from the solid bases of the light
> Abstracted all the letters of the void;
> And from the cloudy bases of the breath
> The word flowed up, translating to the heart
> First characters of birth and death.

Just as in "The Mouse and the Woman," the landscape is representative of the text; the universe here is written. The "first characters of birth and death" suggest both Adam and Eve and the letters of the alphabet – specifically the alpha and omega of the beginning and end – which here again, as in other works, are coterminous. The word that "flowed up, translating to the heart / first characters of birth and death" may be the very word that the madman deciphers; what he reads then, embodied in the "word," could be his own story.

The poem "Today, this insect" (*CP* 38) also pairs birth and death, and links both to language acquisition and the development of meaning, where the creation of form in symbol, poem, or story is both generative and destructive. The speaker is a godlike creator/writer. Symbols and tales act as "witnesses" to creation; they also cause the division of sense and act as witness to the loss of Eden:

> Today, this insect, and the world I breathe,
> Now that my symbols have outelbowed space,
> Time at the city spectacles, and half
> The dear, daft time I take to nudge the sentence,
> In trust and tale have I divided sense,
> Slapped down the guillotine, the blood-red double
> Of head and tail made witnesses to this
> Murder of Eden and green genesis.

The poem structurally enacts the problem it describes, the disjunction between words and things that accompanies the "murder of Eden." Going beyond the essential language of Adam we move into the symbolic order of "tales," "fables," and "stories" which are a "certain promise" and yet a result of "divided sense." The poem is arranged into three eight-line stanzas intercut with two single lines that, taken together, form a chiasmus: "The insect certain is the plague of fables" becomes "the insect fable is the certain promise." The chiasmus is a formal device used often in the early poems. The reversals, and the pairing of such oppositional ideas as "promise" and "plague," "certain" and "fable" (or truth and lie), beg to be taken apart, and it is in the spaces between the crossings where we look for meaning.

The poem is further complicated by Thomas's mythical allusions. While the first two stanzas seem to foreground the story of Eden and the fall, the third stanza, after the second half of the chiasmus, opens out into multiple mythic possibilities:

> Death: death of Hamlet and the nightmare madmen,
> An air-drawn windmill on a wooden horse,
> John's beast, Job's patience, and the fibs of vision,

Greek in the Irish sea the ageless voice.
"Adam I love, my madmen's love is endless,
No tell-tale lover has an end more certain,
All legends' sweethearts on a tree of stories,
My cross of tales behind the fabulous curtain."

The death and multiplicity of the fallen world accompany the creation of meaning in these "legends" and "tales." The "cross of tales" recalls the cross of Christ's crucifixion, perhaps pointing to the death and redemption inherent in the fallen language necessary to the creation of tales. But the phrase also points to the crossing of tales that creates a chiasmus of meaning, which asks the reader to take apart and recreate the poem for herself/himself, allowing for as many readings as there are readers.

The cross recurs in a number of early poems which are self-consciously about language and writing. "When once the twilight locks" (*CP* 9) is, like "In the beginning," a rewriting of Genesis. The opening image of divine creation being unlocked from the "long worm" of the creator's finger is reminiscent of Michaelangelo's God in the Sistine Chapel, or Blake's representation of Urizen dividing time and space. The early notebook version of the poem uses biblical imagery almost exclusively; the writing motifs were added later to the revised, published version, making the subject a creator in the artistic sense. The speaker of this poem, the god/writer, is, like Blake's god, both a creator and a destroyer, and his powers are transferred to his creations – first the world and then Adam:

> My fuses timed to charge his heart,
> He blew like powder to the light
> And held a little sabbath with the sun,
> But when the stars, assuming shape,
> Drew in his eyes the straws of sleep,
> He drowned his father's magics in a dream.
>
> All issue armoured, of the grave,
> The redhaired cancer still alive,
> The cataracted eyes that filmed their cloth;

> Some dead undid their bushy jaws,
> And bags of blood let out their flies;
> He had by heart the Christ-cross-row of death.

Images of decay enter the poem when Adam learns "by heart the Christ-cross-row of death." The "Christ-cross-row" is the alphabet, so called from the figure of the cross preceding the alphabet in old hornbooks used to teach children to read. The letters are the most elementary form of learning from which all later writing derives; once mastered, the child, or Adam, must put the letters together to create meaning – and this is the beginning of the fall into language. The cross at the beginning of the alphabet is to remind us of the crucifixion of Christ; Dr Johnson tells us that "the cross is placed at the beginning, to shew that the end of learning is piety" (Tuer 64). But for Thomas, the cross is a reminder of more practical concerns, for his is a "Christ-cross-row of *death*." One might imagine a graveyard of stories, reminiscent of a row of headstones, created by an alphabet of death. As in "The Mouse and the Woman," a fully created fiction kills the creative process, and therefore must be decreated; but the resurrection implied by the cross of crucifixion means the possibility of renewal. Recalling the "first characters of birth and death" from "In the beginning," this poem presents birth and death as inseparable, and each letter of the alphabet holds within it potential for creation and seeds of destruction.

Similarly, in "From love's first fever" (*CP* 21) writing is a violently creative act derived from the "first characters of birth and death." Language acquisition is paradoxically both empowering and destructive:

> And from the first declension of the flesh
> I learnt man's tongue, to twist the shapes of thoughts
> Into the stony idiom of the brain,
> To shade and knit anew the patch of words
> Left by the dead who, in their moonless acre,
> Need no word's warmth.

"Declension" as defined by the *OED* means a "deviation from uprightness," recalling once again the fall of man; it also means "deterioration," implying the decay of temporal existence. "Declension" also refers to case inflexion, making man ("flesh") a part of speech.[14] Hence language acquisition parallels the story of man, in a cluster of images echoing "When once the twilight." From the beginning of language there is a movement outward to plurality in the last two lines of this stanza, where "The root of tongues ends in a spentout cancer, / That but a name, where maggots have their X." The beginning, the alphabet, the "root of tongues," gives way to multiple languages and to death. The last word, pronounced "cross" in Thomas's live readings, is on the page written as an X, making it both aurally and visually reminiscent of the cross preceding the alphabet in the Christ-cross-row. The cross accompanying a signature, as Dr Johnson noted, is a pledge of piety. It is also often the anonymous signature of one who cannot write; the maggots' signature, death, is hence an erasure in more ways than one, for it denies both life and literacy.

In spite of such images of deterioration, "From love's first fever" ends with a return to multiplicity and to images of life, suggested by such words as "womb," "bud," "sun," and "manna." "When once the twilight" ends indeterminately with an image, similar to the "cross of tales" and "tree of stories" in "Today, this insect," of "worlds hang[ing] on the trees." The poem, and the reader, are left dangling from the chiasmus; there is no clear border between the edenic and the fallen world, and the poem occupies a space in an overlapping region common to both. This space seems to be the natural area of habitation for most of the early poems and stories, in which a movement toward origins occurs at the same time as a push toward generation, and creation is coterminous with decreation. It is shared ground between the edenic world, where there is no disjunction between word and thing, and the post-lapsarian, where a breach has been effected between being and meaning.

The images in Thomas's poems which cause the critics so many interpretive problems seem to occupy this intermediary poetic space. They do not fully participate in meaning because there is neither a complete linguistic system nor a single discourse to support them – there are many possibilities which might give them meaning, but all are potential rather than actual. Most readings push these images into the world of meaning and binary signifiers. The actual state of the poem is the process previous to this order, and is characterized by contradiction, plurality, fluidity, and what Kristeva calls a "pleasurable excess" over precise meaning that is disruptive for the reader.[15] No poem, or linguistically formed utterance, could actually inhabit this space. As in Kristeva's account, poetic language may bring the semiotic into the symbolic in a subversive capacity, but it does not precede the imposition of symbolic order. Yet Thomas's language remains akin to this pre-symbolic space. It is a semiotic language which undermines the relatively secure meaning of the symbolic order, pressing the linguistic sign to its extreme limit and setting up a play of drives within the text which threaten to split apart received meaning. It is a language which values its material properties: its tone, rhythm, and what Thomas called "the shape of sound," those elements of language which bring it closer to its essential, pre-fallen state.

An acceptance of the nature of fallen language makes the act of interpretation less problematic; by its very nature such an approach overcomes the impediments facing New Critical readings, and opens up a playfulness more common to postmodern works. Thomas's emphasis on process, not only in the natural world but also in language and the creation of meaning, is central to an understanding of his work. By foregrounding the creative/decreative properties of signification, Thomas offers a much-ignored key to readers impelled to find sense in his poems; when seen through the lens of linguistic self-reference, the bulk of Thomas's work takes on new meaning – or meanings.

TRANSITION AND THE AVANT GARDE

Thomas's theories of poetic language apply equally to his early prose works, of which "The Mouse and the Woman" is representative. "The Mouse and the Woman," originally written sometime between late 1932 and early 1933,[16] was first published, along with the poem "Then was my neophyte," in the avant-garde quarterly *transition* in the fall of 1936. Thomas describes it to Pamela Hansford Johnson as "a story set in no time or place, with only two characters, a man and a woman. And the woman, of course, is not human. She wouldn't be" (*CL* 35); he warns Johnson that the story is not an example of mainstream realism. [17]

Thomas found in *transition* an ideal forum for his experimental fiction, for the editors and contributors subscribed to a poetics very similar to Thomas's own. Thomas's letters give evidence that he had read *transition* at least as early as March, 1934 (*CL* 98), and it has been suggested that the magazine's theories, gleaned from borrowed back issues, had some influence on his work. [18] During 1934 Thomas was reworking the manuscripts of his poems for his first volume, *Eighteen Poems*, and this was also the period in which he made most of his entries into the "Red Prose Notebook," from which much of his early prose and many of his intricate poems were derived. In July 1934, Thomas reworked "Uncommon Genesis," cutting its length in half (*CL* 145). Two years later, shortly before publication, he expressed a desire to rename the story "The Woman and the Mouse," but settled on its inverse, "The Mouse and the Woman," when it appeared in *transition*. An interesting subtlety can be discerned in this change in the title: the mouse in the tale plays a relatively minor role when compared to the woman; symbolically the mouse represents a subconscious fear for the central figure in the story, and although secondary to the woman, who represents a type of wish-fulfilment, it takes on a more important role when given prominence in the title. This change aligns Thomas's tale even more closely with the directive of *transition* to explore the "night world" of the mind. Whether or not an influence can be claimed, it can certainly be seen that Thomas's work at this period found a congenial home. *transition* published a wide variety of experimental poetry, prose essays, and photographs, ranging among such movements as Dada, surrealism, expressionism, and German neoclassicism. A list of contributors includes James Joyce, Gertrude Stein, Samuel Beckett, Franz Kafka, Kay Boyle, Hugo Ball, Laura Riding, William Carlos Williams, André Gide, Hart Crane, Rainer Maria Rilke, and C.G. Jung (in translation).

transition's mandate was to create a forum for original and experimental art that "disintegrated the philistine notion of a pragmatic world" by searching into the "prelogical" or instinctive world represented by dream, magic, and the unconscious for a deeper language. Its editor, Eugene Jolas, saw the magazine's primary function as re-establishing the pre-eminence of the Word. Jolas himself developed new words to describe the products of a new poetic, words such as "anamyth" ("a fantastic narrative that reflects preconscious relationships") and "psychograph" ("a prose text that expresses hallucinations and phantoms").[19] Jolas also postulated a type of poetry that he called "vertigral"; because he believed that poetry should be "Orphic," he invented a term that suggested an upwardly moving, transcendent quality, combining the word "vertical" with *graal,* the French word for "grail," the symbol of religious experience and of the ultimate quest. Thomas's poem "Then was my neophyte" was published under a section of *transition* titled "vertigral," clearly identifying it, in Jolas's view, as an example of poetry approaching revelation. The poem presents a "neophyte" – a novice or recent convert – who is able to see below the surface of symbols, and who is not fooled by "green myths," but yet, like Beth Rib and Reuben, or the boy in "A Prospect of the Sea," is able to enter into them:

> Stretch the salt photographs,
> The landscape grief, love in His oils
> Mirror from man to whale
> That the green child see like a grail
> Through veil and fin and fire and coil
> Time on the canvas paths.

Cinematic metaphors ("He films my vanity. / Shot in the wind, by tilted arcs ...") juxtapose the true nature of the world in flux with the lies of the static image. This poem is characteristically autobiographical and self-reflexive, even solipsistic, describing the artist watching himself in a photographic image. The suggestion of a mystic revelation of something beyond the photograph, beyond the veil in the grail quest, is, however, not clarified; there is no easy acquisition of secrets, as the boy in "The Tree" would wish. The poem ends with the enigmatic statement of the poem that "I saw time murder me." In order to witness his own death the viewer must be outside of the so-called "realistic" temporal world.

This type of poetry, "vertigralist" in Jolas's view, is quite similar to a form of prose that Jolas dubbed the "paramyth." In one of many manifestos appearing in *transition*, Jolas closely aligns the writer of prose with the poet – as Thomas saw himself – and he defines the paramyth:

> The literature of the future will have no interest in competing with the possibilities for photographic and acoustic realism ... the literature of the future will tend towards the presentation of the spirit inherent in the magic tale and poetry, towards the poet's exploration of heretofore hidden strata of the human personality. It will probably express the irruption of the supernatural, the phantastic, the eternal into quotidian life ... I suggest the paramyth as the successor to the form known heretofore as the short story or nouvelle. I conceive it as a kind of epic wonder tale giving an organic synthesis of the individual and universal unconscious, the dream, the daydream, the mystic vision. In its final form it might be a phantasmagoric mixture of the poem in prose, the popular tale of folklore, the psychograph, the essay, the myth, the saga, the humoresque.
>
> The language of the paramyth will be logomantic, a kind of music, a mirror of a four-dimensional universe. (*transition* 23 July 1935, 7)

Jolas's description resembles, in some significant ways, Kristeva's account of poetic language. It is under the rubric of "paramyth" that "The Mouse and the Woman" appeared in the same issue of *transition* as "Then was my neophyte." While this short story or "paramyth" is not specifically a reworking of "Then was my neophyte" as "poem in prose," it does bear many similarities to the poem. Like "Neophyte," "The Mouse and the Woman" focuses on someone of unusual vision whose special status is used to explore the discrepancies between image and reality – or at least psychological reality. Both works are concerned with a "four-dimensional universe" – a world in time – and both the poet in "Neophyte" and the madman in "The Mouse and the Woman" witness the destruction that time brings. Each witnesses the "murder" of an image, and potentially the murder of their selves: for the poet in "Neophyte," the artist is both outside and inside the film, and the photographic image is an extension of himself. For the madman, the woman he creates in his dream, on paper and imaginatively in the world to accompany him is, like Eve to Adam, also an extension of himself.[20]

"The Mouse and the Woman," having much in common with the Jarvis Valley stories, is characteristic of the paramyth; it explores the "hidden strata of the human personality" through "the dream, the daydream, the mystic vision," and the hallucination of the "psychograph," the "irruption of the supernatural" and the "phantastic," all combined with the "individual and the universal unconscious." It begins with a contrast, first between the world of the asylum and the world "outside," and then between this collective real world and the world inside the head of the madman. There is then a further contrast between the safe, calm appearance of the lunatic asylum and the sinister reality inside its walls: "The building, too, had a sweet expression, as though it knew only the kind things of life and the polite emotions. In a middle room sat a child who had cut off his double thumb with a scissors" (72).[21]

Yet the existence of this physical, external world is, for the central character, at times dependent upon his perception of it (as it is for the characters in "Fern Hill" and "The Hunchback in the Park"), for when he does not look at it, the world ceases to exist, and he enters a new place in his mind: "Opening his mouth wide, he bayed up at the sun, listening to the inflections of his voice with a remorseless concentration. With his unseeing eyes fixed on the green garden, he heard the revolution of the years as they moved softly back. Now there was no garden. Under the sun the iron bars melted. Like a flower, a new room pulsed and opened" (72). The madman goes back in time and sees a springlike image of rebirth in this new room in his mind. It will later take on mythic overtones, resembling the garden of Eden. Not surprisingly, the madman is also a writer. For Thomas, the inner world of the mind is an important place for the artist. In his letters he often writes of the juxtaposition of the "inner" and "outer" worlds, as when he says to Trevor Hughes, in a letter written around the same time as the composition of "The Mouse and the Woman": "Words are so misleading. I don't urge a monastic seclusion, & preoccupation with the invisible places. ... You must *live* in the outer world, suffer in it & with it, enjoy its changes, despair at them, carry on ordinarily with moneymaking routines, fall in love, mate, & die. You *have* to do that. Where the true artist differs from his fellows is that *that* for him is not the only world. He has the inner splendour. ... The outer & inner worlds are not, I admit, entirely separate" (CL 12).

In the early sections of the tale this inner world is characterized by creation and possibility. The woman of the madman's dream, brought forth from his subconscious, becomes something alive as she enters into the madman's waking reality: "He could no longer listen to the speaking of reason. The pulse of a new heart beat at his side. Contentedly he let the dream dictate its rhythm" (73). The madman's artistic intentions are only partially responsible for her creation, for he lets the vision develop naturally on its own. The reality of the creation brings conflict for the madman; "caught between believing in her and denying her," he nonetheless does not stop her creation. Confusion regarding her reality increases as the madman/writer attempts to translate his dream onto paper. She then can possibly be fictional on two levels, psychologically and linguistically: "another voice told him that she was dead. She was a woman in a mad story" (74). Her origin in "story" would imply that she is fictitious, but her "death" would imply that she was once alive, and therefore real. He initially attempts to deny her, and when the urge to write her comes upon him, he rejects it, until he can no longer fight her presence: "One winter morning, after the last crowing of the cock, in the walks of his garden, had died to nothing, she who for so long had dwelt with him appeared in all the wonder of her youth. She had cried to be set free, and to walk in his dreams no longer. Had she not been in the beginning, there would have been no beginning. ... He at last gave birth to her who had been with him from the beginning" (74–5). She is both a part of him and something separate, a duality symbolized by the birth metaphor. She is connected to him in the world of his mind; in a seemingly endless series of reflections, she dreams what he dreams, seven images of herself. The interconnection of the man and his creation begins to resemble the problematic relationship that Alice faces in her journey through the looking glass: when she encounters the sleeping Red King, she is faced with the possibility that she is a creation of *his* dream. Likewise the question of "which dreamt it" arises for the madman and the woman, who is herself partly responsible for the dream, for "the changes of the details of the dream and the celestial changes, the levels of the trees and the toothed twigs, these were the mechanisms of her delirium" (73). As she slowly takes on a life of her own, the man and the woman appear to separate and to exchange roles. He seems to become a "voice" who visits her as a disembodied spirit. To the woman the madman might become "the still small voice" that she "must not listen to." Eventually she begs for a separate identity apart from him. She cries to be set free from the imprisonment of his dreams, to be brought forth into the "real" world. He does this by putting her into writing.

Words have both a capacity to make things real and a revelatory function. The creation of the woman is described as if it were something mystical, to be undertaken away from the eyes of mortals. There is something sacred in the "absoluteness" of the writing, and something awe-inspiring in "the telling of a creation." Aware of the responsibility of creation, the madman/artist – like Sam Rib and Mr Owen – sees himself as godlike. The oracle in the pencil suggests that the writing itself is somehow divine or prophetic, perhaps illustrating what Jolas meant by "logomantic" language – words that, like oracles, give insight into the unknown. Because, as with many of Thomas's poems, writing is analogous to giving birth, the creation of the woman is also more generally about the creation of a poem or story. The literary creation is something that emerges from within, "out of the soul and the spinning head," an idea begging to be given a form. It is at once a part of the writer, and, once written, a separate entity. For Thomas, the poem compels and controls the poet, having to some extent a life of its own.

In "The Mouse and the Woman," as in many of Thomas's works, the word here is made flesh, and the creation of the woman, analogous to the creation of the Word, is closely linked to the creation of the world itself. Yet in inverse relation to the decreative flood in "A Prospect of the Sea," the springlike world holds the seeds of destruction: "There was nothing to see in her but the ebb and flow of creation, only the transcendent sweep of being and living in this careless fold of flesh from shoulder bone to elbow. He could not tell, after the horror he had found in the translating symbols, why the sea should point to the fruitful and unfailing stars with the edge of each wave, and an image of fruition disturb the moon in its dead course" (78–9). Consistent with Simone Weil's view of decreation as a holy metaphysical transformation, the "translation" of the symbols implies a movement from one spiritual condition to another without dying. The "translating symbols," as well as emphasizing the constant change that takes place, are a reminder that the Word is something to be read as well as written. For the madman, "horror" and images of death mar the image of fruition. His double impulse to accept and deny the woman is matched by his awareness of the oracular capacity of language and his fear of actually decoding the mysteries offered. Early in the story the positive visions in the madman's dream are tainted by a vague fear as he tries to decode the dream's symbols: "Waking up when it was still dark, he turned the dream over and over on the top of his brain until each little symbol became heavy with a separate meaning. But there were symbols he could not remember" (72). The external world is also full of symbols to be decoded, even more explicitly associated with language. The universe is for the madman literally an embodiment of the Logos, the "pattern of letters spelling a word" in the stars. The woman senses his unspoken fear of deciphering the mysterious message, for she then "kissed him and calmed his fears" (75).

Although the madman's fears are never fully explained, they are embodied in the mouse that, like something from the subconscious, claws its way to the surface bit by bit, trying to break through into the madman's world. The madman does not directly encounter the mouse, but, perhaps even more frighteningly, only sees hints of it, such as the mousehole that he attempts to nail shut. The "sinister" mouse is a threat to the beatific vision of the woman, and its presence is felt more strongly as the madman gets closer to decoding the word of the world: "He could remember little else except the odds and ends of sentences, the movement of a turning shoulder, the sudden flight or drop of syllables. But slowly the whole meaning edged into his brain. He could translate every symbol of his dreams, and he lifted the pencil so that they might stand hard and clear upon the paper. But the words would not come. He thought he heard the scratching of velvet paws behind a panel" (78). When the mouse emerges, creation gives way to destruction, as it always does in Thomas's world. The madman's ability to write returns, but he seemingly has no control over it, as he "wrote upon the block of paper, not knowing what he wrote, and dreading the words that looked up at him at last and could not be forgotten." Fulfilling the words of the prescient voice earlier in the story, he writes the "murder" of his dream-woman: "Gradually the chaos became less and the things of the surrounding world were no longer wrought out of their own substance into the shapes of his thoughts. Some peace fell about him, and again the music of creation was to be heard trembling out of crystal waters, out of the holy sweep of the sky down to the wet edge of the earth where a sea flowed over. Night came slowly, and the hill rose to the unrisen stars. He turned over the block of paper and upon the last page wrote in a clear hand: The woman died" (84–5). The madman sees the death of the woman as a necessary and "holy" sacrifice: "There was dignity in such a murder. And the hero in him rose up in all his holiness and strength" (85).

One might recall here a statement that Thomas made in a letter to Trevor Hughes, written about the same time that he was reworking this story: "The best in a man comes out in suffering; there is a prophet in pain, and an oracle in the agony of the mind" (CL 93). The woman's death is coincident with the madman's decoding of the message and fulfilment of an unspoken prophecy: "Acquainted with the last grief, he stood at the open window of his room. And the night was an island in a sea of mystery and meaning. And the voice out of the night was a voice of acceptance. And the face of the moon was the face of humility. … There were a million stars spelling the same word. And the word of the stars was written clearly upon the sky" (85). Because the vision of the woman was a part of himself, his murder of her becomes a self-sacrifice. As with Galahad's vision of the grail, the revelation of the mystery is coincident with the death of the hero. We are not told what the word in the sky is, or precisely what happens to the madman; we are left only with an image of the mouse crawling back into its hole after surveying the destroyed furniture and china in the "room" in the madman's mind. As the madman decodes the message in the sky, he too dies in his own mind, returning to the asylum, the land of the living dead.

The last image of the story is a return to the beginning, with the madman behind bars baying up at the sun: "Spring is come, said the warders." The irony of this final line is not out of place in Thomas's destructive/creative universe, as death always leads to new life and creation. The circularity of the story recalls the writer of "Then was my neophyte," who, being both outside and inside the image that he witnesses, has survived his own murder in order to write about it. (Indeed, "Then was my neophyte" may be considered the converse of "The Mouse and the Woman" if we consider the point of view; that is, the story of the "creative murder" is told from the "child" or artwork's perspective, and the "villain" is Time.) For the madman, spring will bring a return to life, if only in his mind. Perhaps the decoding of the mystery led to his madness in the first place, or perhaps its continual decipherment is what sustains him. Either way, language and the written world – its writing and reading – is inescapable for him.

Like the Jarvis Valley stories, "The Mouse and the Woman" follows Jolas's definition of the paramyth by illustrating a "synthesis of individual and universal unconscious" forces. The mouse and the woman, the two contrary symbols within the artist/madman's mind, have mythic parallels, if not origins. The madman is influenced alternately by the heavenly and the satanic. First he thinks that the source of his inspiration is evil: "I have a devil, but I do not tell it what to do. It lifts my hand. I write. The words spring into life. She, then, is a woman of the devil" (77). He then decides that "her beauty could not have sprouted out of evil. God, whom he had searched for in his loneliness, had formed her for his mate as Eve for Adam out of Adam's rib" (77). The garden of the asylum disappears, to be replaced by a garden in his mind, which soon is conflated with the mythical garden. The madman tells the woman the story of Adam and Eve and of their "love in the garden of Eden"; walking in their own garden, "they remembered how they had walked in the garden for the first time" (79). Remembering themselves and repeating previous actions, they also repeat the story of the fall, first in story-telling and then in their own consummation.

Accompanying their fall is the appearance of the mouse, who is equated with the devil. The devil within the madman parallels the woman within him; like the opposing voices in "A Prospect of the Sea," the positive and negative forces are equal and have the same source. The mouse's appearance echoes the genesis of the woman, who first appears in a dream of seven images of herself, "in a mad play by a greek":[22] " 'Welcome' said the devil to the madman. 'Cast your eyes upon me. I grow and grow. See how I multiply. See my sad, Grecian stare. And the longing to be born in my dark eyes'" (80). His longing to be born also parallels that of the woman. There is the suggestion that negative images – equally capable of being made into writing, like beautiful ones – are there from the beginning: "Ever since the evening of the second day after their love in the garden, when he told her that her nakedness was not good to look upon, he had heard the welcome ring out in the sliding rain, and seen the welcome words burnt into the sea. He had known at the ringing of the first syllable in his ears that nothing on the earth could save him, and that the mouse would come out. But the mouse had come out already" (80). Curiously, the mouse's greeting becomes "welcome words," perhaps because the powers of destruction ironically offer the promise of creation in the newly fallen world. The fall from grace is in fact desired, for initially "it was not the sickness of sin that was upon her face. Rather it was the sickness of never having sinned" (73). The movement out of the garden is accompanied, as the mouse promises, with a movement toward change and multiplicity. Along with a linguistic genesis, a search for the Logos and exploration of word as spirit and flesh, Thomas also explores, in works such as "The Mouse and the Woman," the necessary fall of language that always follows from any beginning. The quest for a beginning always moves "in the direction of the beginning" only, because of an equally compelling movement in the opposite direction, in which the genealogies necessarily born out of the origins move away from their source. On its own the "garden" becomes a symbol of stasis and restriction. Because the generative possibilities of origins are seen as positive, the world outside the garden is one to be explored; the fall into language becomes an opening up of possibility. Both the restriction of fluidity and constant change, and the freedom to create within the boundaries set by language, accompany this fortunate fall, as can be seen in the destructive-creative events in stories such as "The Mouse and the Woman." The artist figures who undergo such a fall in Thomas's early stories are like Adam with his newly acquired linguistic powers, who both partially masters the world through language and becomes entrapped by it.

2 Solipsistic Adam

The few studies concerned with the early prose works make very little mention of the predominant artist figures within them. Even the more extensive studies to date, such as those by Annis Pratt and Linden Peach, make little or no reference to the self-reflective nature of these stories. Although signs of intertextuality are sometimes noted (in some cases as examples of Thomas's literary inferiority), critics generally have not viewed these similarities as central to a Thomasian poetic. The present study regards both the intertextuality and the self-reflexivity as characteristic of Thomas's central concern with the Adamic artist, linguistically taking possession of the world around him.

While all of the early stories concern the act of artistic creation, and many allude to a written world, two stories in particular, "The Orchards" and "Prologue to an Adventure," are noticeably rich in self-conscious references to artistic creation, and to the difficulties facing the writer who must work with the slippery medium that is language. Both of these works have as their protagonists artist figures obsessed with linguistic creation to the exclusion of any world outside of their fictions. Their creations are extensions or reflections of themselves, and they are solitary artists who write their worlds into existence. Such solipsistic "Adams" represent a type that appears in many of the early poems as well as in the stories. The stories and poems often read as translations of one another. "In the beginning" and "I, in my intricate image," for example, read almost as versified versions of some of the early stories. Thus, an intensive study of these two central prose works, with their self-conscious Adamic artists and their fictive worlds, contributes to our understanding of the poetry as well as the prose.

"THE ORCHARDS"

"The Orchards" appears in an early form as "Anagram" dated October 1934 in the "Red Prose Notebook"; revised in 1935, it was first published in *Criterion* (1936), then in *The Faber Book of Short Stories* (1937) and *Welsh Short Stories* (Faber, 1937), and later included, as was "The Mouse and the Woman," in *The Map of Love* (1939). Its inclusion in anthologies marks it as a representative short story of the period. Interesting on its own, and in the context of other modernist works, it is also valuable for the conceptual elements which reveal Thomas's attitude to his own work, to language, and to the relationship of art and the artist to reality. The hero of the story is a questor/writer named Marlais, and the story is clearly about writing, most obvious in a self-conscious image of a hand holding a pencil: "He raised his pencil so that its shadow fell, a tower of wood and lead, on the clean paper" (43). The difficulties which Marlais encounters offer a number of entrances into the workings of his mind, which is as complex as the story itself.

"The Orchards" begins with Marlais's apocalyptic dream of burning apple orchards that are extinguished by a wind. This was a dream "that ended as it began: with the flesh-and-blood ghost hand of a woman pointing to the trees." The circular nature of this dream sets the stage for a number of repetitions to follow. The woman of the dream, like many of Thomas's symbolic figures, has a dual nature: she is a "scarecrow lover" who is both real and unreal, both "flesh" and "ghost"; in fact, she is one of two scarecrow lovers, neither of whose symbolic functions is simple. Marlais has some awareness of the mythic potential of his dream. It is a dream that is repeated, and it attains the level of a "story" that he tells himself. He also places his dream/ story among the ancient myths of his heritage (albeit a Thomasian personalized Welsh heritage), juxtaposing it to "the stories of the reverend madmen in the Black Book of Llareggub."

After apparently waking from this dream, Marlais looks out of his top-storey window onto a landscape of roofs that very much resembles the view from the Thomas home on Cwmdonkin Drive, Swansea. Shutting out this outside world, Marlais sits down to write a story: "He sharpened his pencil and shut the sky out, shook back his untidy hair, arranged the papers of a devilish story on his desk, and broke the pencil-point with a too-hard scribble of 'sea' and 'fire' on a clean page" (42). While he is trying to write this story, images from his dream and other stories inflict themselves upon him and he, or more precisely the story, ends up defeated: "The story was dead from the devil up; there was a white-hot tree with apples where a frozen tower with owls should have rocked in a wind from Antarctica; there were naked girls, with nipples like berries, on the sand in the sun, where a cold and unholy woman should be wailing by the Kara sea or the Sea of Azov. The morning was against him." The external, or alternative inner, world that he had tried to shut out impinges on his imagination, and the cloudless summer sky defeats his desired vision of gloom. Watching himself grapple with his words, as things, he is aware that he is losing: "He struggled with his words like a man with the sun, and the sun stood victoriously at high noon over the dead story." The verbal structure that he attempts to impose on his dream-vision interacts with the external world, transforming even that into a linguistic entity. He comes to the conclusion that "the word is too much with us."

Dismayed at the predominance of images over reality in the workings of his mind, he admits defeat; and, since he cannot shut out the images of the external world, enters into it. Imagining even himself as "an image of man," he steps out through the window onto the roof, into what seems to be another world, like the one in his room, created out of words. Moving from his dream to his writing to the rooftop landscape, he is simply moving from one fiction to another. Marlais becomes a questor, and self-consciously sees himself as a "legendary walker" on a grand mission, searching for "the last answer." Yet his heroic stance is undercut as he is mocked by various figures on the rooftops, creations of his own imagination. After this abortive beginning his actions are repeated, and for a second time he steps out of the open window without apparently having returned to the room. This time he emerges into the dream that opened the story: "The woman pointed to the hundred orchards and the black birds who flocked around the sister, but a wind put the trees out and he woke again. This was the intolerable, second waking out of a life too beautiful to break, but the dream was broken." The hint that Marlais awakes from a dream does not clarify how much of his previous experience was in fact a dream, problematizing the usual dream-waking distinction.[1] Following this second waking, Marlais takes what appears, at first at least, to be a real walk, telling those he meets along the way that he is walking to the sea. Seeing himself self-consciously now as "the poet," he is again taken over by his imagination, and the legendary walker pursues his quest over a mythic landscape that is shaped and transformed by his mind. He ends his journey not at the sea, but in the orchards of his dream, having tea with his scarecrow lover. He watches as the trees burst into flame, and the story ends the way the dream does, "as it began." Like the rest of the tale, the end does not clarify whether Marlais's adventure is dream, vision, or the story that he attempted to write. At the end we are only told cryptically that "this he had dreamed": "a dream that was no dream," that "was a dream no longer."

In a letter to his publisher regarding the publication of *The Map of Love*, Thomas describes "The Orchards" and similar stories grouped with it as "short imaginative stories or fables" (*CL* 357). Like many of his contemporaries, Thomas opted for a subjective form that broke with the tenets of realism; the fantastic possibilities of the fable allowed for the free play of images that Thomas seemed naturally inclined toward. The resurrection of the fable was not unique to Thomas: it was in fact a form advocated by Eugene Jolas in *transition*, along with the new fantastic forms like anamyth and psychograph, and was employed by many of *transition's* contributors, since it was a narrative form that had much in common with their manifesto. The fable is an imaginative work that bears its resemblance to reality on a symbolic rather than representational level, often employing types rather than individualistic characters to reveal universal truths. Usually, as with those of Aesop, fables are concluded with a moral tag, often in the form of an epigram; however, Thomas, like other modern fabulists, omits the express moral, leaving it up to the reader to determine the significance of the symbols. One consequence of the lack of a moral is that closure disappears from the fable when there is nothing that seems to sum it up. For interpretation, then, the reader has to plunge back into the tale. The circularity of the story reflects the interpretive act of the reader. What makes this particular fable even more interesting is the way in which Thomas surpasses the work of his contemporaries, employing what now may be seen as a postmodernist tendency to go beyond a subjective view of reality, and to view reality itself as constructed in and through language. Thomas liked to say that he was a poet who lived "inside language"; the plot of "The Orchards" is a reflection of the writer's sense of his own situation among words. In this story the word literally shapes the world; Marlais's world is a text over which he does not have complete control.

Marlais dreams about himself, and then perpetuates the fictionality of the dream by attempting to write about it, to tell stories about himself. In one work he creates not one but multiple fictions, one of which is himself. In a world that is constantly shifting, Marlais is on a circular quest that remains unfulfilled. The reader cannot clearly delineate where the dream ends and the story begins, or where the dream world and the waking world separate, for the strategy of moving from dream to dream eliminates such dualities. At bottom, Thomas's fable registers his awareness of his inability to attach set signifieds to signifiers; the text remains indeterminate for the reader because it is so for the writer. The converging multiple fictions foreground the instability of language and the world.

"The Orchards" resonates in some ways with many of Thomas's letters, in which he demonstrates an acute awareness of the strengths and weaknesses of his own work. This story also contains many elements characteristic of the poems: images conflict and merge in a multiple space in which process and the notion of destructive creation are central. It focuses on the inner world of the self, what Thomas called his "bone-bound island." Yet the short-story form allows Thomas a level of commentary additional to those of the poems. The autobiographical model allows him to be both author and subject at the same time, and, as author, he allows himself a critical distance from which he can comment on and even mock the subject's work and sense of importance.

The protagonist of "The Orchards" is a parody of the modernist alienated artist who believes that his artistic calling somehow places him above the ordinary world. Marlais, the mythic folk-man, has aspirations akin to those of Joyce's self-exiled Stephen Dedalus, the model of a modernist author. However, Marlais's attempts to withdraw are undermined. Marlais cannot escape because of the extent of his reliance, as a poet, on language: for Marlais, there is no ordinary world other than that created by language. This places him in what now may be seen as a typically postmodern, rather than modern, dilemma, especially when he attempts to write about himself – for even his own life is created by language, and there is no assurance of any stable referent against which he can measure himself. His life seems to be merely a story among countless other stories; furthermore, it is a story that somehow evades structuration. By employing autobiography, by attempting to write about himself, Marlais, mirroring Thomas, is trying to impose a retrospective organization on experience that is continually defeated by the processes and changes which characterize that experience. Further, the very emphasis on the writer writing places the text in a type of continuous present tense whose essence is transformation. When the outside world and the emerging story intersect, Thomas suddenly shifts from the third-person past tense to the present imperative, co-opting the reader into the process as well: "he sharpened his pencil ... Put a two-colored ring of two women's hair round the blue world, white and coal-black against the summer-coloured boundaries of sky and grass, four-breasted stems at the poles of the summer sea-ends, eyes in the sea-shell, two fruit-trees out of a coal-hill: poor Marlais's morning, turning to evening, spins before you. Under the eyelids, where the inward night drove backwards, through the skull's base, into the wide, first world on the far-away eye, two love-trees smouldered like sisters. Have an orchard sprout in the night, an enchanted woman with a spine like a railing burn her hand in the leaves, man-on-fire a mile from a sea have a wind put out your heart: Marlais's death in life in the circular going down of the day that had taken no time blows again in the wind for you" (43). Thomas's, and Marlais's, writing draws attention to itself as writing. This paragraph reminds the reader that the story is something created, and furthermore, arbitrarily so. Character and plot can be inserted like interchangeable ingredients, and the final product materializes autonomously for the creator: woman + orchard = "Marlais's death in life." The curious point of view of this passage complicates matters even further, for the reader is implicated in the act of creation. Not only are we compelled to witness the turbulence of the writer's mind working itself out in visible verbal performance, but we are also invited to be co-creators. The use of the imperative and the address to the second person are ambiguously directed. In one sense we can read this passage as if it were Marlais directing himself in his writing. But Marlais is referred to in the third person, causing a doubling effect in which we see him as both the writer and a separate character he is writing about. At the same time, the third-person references to Marlais complicate the identification of the second person: it is possible that "you" is the reader. In this case we are both audience – "Marlais's morning, turning to evening, spins before you" – and the creator of the scene to be witnessed, for we are the ones being told to put the images together. Just as Marlais/Thomas is simultaneously inside and outside of the text, being both the author and subject of the autobiographical study, we as readers find ourselves in a dual relationship to it. Indeed, such a strategy of reader involvement makes the story equally about readership and about writing.

What Thomas, Marlais, and perhaps even we are creating in this sequence is, of course, a story. This story, because of its circular nature, is one that can be repeatedly read. It can also be repeatedly created, as evidenced by the pattern Marlais finds himself in. Yet because the creation of the story is both arbitrary and subject to transformational forces, what we are reading is not the final version of the story. The evolving continuous present produces an unstable and eternally unfinished world inside the text that Marlais is unable to leave. Thomas said in a letter to Vernon Watkins that a poem, in its "forming phases ... is not ... itself until the poet has left it" (CL 383). In this case, it is the unfinished written work that is in control, holding the writer captive.

Marlais's predicament is a manifestation of a paradox that many twentieth-century writers find themselves facing: in order to write in any communicable form they must employ a language which by its very nature limits and even controls their formulations. Thomas takes the writer's situation to its logical (and perhaps absurd) extreme. As in some of his poems, language is seen as a living thing. In "The Orchards" Marlais mock-heroically confronts language as an enemy, in an Olympian battle that dwindles into a parody of a Western: "He struggled with his words like a man with the sun, and the sun stood victoriously at high noon over the dead story."[2] Believing himself unable to write, Thomas satirizes his own dilemma and creates a work about the inability to create. As in the poems "A Refusal to Mourn" and "On no work of words," in which Thomas "take[s] to task [his] poverty and craft," Thomas does exactly what he says he cannot do. "The Orchards," of course, is clearly a work of metafiction – for a creation such as this, arising out of self-parody, becomes fiction about itself rather than about objective reality. Being a representation of representations, it exploits the labyrinth of life and art in which Marlais/Thomas is trapped. Rather than despairing about the limits of fictive language, Thomas focuses on the power of story-telling to create worlds. Where Thomas differs from many of his contemporaries is in his ability to turn language against itself in this way. Rather than Beckett's exhausted world in which verbal play leads to nihilism, Thomas creates a more positive play enabling limitless occasions for liberating parody and subversion.

Thomas's letters clearly illustrate his talent for self-subversion. The letters offer numerous examples of his awareness of potential defects in his work; they also reveal his crafty ability to turn such problems to his advantage. In a letter to Trevor Hughes, Thomas abdicates responsibility for his creative imagination, saying with perhaps false modesty that "such is the horribly argumentative, contradictory nature of my mind. Give me a sheet of paper and I can't help filling it in. The result – more often than not – is good and bad, serious and comic, sincere & insincere, lucid or nonsensical by the turns of my whirligig mentality, started from the wrong end, a mentality that ran before it walked, & perhaps will never walk, that wanted to fly before it had the right to even think of wings" (CL 12). Thomas is able to maintain an ironic distance from his work while at the same time firmly believing in its integrity. An even more telling self-awareness is revealed in a letter to Edith Sitwell, in which he expresses the fear that his poems "caricature themselves" (CL 258). We cannot be sure whether Thomas truly believed this, or whether this is simply a conscious play at humility to deflect criticism before it is applied. Many of Thomas's poems do have a consistency in their style and imagery that might merit such criticism. However, the fact that Thomas was able, when the spirit arose, deliberately to caricature his own work suggests a subversive sense of humour lurking dangerously close to the serious voice. We can see this clearly in Thomas's letters to Pamela Hansford Johnson, which are both playful and revealing. Taking such varied forms as parodic poems, stories, autobiography, plays, and diaries, they are also serious commentaries on Thomas's views about literature and language. Above all they show that from a very early date Thomas was intensely aware of the characteristics of his work. Responding to a review by Victor Neuberg, Thomas defends himself through self-parody:

... I write in the only way I can write, & my warped, crabbed & cabinned stuff is not the result of theorizing but of pure incapability to express my needless tortuities in any other way. Vicky's article was nonsense. If you see him, tell him I am not modest, not experimental, do not write of the Present, and have very little command of rhythm ... tell him too, that I don't know anything about life-rhythm. Tell him that I write of worms and corruption, because I like worms and corruption. Tell him I believe in the fundamental wickedness and worthlessness of man, & in the rot in life. Tell him I am all for cancers. And tell him, too, that I loathe poetry. I prefer to be an anatomist or the keeper of a morgue any day. Tell him I live exclusively on toenails and tumours. I sleep in a coffin too, and a wormy shroud is my summer suit.

"I dreamed the genesis of mildew John / Who struggled from his spiders in the grave" is the opening of my new poem. So there. (CL 134)

This of course is a parody, or perhaps even an early version, of his poem "I dreamed my genesis."

In another letter to Johnson, Thomas imposes a narrative element on an insignificant event, turning his life into a story. Called "A Touching Experience," this story satirizes, among other things, his flair for the melodramatic and his sense of self-importance:

After my last letter to you, written from the despondency of a Welsh hill cottage, I ran out of cigarettes and walked three miles to the nearest village, Llanstephan, to buy some. It was a fool of a night. The clouds were ass's ears. The moon was ploughing up the Towy river as if it expected it to yield a crop of stars. And the stars themselves: – hundreds of bright-eyed urchins nudging each other over a celestial joke. It is a long road to Llanstephan. ... I found the madness of the night to be a false madness, and the vast horseplay of the sky to be a vaster symbol. It was as if the night were crying crying out the terrible explanation of itself. On all sides of me, under my feet, above my head, the symbols moved, all waiting in vain to be translated. The trees that night were like prophet's fingers. What had been a fool in the sky was the wisest cloud of all – a huge, musical ghost thumping out one, coded tune. It was a sage of a night, and made me forgive even my own foolishness. There was, of course, no cigarette machine in Llanstephan. (CL 43–4)

In many of Thomas's poems, such as "In the beginning" and the "Altarwise by Owl-light" sonnets, as well as many of the short stories like "The Mouse and the Woman," the concept of the Logos is central – the word is seen as a mystic signature stamped upon the world; the world is a system of signs to be deciphered, "translated." Yet in Thomas's bathetic rendition of his journey to Llanstephan, as in Marlais's experience in "The Orchards," the questor either misreads or is unable to read the hieroglyphic world, and is even chastised by it, ending up the butt of a celestial joke. Marlais, a potential Ulysses, heads out on a journey to the "wine-coloured sea," but his heroic mission is reduced to a domestic scene: rather than to sea, he ends up going to tea. Because of the interdependent relationship between words and the world, the linguistic transformation inherent in the rhyme transforms Marlais's adventure, and he is deflected from his goal, being once again at the mercy of his own images.

Thomas's stories and poems are full of hints that there are mysteries to be unravelled. His questing heroes inhabit romantic landscapes where portents of hidden forces abound. Often there is a grail-like quest for revelations of the meaning of life. Marlais hears prophetic voices in the landscape, and tries to read the world and to decipher his cryptic dream: "High above the hum of the houses, far from the sky and the frozen fence, he questioned each shadow; man among ghosts, and ghost in clover, he moved for the last answer." The reader, like Marlais, gropes to unravel the dense elliptical and shifting images of the text, searching for meaning. Thomas's description of such stories as "fables" teases the reader with the belief that there may be a moral hidden somewhere. However, Marlais's search is never satisfied, for his adventures are transformed before any conclusions can be made; as with Marlais, the reader's task of decoding is next to impossible. There is in fact no "last answer."

An interesting clue may be found in the original title of this story, "Anagram." As he did with his poems, Thomas omitted this title because it provided too easy a key to interpretation for the reader. In the Red Notebook, "Anagram" is also given the alternate title "Mr. Tritas on the roofs." Tritas, an anagram of "artist," is removed from later versions of the story to be replaced by Marlais. Anagrams, words or phrases composed of the transposed letters of known words, are linguistic puzzles created sometimes simply to display the writer's ingenuity, and sometimes to veil messages. In a general sense, this title is apt because transformation is central to the story. More specifically, however, Thomas uses the anagram to derail the reader's search for meaning. The most prominent anagram in "The Orchards" is the name "Llareggub," a favorite word of Thomas's that appears on numerous occasions throughout his career, from the early stories "The Burning Baby" (September 1934) and "The Holy Six" to the developing versions of *Under Milk Wood* (1944–54). Thomas's meaning is not lost to anyone familiar with this anagram: when we try to unravel the mysteries of the text/world, what we get is "buggerall."

Nevertheless, Marlais represents the questor-poet who continues in spite of imminent failure. In fact, there may even be some consolation in the fact that he reaches no conclusion, for each repetition and new beginning allows his own continuation, and the possibility of endless creation. As with Thomas's poems, the life-force works itself out through processes of "destructive creation, creative destruction." So too with language, for the breaking down of images leaves the material out of which new creations may be built. When Thomas says in a letter to Vernon Watkins that "I build a flying tower, and I pull it down" (CL 278), he does so happily. Images of towers abound in Thomas's work, and they are most often metaphors for poems, such as when he says that he is "shut in a tower of words" ("Especially when the October wind").[3] The tower, in its order and solidarity, once created, becomes something static that must be submitted to the forces of change – and hence destruction. In "The Orchards," the tower metaphor appears as Marlais is caught at the moment when creation and destruction converge: "The word is too much with us. He raised his pencil so that its shadow fell, a tower of wood and lead, on the clean paper; he fingered the pencil tower, the half-moon of his thumb-nail rising and setting behind the leaden spire. The tower fell, down fell the city of words, the walls of a poem, the symmetrical letters. He marked the disintegration of the ciphers as the light failed, the sun drove down into a foreign morning, and the word of the sea rolled over the sun. 'Image, all image,' he cried to the fallen tower as the night came on. 'Whose harp is the sea? Whose burning candle is the sun?' An image of man, he rose to his feet and drew the curtains open" (43). For any vision, poem, or even person to exist, there must be some outline necessitating physical restraint, and an acceptance of limits. Thomas is always acutely aware of the opposition in writing between language as structure and as "flow"; of the dual tendencies inherent in the urge to "craft" a poem while allowing it to be like "a stream that is flowing all ways" (CL 282).[4] He rejects the forms of language employed by his literary ancestors, the use of which would be severely constraining. But having to accept the necessity of form, he breaks down the old forms to create new ones of his own. Marlais struggles with a language which is perpetually solidifying into image, and as he creates, he has to live within the confines of his own story. He creates a "city of words" on the page which he as writer is outside and above, one he can then watch disintegrate. Yet when he leaves pencil and paper to go out of the open window, he encounters another lexical city: "Below him, in a world of words, men on their errands moved to no purpose but the escape of time." It is into this world that Marlais must journey. Marlais illustrates Thomas's awareness that the writer's need to assert his own patterning powers is always fraught with the possibility of his being imprisoned in his own system. For this reason, Marlais witnesses the destruction of his linguistic towers. Yet with each repetition of his vision there is another creation of a tower, and a new version of story or poem.

Marlais walks through his "ancestral valley" leaving behind him the dead forms of his inheritance. Rather than the mythic Jarvis Hills, this is now the "Whippet valley," both a metaphoric landscape and a wasteland like industrial South Wales: "the trees, forever twisted between smoke and slag, tore at the sky and the black ground. The dead boughs prayed that the roots might shoulder up the soil, leaving a dozen channels empty for the leaves and the spirit of the cracking wood, a hole in the valley for the mole-handed sap, a long grave for the last spring's skeleton that once had leapt, when the blunt and forked hills were sharp and straight, through the once-green land. But Whippet's trees were the long dead of the stacked south of the country; who had vanished under the hacked land pointed, thumb-to-hill, these black leaf-nailed and warning fingers. Death in Wales had twisted the Welsh dead into those valley cripples" (45). Marlais, who cannot but see the world in terms of metaphor, imagines a landscape shaped in images of disease and death: "Marlais passed out of the tubercular valley on to a waste mountain, through a seedy wood to a shagged field" (46). Once again his experience is transposed onto the level of myth, and he is guided by the disembodied voices of travellers, or rather the inverted "travellers of voices," the "dusty journeymen," his path leading him to "a hill's v balancing on the grave that proceeds to Eden" (46). The vision of the orchard on fire becomes a simultaneous Genesis, Fall, Crucifixion, Apocalypse, and Resurrection, a synchrony that outfoxes time: "Winds on fire, through vault and coffin and fossil we'll blow a manful of dust into the garden. Where the serpent sets the tree alight, and the apple falls like a spark out of its skin, a tree leaps up; a scarecrow shines on the cross-boughs, and, by one in the sun, the new trees arise making an orchard round the crucifix." Marlais enters into the heritage of biblical stories contained in this landscape: "He was a young man no longer but a legendary walker, a folk-man walking, with a cricket for a heart; he walked by Aberbabel's chapel, cut through the graveyard over the unstill headstones, spied a red-cheeked man in a nightshirt two foot above ground." While the dead are being resurrected around him, the world continues to transform, breaking apart and coalescing. The name "Aberbabel" reminds the reader of yet another tower, one which significantly represents fragmentation and multiple voices. Although a symbol of the fallen world, like the serpent in the garden, the tower of Babel here may be representative of a "fortunate fall," not only because of Thomas's view of positive destruction but because multiple voices are superior to one authoritative voice that can impose an enslaving system. The prefix "Aber" is a Welsh word meaning "at the mouth of (the river)" – the pun on the word "mouth" again reminds us of voices, and the voices of Babel can create an endless number of unique poems and stories. "Aberbabel" is itself onomatopoeic, and represents a crossing of "natural" language (as in "babbling brook"); like the voices of the Jarvis Hills, a voice associated with place and the language it speaks are inseparable from the natural world. Marlais does not stop on his journey through this biblical landscape, because it too is only one of many fictional worlds. Having become a legend, he becomes a part of the folk tradition that encompasses all sorts of stories.

After passing through the valley of Aberbabel, Marlais encounters another tower, and another story, when he suddenly finds "to his both sides the unbroken walls, taller than the beanstalks that married a story on the roof of the world." Later the trees of the orchard also become "towers" in the story's final repetition of the apocalyptic vision: "lame like Pisa, the night leaned on the west walls; no trumpet shall knock the Welsh walls down before the last crack of music" (48). The vision becomes a metaphor for many stories conflated, from the story of Jericho to the folk-tale of "Jack the Giant-Killer."

The repetition of the tower image suggests further parallels, in tone as well as substance: among all the legendary travellers whose company Marlais joins, perhaps the most extended comparison may be made to the hero of Browning's "Childe Roland to the Dark Tower Came." Both works combine elements of surrealism with myths of the quest. Their disillusioned heroes search through a wasted world, and neither the meaning of their search nor its goal is made clear. Browning claimed that his poem came to him "as a kind of a dream," and indeed it has the same sort of elusive dream-logic that Thomas foregrounds in his story. Browning's contemporaries tried to interpret the poem as a moral allegory, although Browning claimed that he had no allegorical intention when he set his dream into a poem. The ambiguity of "Childe Roland" raises more questions than it answers, and it leaves the poem open to any number of interpretations, prompting Browning to say of it that every reader can be his own allegorist (Whiting 261). This is the same task that Thomas sets for his reader, not only in "The Orchards" but in a good number of his poems as well. More specifically, however, Marlais and Childe Roland represent the same literary type: an as yet unproven adventurer setting out after something that eludes him, yet something he must continue to seek. They may both be seen as metaphors for the artist who paradoxically reaches his goal in spite of his apparent inability to do so.

Parallels may also be seen in the details of the two works. Roland is a "Childe" because he is an unproven knight; Marlais is mocked by the stone boy and the gossips on the roof for being a virgin. "The Orchards" begins with a vision of a scarecrow pointing the way for Marlais to follow, as "Childe Roland" begins with the guidance of the "hoary cripple." Childe Roland's inner vision always turns dark; journeying along a "darkening path," as Marlais does, he imagines all sorts of horrors, couching the landscape in metaphors of sickness, and even imagining a spiteful world rising up against him. Roland concludes that "'tis the last judgement's fire must cure this place." Marlais's vision of the orchards on fire briefly resembles the "last judgement's fire," although it is not a cure. Roland, like Marlais, is subjected to transformations around him that leave him "just as far as ever from the end." The landscape surrealistically changes, and the plain gives way to mountains which stop his progress. Roland does not recognize the place he has been searching for when he comes upon it, despite a "life spent training for the sight." At this point there is a curious interjection in Roland's monologue: "solve it, you!" – and it is ambiguous whether Roland or the reader is being addressed. As with the imperative directions in Thomas's address, it may in fact be both Roland and the reader who are challenged to make sense of an unfathomable situation. At the culmination of Roland's adventure "one moment knelled the woe of years," just as, for Marlais, time, and all previously created stories, conflate. Like the "travellers of voices" in "The Orchards," Roland hears the "names in my ears / of all the lost adventurers my peers"; seeing his predecessors "ranged along the hillsides," he attains the goal of his quest as he joins the band of the "lost." Blowing on his horn "Childe Roland to the Dark Tower Came," he becomes to his predecessors who witness the moment "a living frame for one more picture." Coming "very near the end of the indescribable journey," Marlais is "a folkman no longer but Marlais the poet walking, over the brink into ruin, up the side of doom," and he becomes "a man-in-a-picture Marlais." His scarecrow lover pours tea for him at "the end to the untold adventures," as Marlais too realizes that other questors had gone before him to the same fate: "Her many lover's cups were empty on the flat stone." He too joins his peers, "all the lost adventurers."[5]

Yet the similarities between the two works are perhaps not as significant as the differences. Whereas Roland is "a living *frame* for one more picture," Marlais is the "man *in* the picture." This distinction illustrates a difference in the characters' views of themselves in relation to their adventures, as well as a difference between Browning's and Thomas's relationships to their texts. "Childe Roland" is widely regarded as an ironic comment on the traditional role of the hero and on the impossibility of finding meaning in modern heroic action. But the poem may also offer commentary on Browning's conception of the role of the artist. Like many of Browning's poems, "Childe Roland" is considered a remarkably modern work, resembling those of W.H. Auden in its objectivity, at least as Browning used the term. Browning objected to what he felt was an oversimplified view of the morality of art in the Victorian sensibility; in poems such as "Childe Roland" he developed an objective form of art that simply presents without moralizing and that reveals individual rather than universal mores. Browning calls the artist who takes an objectifying approach to ethical problems the "fashioner" and he says that "the thing fashioned, his poetry, will of necessity be substantive, projected from himself and distinct."[6] For the objective poet, the work speaks for itself: "The man passes, the work remains." Browning's use of the dramatic monologue enables him to disappear from the work, his personae presenting thoughts and feelings that we cannot specifically trace back to Browning's own. The dramatic monologue is antithetical to explicit autobiography; through its masks the ego of the creator is all but extinguished. This disappearance of the artist might seem to be analogous to the quest that Roland undertakes, for he faces possible extinction with the attainment of his goal. Yet Roland expresses a wish to be "fit" enough to join the band of "failures": "that just to fail as they seemed best, / And all the doubt was now – should I be fit?" Although his identity is snuffed out, like the ego of the objective artist, he leaves behind him a "picture" (vision, work of art) frozen in time like the eternal stories of his questing peers. If heroic action is merely part of a mythic past, Roland attains an odd sort of "success" by joining his predecessors in myth.

71 Solipsistic Adam

Marlais, in contrast, is a purely subjective artist who cannot separate himself from his art. Rather than being a frame outside of the picture, he is within the picture; likewise the mask of the protagonist which Browning utilizes is for Thomas made transparent, and we see the primary artist Thomas in the figure of Marlais. In Marlais's case the work does not speak for itself. In fact, as autobiography the work cannot exist without the author who is – continually – creating it while living it. While Marlais's own identity or even existence is brought into question, being an image he does not enter into a void when he arrives at the heart of his quest; instead, he enters into a work of art, and his success is coterminous not with death but with continuation. Marlais's quest, unlike Roland's, does not conclude, and therefore the work of art from which he is inseparable resists closure, ensuring his own continued existence. He becomes a part of his own dream, and he interacts with his creations: "This he had dreamed before the blossom's burning and the putting-out, before the rising and the salt swinging-in, was a dream no longer near these orchards. He kissed the two secret sisters, and a scarecrow kissed him back. He heard the birds fly down on to his lovers' shoulders. He saw the fork-tree breast, the barbed eye, and the dry, twig hand" (48). The tone is ominous as Marlais seems to wake up to discover that his lovers are lifeless scarecrows. But he does not wake up from the dream; he merely enters into it. Marlais and Thomas live what Roland and Browning merely present. Marlais explores and in part defines a postmodernist conception of the artist and his text, as Roland does for modernist conceptions. Thomas continues in the Victorian-Modern tradition which depicts the artist alienated from society, but he goes further: the artist does not also have to be alienated from art, and borders can be crossed.

"PROLOGUE TO AN ADVENTURE"

The protagonist of the short story "Prologue to an Adventure," and the environment in which he moves, bear many similarities to Marlais and his dream/text. The unnamed first-person narrator is on an ambiguous quest through the "wilderness" of a strange city, which is a shifting symbolic landscape. The narrator may in fact actually be Marlais himself, describing his walk through the City of Words in "The Orchards." The story begins with what are actually three beginnings, a phrase being repeated with variations as if it were a writer's attempts to begin a story: "As I walked through the wilderness of this world, as I walked through the wilderness, as I walked through the city with the loud electric faces and the crowded petrols of the wind dazzling and drowning me that winter night before the West died, I remembered the winds of the high, white world that bore me and the faces of the noiseless million in the busyhood of heaven staring on the afterbirth" (104). The wandering protagonist resembles Thomas's descriptions of himself in his brief early career as a newspaperman, aimlessly prowling about and loafing in pubs looking for sordid stories: "the news of the world is no world's news, the gossips of heaven and the fallen rumours are enough and too much for a shadow that casts no shadow I said to the blind beggars and the paper boys who shouted in the rain" (104). The narrator is not alone, as Marlais was, but is accompanied by the "sinister" Daniel Dom, who, like the narrator, is vaguely mythic, at least in his own self-conception. The two characters are "the dreamer and the pilgrim" (107), and they are contrasted to the rest of the city's mundane inhabitants, who resemble the men rushing to escape time in "The Orchards": "They who were hurrying by me on the narrow errands of the world, time bound to their wrists or blinded in their pockets, who consulted the time strapped to a holy tower, and dodged between bonnets and wheels, heard in my fellow's footsteps the timeless accents of another walking" (104). The timelessness of Daniel Dom contrasted to the men enslaved by time is important, for at the end of the story Daniel and the narrator are left alone to watch aloofly as the "holy tower," the men, and everything else in the city in time are destroyed.

Once again, as in "The Orchards," the tower may be analogous to a written creation. This wilderness is a world of images and representations: "No, not for nothing did the packed thoroughfares confront me at each cross and pavement's turning with these figures in the shapes of sounds, the lamp-chalked silhouettes and the walking frames of dreams, out of a darker allegory than the fiction of the earth could turn in twelve suns' time" (105). Like Marlais, the narrator himself is described as if he too were an image. He is not quite real, a reflection or transparency, a "shadow that casts no shadow," but he is at the same time a creator, and a creation dependent upon the perception of others: "they who nudged me through the literate light of the city, shouldered and elbowed me, catching my trilby with the spokes of their umbrellas, who offered me matches and music, made me out of their men's eyes into a manshape walking" (104). His companion Daniel, "he who played the sorcerer," is described as "a symbol in the story of man's journey through the symboled city" (106).

All, it seems, is fiction, yet the unreality of it all is not analogous to meaninglessness: "there was more than man's meaning ... to the dead man, smiling through his bandages, who laid hand on my sleeve, saying in no man's voice, There is more than man's meaning in a stuffed man talking ..." (105). The repetition is of the quality of two mirrors reflecting each other in infinite regress. The self-reflecting echo in this statement offers the possibility of meaning without offering the meaning itself. All that we are told of the meaning is that it is "ungodly." Once again Thomas seems to set the reader on an ambiguous quest resembling Roland's to find it. Because it is "ungodly" we might suppose that we should not look to the transcendent – for the "holy" tower is among those that are destroyed at the end of the story. Yet at the same time Thomas does not leave us merely with a void, and there is the suggestion of meaning, however elusive, in the decreative act, for the destruction of the tower is less a negation than a reduction of fixed materials to raw ones.

Just as the symbols seem to coalesce, the reader is suddenly thrown off guard by an oracle above a mirror that interjects with the non sequitur, "What is the colour of the narrator's blood?" The "narrator" is looking in the mirror, so we might suppose that he is asking himself this question about himself, in what may be a parody of a literary discussion. The question resembles a riddle, such as "What is the colour of the bear?", which ends a convoluted story that has nothing to do with a bear – a question that has less to do with logic than with throwing the subject off track. The focus is returned to the world of man, to the narrator himself, rather than to a transcendent truth outside of himself after which he may be striving. The reflection of the oracular mirror is analogous to the self-perception of Thomas, who in "Prologue" sees himself as "the narrator of echoes moving in man's time" (104). The temporal world is doubly emphasized in "man's time" and in the "echoes" which are both repetitive and fleeting. We also see in this characterization a writer whose primary function, as a "narrator of echoes," is to rework other voices, to retell existing stories (including his own): "Walking into the Deadly Virtue, we heard our names announced through the loudspeaker trumpet of the wooden image over the central mirror, and, staring in the glass as the oracle continued, we saw two distorted faces grinning through the smoke. Make way, said the loudspeaker, for Daniel, ace of Destruction, old Dom the toper of Doom's kitchen, and for the alderman of ghosts. Is the translator of man's manuscript, his walking chapters, said the trumpet-faced, a member of my Deadly Virtue?"(107).[7]

As the "translator of man's manuscript" the writer-narrator performs a number of tasks: he is at once a reader, a writer, and a transformer of existing stories, most specifically the living story of the history or fictions of man, his "walking chapters." The "translator" is the interpreter of signs and the conveyor of ideas from one language or art form to another; he retransmits messages in another voice. For the narrator, the "symboled city" is to be read and translated, rendered into another story. Yet the writer must yield to the nature of symbols not as something static and universal, but as signs that are forever shifting and pointing in new directions. The symbols, like the riddle of the oracle, beg to be decoded; yet at the same time any final meaning is elusive. As with the landscape in "The Orchards," "the symbols of the city writhed before [him]" (106). Man himself, like the world, is also a shifting symbol, the "shadow that casts no shadow," perpetually a sign of "something else" which is in turn a sign of yet another something. With this endless deferral, Thomas further complicates the representational nature of signs by bringing all symbols back to their linguistic function: "We are all metaphors of the sound of shape of the shape of sound, break us we take another shape"(106).

The "sound of shape" and the "shape of sound" are apt descriptions of poetry, and are recurrent images in Thomas's work, as in the "Altarwise" sonnet VII, where "Time tracks the sound of shape on man and cloud" (CP 61). He frequently crosses phonic and graphic divisions, revelling in synaesthetic images that create linguistic cruxes. Creation occurs in the Saussurian gap between the sign and the signified, the poem's "witnesses" of the crossings between form and meaning, as in "When all my five and country senses" (CP 70) where the heart "sees," eyes "break," and ears "watch." Thomas characterizes his view of language, poetry, and the world as subject to the shaping impulses that war against destruction. Language, signs, poems, and myths can all be broken down and rebuilt into new forms: "break us we take another shape." "We" are also included in this creative destruction. The destruction of the symboled city leaves man – or the self – as the least elusive of ephemeral signs, and the view in the mirror is the easiest read and has the richest possibility for reshaping.

The man-in-the-mirror, like Marlais's man-in-the-picture, is the living, transforming subject. The autobiographical dualism of the character/author Marlais becomes apparent in the narrator and his companion in "Prologue to an Adventure": "We were forever climbing the steps of a sea-tower, crying aloud from the turret that we might warn us, as we clambered, of the rusty rack and the spiked maiden in the turret corners" (106). The instruments of torture, no less than the tower itself, might remind us again of "Childe Roland to the Dark Tower Came." If, as in previously mentioned works, the sea-tower can be equated with art, Daniel Dom and the narrator, like Marlais, are simultaneously inside and outside it – for their identities are split, being both on top of the tower and calling down warning to their same selves below, still climbing.

Daniel Dom, the "ace of destruction," both laments the end of the world and waits impatiently for it, crying, "how long, how long, lord of the hail, shall my city rock on, and the seven deadly seas wait tidelessly for the moon, the bitter end the last tide-spinning of the full circle" (106).[8] Daniel becomes a story-teller of the past and a prophet of future destruction at the same time: "It was then, in the tangled hours of a new morning, surrounded by the dead faces of the drinkers, the wail of lost voices, and the words of the one electric image, that Daniel, hair-on-end, lamented first to me of the death on the city and the lost hero of the heart" (107). The telling of the story becomes concurrent with its happening, in an apocalyptic vision similar to that in "The Orchards": "Now a wind sprang through the room from the dead street; from the racked tower where two men lay in chains and a hole broke in the wall, we heard our own cries travel through the fumes of brandy and the loudspeaker's music; we pawed, in our tower agony, at the club shapes dancing, at the black girls tattooed from shoulder to nipple with a white dancing shape, frocked with snail-headed rushes and capped like antlers. But they slipped from us into the rubber corners where their black lovers waited invisibly; and the music grew louder until the tower cry was lost among it ..."(108). Although initially within the "tower agony," Daniel and the narrator are suddenly outside of the destruction. Like Marlais, they are both in the city and above it. Looking out of the window they see the city beneath them, and they watch as it is destroyed by a flood, or at least a surrealistic vision of one:

Beneath him lay the city sleeping, curled in its streets and houses, lamped by its own red-waxed and iron stars, with a built moon above it, and the spires crossed over the bed. I stared down, rocking at his side, on to the unsmoking roofs and the burned-out candles. Destruction slept. Slowly the room behind us flowed, like four waters, down the seven gutters of the city into a black sea. A wave, catching the live loudspeaker in its mouth, sucked up the wood and music; for the last time a mountainous wave circled the drinkers and dragged them down, out of the world of light, to a crawling sea-bed; we saw a wave jumping and the last bright eyes go under, the last raw head, cut like straw, fall crying through the destroying water. Daniel and I stood alone in the city. The sea of destruction lapped around our feet. We saw the starfall that broke the night up. The last light on iron went out, and the waves grew down into the pavements. (108)

Daniel Dom and the narrator are witnesses to the destruction. They are also survivors of it, as must be implied by the use of a first-person point of view. The title of the story attests to the fact that this flood is not the end, for it is a "*Prologue* to an adventure." We may deduce that the adventure proper is the creation that, in Thomas's scheme of the world, is sure to follow the destruction. Like the flood in the later poem "Prologue" (itself a "coming before," an introduction to the collected poems), the deluge ushers in a "flowering" of possibility from the fragments left by the decreative act. The "translator of man's manuscript" is merely presenting a preliminary narrative which offers a beginning inherent in the image of an ending.

In the early prose works, images of separation and multiplicity in the stories of Adam and Eve, the tower of Babel, and the flood override any attempt at unity that might be supposed from the idea of a beginning. Thomas's search for the primal generative principle always leads to generation, and therefore a necessary movement outward. As Adam and Eve must move out of the garden, the singleness of the innocent word must always move outward to the multiplicity of experience. There is always a movement outward, a movement toward multiplicity rather than the unity inherent in a return to source. The primal "Word," once made into a system of language, becomes fragmented. Yet the Babel that is created is full of more potential in multiple relationships than is possible in a single system of association. As many of Thomas's questing heroes find out, the search for a virgin word proves illusory. Their initial commitment to a belief in some ultimate origin or end, whether word, truth, or presence, that will act as a foundation for all their experience is undermined, and they are left only with ever-increasing unanswered questions. The best they can do is grope "in the direction of" the ultimate word. Images of floods become symbols for new beginnings, new generations, and ever-increasing circles of meaning. Since there are always new beginnings inherent in every apparent ending, closure becomes impossible.

Thomas describes his method of creating a poem as a "breeding" of signifieds and signifiers in a weblike rather than a linear development of signification: "A poem by myself needs a host of images, because its centre is a host of images. I make one image, – though 'make' is not the word, I let, perhaps, an image be 'made' emotionally in me and then apply to it what intellectual & critical forces I possess – let it breed another, let that image contradict the first, make, of the third image bred out of the other two together, a fourth contradictory image, and let them all, within my imposed formal limits, conflict. Each image holds within it the seed of its own destruction and my dialectical method, as I understand it, is a constant building up and breaking down of the images that come out of the central seed which is itself destructive and constructive at the same time" (*CL* 281). The shaping impulse is met by Thomas's "destructive creation" as each image lends itself to multiple possibilities of meaning that keep opening outward. Poems and stories end either with questions or with ambiguous events that stop without being conclusive or explanatory. Warring forces of signification within the text deter the possibility of adding up the sum of its parts to reach any integrated whole. Every poem for Thomas is seen to some extent as an indeterminate moment extracted from constant and conflicting movement. Only briefly can any idea or image be contained within the boundaries of a poem; Thomas admits that much of his early work can be seen as multiple efforts to contain the same image or idea, just as the "Owl-light" poems are both self-contained poems and fragments of a larger work. Writing to Henry Treece, Thomas says: "a poem of mine is, or should be, a watertight section of the stream that is flowing all ways; all warring images within it should be reconciled for that small stop of time. I agree that each of my earlier poems might appear to constitute a section from one long poem; ... images were left dangling over their formal limits, and dragged the poem into another; the warring stream ran on over the insecure barriers" (*CL* 282).

Thomas's letters, while offering valuable insight into his poetics, must also be read with a grain of salt, for he adopts different masks according to his intentions and the recipient of the letter. Rather than being a result of error, as Thomas suggests to Treece, this "dangling over ... formal limits" is just the opposite: consistent with Thomas's ideas of paradox, indeterminacy, and dialectic and generative language, these poems were written at a time when the "warring stream" was central to his consciousness, and the lack of "fullstop armistice" was therefore deliberate.

INTERPRETIVE BEARINGS OF THE EARLY STORIES ON THE POEMS

Reading the early prose as the recording of artistic autobiography sheds light on many of the cryptic poems written during the same period. The central motif of "In the Beginning," for example, while obviously referring to the beginning of the world as Logos, reveals Thomas's own personal interpretation of the myth. The first word is regarded as the seed of all that follows, including death. As he does in his stories, Thomas foregrounds images of writing when dealing with the physical universe. Creation and destruction – artistic and otherwise – are the driving force of the written world. First composed in 1933, "In the Beginning" was revised in April 1934 and then in 1935, concurrent with the revisions of "The Orchards" and the writing of a number of the early stories.

"In the beginning" distils the creation myth, often rearranging phrases taken directly from the book of Genesis. The creating spirit, the holy trinity (symbolic of multiplicity in unity, and vice versa), both spirit and flesh, is as a physical entity a "three-pointed star" and a less tangible word, "three-syllabled and starry as the smile." The "spirit of God" that "moved upon the face of the waters" in the Old Testament becomes "one smile of light across the empty face," suggesting both the personification of the world as a living thing and the artistic rendering of it as if by brushstrokes on a canvas. The artistic metaphor is made more explicit, as the God, the artist, is transformed into a writer, and material substance is created by God literally writing upon the blank page of the void, "burning ciphers on the round of space." These "ciphers" (the word also appears in "The Orchards")[9] are the mark of God's name:

> In the beginning was the pale signature,
> Three-syllabled and starry as the smile

> And after came the imprints on the water,
> Stamp of the minted face upon the moon;
> The blood that touched the crosstree and the grail
> Touched the first cloud and left a sign.

All the world bears the "stamp" of God's identity, like the "minted face upon the moon"; the man in the moon is likened to a coin bearing God's "imprint," which is a reflection of himself. God's "signature" is at the same time a written word and a picture of a human face, suggesting not simply that God created man in his own image, but that the universe possesses a "human" form, like the Jarvis Hills in the early stories.

The signature, a written word that is representative of one's identity, then becomes the original of which copies are made. "Imprints," suggestive of printed copies, is significantly plural, as the one original leads to many. Everything created is a different edition of the first work. Like the signature which stands for the person, the imprints also stand for something beyond themselves, for they are signifiers pointing to signifieds. Like the lights in the firmament which God left for signs, the imprints point back to their original source; but they also, as the complex imagery of the poem suggests, point away from their source as copies, for the original leads out to multiplicity. However, "imprints on water" suggests impermanence, as in the expression "writing on water." The writing metaphor is even more explicit in the fourth stanza:

> In the beginning was the word, the word
> That from the solid bases of the light
> Abstracted all the letters of the void;
> And from the cloudy bases of the breath
> The word flowed up, translating to the heart
> First characters of birth and death.

All the letters are present in the void from the beginning, and from them all subsequently created words, not just the "first." Therefore, Thomas is not presenting a modernist universe which is a fragmentation of an original unity; instead, he offers a world fragmented from "the beginning" in intangible and shifting "cloudy bases." When the imagery of the above stanza is unravelled, the events are seen to be cyclical with no determinate beginning or end, for the word derives not only from the "cloudy bases" but also from the "solid bases" which themselves were created of an abstraction, a "thought" in the "secret brain." The phrase "in the beginning" is repeated at the beginning of each stanza in the poem, and functions in much the same way as the repetitive phrase opening the fragmentary prose piece "Prologue to an Adventure": the many beginnings ironically undercut the possibility of one definitive beginning. By apparently creating a poem about the conventionally described creation myth of the Bible, Thomas in fact negates its certainty and complicates its simplicity.

The inversion of the accepted myth is further evidenced in the fact that the word not only begins in thought to be made tangible, but also moves from the "solid" to become "abstracted," and is translated from sound into meaning. Thus as the word is written it is also read, or translated, and the simultaneous writing and reading is a continually transformational act. We are once again brought back to Thomas's idea of "destructive creation" in which building up, implied in the writing process, is concurrent with the breaking down necessary to reading comprehension. Images of division in the poem reinforce this duality, from the "substance forked" in the first stanza to the division of mankind in the last. The last lines, in which the "original" is "scattered," refer again to Genesis, this time in Thomas's favoured theme of the fall. Adam and Eve are alluded to in "the ribbed original of love" and the "bough of bone." They are also countered by allusions to the devil, in the "pitch" "forking," and by an implied allusion to the story of Cain and Abel in the fifth stanza. The blood of Abel echoes the second stanza, which mentions "the blood that touched the crosstree and the grail." Adam and Eve, Cain and Abel, Christ and the Devil are the "first characters of birth and death," opposites that were present from the beginning, for as the "ciphers" spun, "heaven and hell mixed" together before the "division." The "first characters" are human forms; they are also the letters "abstracted from the void," the alpha and omega. Thus all life is inextricable from language.

The poem "I, in my intricate image" raises further ontological questions regarding a world created by language. This poem is presented from the point of view of the creator, who is himself his own creation: "I, in my intricate image, stride on two levels, / Forged in man's minerals, the brassy orator / Laying my ghost in metal. ..." The first-person I, the identity of the speaker, is contained within an "image," which suggests a replication of an original as a physical imprint, the non-physical identity being the original. This image is an "intricate" one, and the nature of the complexity is explored in the narrator's claim to "stride on two levels": the speaker is a "twin miracle" of flesh and spirit, being both a "ghost" and "forged in man's minerals." His dual nature allows him to move through two worlds, one physical and the other immaterial; yet the intricacy of his being makes the so-called non-physical world something more than a simply spiritual one – for, as with the early prose, the "other" world is a world of art, and the speaker, like Marlais in "The Orchards," strides, or forges his way through, a written world. This second world can also be made physical, as suggested by the image of the creator as blacksmith, who, laying his "ghost in metal," may be seen as the artist putting his idea into form. The created work is the poem itself; the speaker of the poem, the blacksmith, is also the "orator." He is both the creator of his proclamation and an image created out of his own decrees, being both the forger and the forged. He says of himself, in his "fusion" as a "metal phantom," that "I ... create this twin miracle." Like the self-created Marlais, he is an "image of images," a fictional creation, moving through his own created world. The word "forged" in fact works on a number of levels, for it means "to make" something, to advance with difficulty, to fabricate or invent, and also to create a fraudulent imitation of something. Thomas, the self-proclaimed "dog" and "crafty devil," in fact openly revels in his ability to steal created images and create other versions of them (as Eliot said, a bad poet borrows, a good poet steals). Although the comparison may seem sacrilegious, the poet, like God, the ultimate artist in "In the beginning," is a forger making "imprints" or successive images in reflection of something already created.

Inside or outside of art, the individual faces the same fate, "the fortune of manhood: the natural peril, / A steeplejack tower, bonerail and masterless / No death more natural." The "natural peril" of death has its equal in art, and it becomes the "natural parallel," the individual locked in his man-made tower of art. Like Marlais, the artist adventures on an ambiguous quest which is circular, bringing him back to his initial point of departure without actually undergoing a definitive beginning or end. The "I" becomes plural as his "intricate image" journeys between land and sea, "voyaging clockwise off the symboled harbour." As in Marlais's story, the speaker's images are deflected from the sea to the hills, and must encounter obstacles such as winds, babbling disembodied voices, and the "undead water." Finally coming "unto sea-stuck towers," the speaker's image of himself gains control over the linguistically self-created landscape. The world becomes a literal recording of the artist's vision; implied in the imperative mood is the artist's ability to manipulate the record physically. As in "The Orchards," the imperative mood also indicates the involvement of the reader: "(Turn the sea-spindle lateral, / The grooved land rotating ... These are your years' recorders. The circular world stands still)." Like the parentheses bracketing this passage, the phonograph record is a physical entrapment of the human voice. Like a written "record," it acts as "witness" and testimony to ephemeral events. The landscape here is the record echoing a voice much the way the voice of Jarvis remained in his valley. Repeating the "shames and damp dishonours," it also resembles the "travellers of voices" that mock Marlais. "The face of voices on the moon-turned table" recalls the face of the creator stamped on the moon in "In the beginning," suggesting that the phonograph record which is capable of mockery is created by the speaker of the poem; like Marlais's, the artist's creations come back to haunt him. But here the record stands still and is silent. The directive to "turn the sea spindle" allows the artist to reactivate the "circular world," to retrieve the voice imprinted on it, and therefore to allow further repetitions of the voice/image to be created.

The speaker gains full possession of the world around him, and is able to do something physical with his images: "thrusting the tom-thumb vision up the iron mile," he not only creates but becomes Godlike in his powers to do so: "I, in a wind on fire, from green Adam's cradle, / No man more magical, clawed out the crocodile." Creating both birth and death simultaneously – for the evil suggested in the crocodile emerges out of "Adam's cradle" – he explicitly proclaims himself the creator known in the Old Testament: "This was the god of beginning in the intricate seawhirl, / And my images roared and rose on heaven's hill." Once again, he makes it clear that all he creates is "image," from the illusion of the grail to the myth of Satan. Yet, as suggested by the "oils and ointments on the flying grail," the myth has healing powers; a "miracle" is created in spite of its fraudulent nature, just as the recorded copy of a voice on the gramophone can still "dazzle" as though it were alive.

Similarities between the poems and the prose of Thomas's early career are not limited to the above comparisons; nearly all of the early poetry makes self-conscious reference to creation, artistic and otherwise. His later work also maintains this focus, but its nature changes significantly. After fully exploring language and the difficulties often imposed by it, Thomas gradually moves toward a focus on the applications of artistic creation. His artist figures gradually attain a sort of compromise with their demanding medium; language and fictive creations become tools to be used as well as merely worlds to be inhabited. Accompanying this compromise is a necessary move away from the solipsism seen in the artists of the early stories toward a more communal stance. The subjects of *Portrait of the Artist as a Young Dog*, *Adventures in the Skin Trade*, and the poems contemporary with these later prose works are very different from the type represented by Marlais, the madman, and the other early artist figures.

3 Portraits of the Artist

PORTRAIT OF THE ARTIST AS A YOUNG DOG AND ITS RELATION TO THE EARLY STORIES

Like the early tales, Thomas's later short stories in *Portrait of the Artist as a Young Dog* reveal much about his changing conceptions of language, literature, the function of art, and art's relation to life. What eventually emerges is a portrait very different in both style and subject matter from those found in the early works. The early stories illustrate a mythologizing of the creative process. The artist is generally depicted as a type, someone of unusual vision whose special status is used to explore the discrepancies between image and reality. A godlike creator-destroyer, he transforms an already written world through acts of translation. In *Portrait*, the artist, a dog rather than a god, loses his special status. He is an ordinary person who explores the correspondences rather than the differences between image and reality. In the early fiction, there is a break from realistic conventions and expectations; in the later fiction, reality may be distorted, because of subjective and idiosyncratic vision, as in "Old Garbo" and "One Warm Saturday," but the realistic premise remains intact. Functioning in a real world rather than a written one, Thomas's later artist hero explores life as well as story.

The early experimental stories may be read as a recording of artistic autobiography, because they are about the creation of art, not about the artist. They reveal little of Thomas himself as a person, or of the world around him. The later stories, deliberately autobiographical, consciously disclose the life of the artist. Thomas described the stories written from 1938 onward as being about his "true childhood" (CL 305), as distinct from the earlier, nightmarish, imagined one. The later works also move away from the earlier egocentrism, being, as Thomas describes them, "stories of Swansea and me" (CL 277) and "stories about Welsh people" (CL 286). Since they are about his "true" self and his Welsh surroundings rather than about a mythic, written world, *Portrait* defines the artist figure, an ordinary human being, by place rather than by image. Indeed, by 1939 Thomas had changed his generic definition of the stories from "autobiography" to "provincial autobiography" (CL 375), shifting the focus away from the self to the place.

Stylistically less dense and difficult, the later stories show Thomas, as both writer and character, gradually accepting the limitations necessary for accessibility, which becomes a primary quality of art. Through an increased use of dialogue and an insertion of other voices, especially as story-tellers, Thomas moves away from the artist as solipsistic Adam. Accepting his social function means that the artist cannot be alienated from society. The growing sense of community, multiple story-tellers, and decentring of the Thomas character in *Portrait* may be seen as steps toward the play for voices, *Under Milk Wood*. By 1953, Thomas was referring to *Portrait* not as an "autobiography," but as "more-or-less autobiography" (CL 861), acknowledging a certain degree of artistic shaping of life that was inescapable for him. *Portrait*, "a growing up told ... in memories of childhood written when grown up" rather than in "stories written while growing up" (CL 862), allows the artist to see his life and his surroundings because he is not, as he was in the early stories, too immediately caught within his tower of words. *Portrait*, like *Under Milk Wood*, depicts not the fictional world in which Marlais and the Madman move, but a "more-or-less" real world tempered by nostalgic reflection and the natural fabulation occurring in everyday life.

Criticism of *Portrait of the Artist as a Young Dog* usually begins by pointing out the striking stylistic differences between the *Portrait* and the early stories, noting Thomas's abandonment of subjective, experimental, or surrealistic convolutions in favour of simple realism.[1] The continued focus on the artist indicates that there is not a total departure from the earlier concerns. Indeed, these stories extend the metafictional bent of the early stories, dwelling on the importance of the creation of narrative in human experience. Thomas uses the autobiographical form and a preponderance of characters who tell stories within the stories, to show us how all life – not just words – is subject to artistic shaping. There are, however, significant differences between the earlier and later stories. The latter, comprising *Portrait,* more closely resemble the genre of the realistic short story. Sometimes defined as middle-class art, realism describes the common, everyday materials of the immediate world, striving for the illusion of actuality in its representation. The early stories clearly belong to a different genre, being fantastic treatments of events that are anything but common.

More intimately connected with the community around the artist, the *Portrait* stories are social in both subject matter and form; Thomas's tales concern others as well as himself, and he presents a setting in time and place for the tales, as we expect from the short story rather than the poem. They are explicit rather than dense and suggestive, taking their time to state and show meaning. While the style is still verbally rich, the word patterns predominant in the earlier poetic prose become less dense, and are interspersed with large blocks of action – in contrast to the early stories, things happen. One can define plots in the *Portrait* stories, while earlier plot was either disjointed or absent, often causing difficulty of interpretation. Events now cause linear movement, unlike, say, the predicament of Marlais, in "The Orchards," who becomes stuck in the circularity of his own created story. The *Portrait* tales are self-reflexive on the level of story rather than on the level of language. Their narrative form is reflected in the change of subject matter, which is often, itself, narrative: where the early prose-poetry is quite frequently about the creation of poems, the later stories are about the creation of stories, and the production of a narrative element in life.

It is appropriate to focus on narrative because it has traditionally been regarded as the art form most closely resembling real life, while lyric, as Sharon Cameron asserts, is the least mimetic form (241). The change in Thomas's work may also be seen in the way he moves from the highly stylized myth-vision, nightmare, and romance of the early stories to the more realistic genres of everyday tragedy and comedy nearer to the unordered raw material of reality. Gone are the gothic towers and madmen, the surreal landscapes and epic figures; instead we see the more benign and everyday madnesses of the grandfather in "A visit to Grandpa's" or the minister's wife in "The Fight," the ordinary eccentrics in the pubs, and the identifiable places such as Rhossilli and Swansea. The later stories are grounded in the real rather than a mythological or fabular Wales.

The early prose-poems are extremely lyrical not only in subject matter but also in structure, being highly patterned and repetitive, often with a circularity reminiscent of the meditative reflections of some lyric poems. The patterns of recurrence, such as we find in the opening of the "Prologue to an Adventure," accentuate the reflective focus. Their fragmentary nature may be seen as a privileging of the lyric moment over the sequentiality of narrative. Time in the lyric is subjective, and can deviate in a number of ways from the diachronic, objective time generally found in narrative structures: subjective, lyric time can rearrange the temporal flow, or stall it to create the illusion of a static present; it can also realize synchronicity by distilling many moments into one. Tensions between lyric time and narrative time arise out of the characters' concerns with creation, as they achieve a kind of atemporality in artistic reflection, and their search for adventure, which is teleological and hence more conducive to being rendered in narrative. But a lyricized structure predominates because of the strong pull toward the world of words; unlike the later tales, the early work resides almost entirely within the head of the central character. Thus, despite the imagistic play of the early stories, and their narrative complexities, they are, to this extent, monologic.

The overall structure of *Portrait* blends lyric and narrative, for it is a retrospective collection of moments, the stories functioning as lyrical markings in time. Although there is an overall pattern of development tracing the growth of the artist from a small child to a young man, there are discrepancies between the story order and the text order: the third story, "Patricia, Edith and Arnold," focuses on a child clearly much younger than he was in the first two stories, "The Peaches" and "A Visit to Grandpa's." The *Portrait* stories, like Thomas's occasional poems, are markings in time that allow one to go back and recreate stories from those moments; thus they can be at once atemporal and historical. While the narrative pattern places the stories in time, their structures double back in a lyric reiterability. Hence the collection of short stories effects a compromise between lyric moment and narrative sequence, both within the individual stories and between them, in the volume as a whole.

The move toward narrative informs most of the developments in Thomas's later career. Concerned with the act and process of story-telling, rather than composition, Thomas again illustrates his concerns with language, but here the emphasis is on language as a communicative tool – for he uses the dialogic capacities of narrative, assuming a listener/reader who interacts with the storyteller. The teller of the tale also becomes important. In the early stories, the composed work had a life of its own: in some stories, such as "The Vest" or "The Visitor," we concentrate on the work and not on the narrator; in others, such as "The Orchards" or "The Mouse and the Woman," the created work leads a life independent of the writer in the tale. While the early short stories are autobiographical, they are so in disguised form. But *Portrait* is explicitly autobiographical, however fictionalized, and we cannot ignore the narrator, who in many of the stories refers to himself in the first person, as the very subject of his story. His voice as narrator is as central as his position as character within the stories. In turn, the other characters in the book, such as Tom in "Just Like Little Dogs" or Mr Evans in "Where Tawe Flows," are both written about and allowed their own internal narratorial voice. Thomas, as a character within the book, is both a listener to the others' stories and a future teller who will write the stories we are now reading – "I'll put you all in a story by and by" ("Old Garbo" 208). Thomas (the author) moves away from the monologic inner dialogues of the early stories and allows the people around him a voice too. He tempers the egotism of his earlier self, and allows artistic, imaginative creation to become communal – a development that becomes most fully realized in his last created work, *Under Milk Wood,* the "play for voices," where all the characters serve the function of tellers.

As in many künstlerromans, we are given a double portrait, the later mature Thomas looking back on his earlier self or selves as he traces the development of the artist. While the stories are entertaining on their own, an acquaintance with the early short stories greatly enriches our awareness of the irony of the narrator, for the *Portrait* contains many references, if not to the early stories themselves, then to the young Thomas who wrote them, or to a similar sort of experimental young writer. The boy in "The Peaches" has a morbid imagination with the potential to slip into the nightmare world of the early stories, as he does when offered the raw material of a darkened window, a "hangman's house," a "mad" cousin, and a demonically foxlike uncle. But the potentially nightmarish events are reduced to the tiny domestic tragedies of everyday life. As in "The Mouse and the Woman," "The Orchards," or "A Prospect of the Sea," reality intermingles with dream and fiction; in "A Visit to Grandpa's," the noises the grandfather makes while dreaming of horses partly create the dreams of the child, and the child and the grandfather momentarily inhabit a communal fictional world. The reality of dream here does not seem surreal, as it does in the early tales, but is rather commonplace. In tales like "The Peaches" madness is benign: a parson puts up a sign to direct ducks to a pond, and only the "innocents" are elected mayor.

Unlike the early stories, where the character of the artist/protagonist remains relatively fixed, the *Portrait* ensures character evolution in its künstlerroman structure. The narrator/hero of the *Portrait* develops from a child playing with words for their sound value to a young adult who learns to manipulate words for various uses. When he first realizes his vocation as an artist he does so for the purposes of self-aggrandizement ("The Fight"); later, with a growing concern for others, he uses words to heal individuals ("Who do you wish") or to heal rifts in a community ("Old Garbo," "One Warm Saturday"). As the hero matures, he acquires the ability to objectify himself and watch himself, as in "The Orchards," where he is the "Poet" and "lone walker." In "The Fight," both Thomas and his friend Dan are seriously and self-consciously artists, but their stance is continually deflated. The lone wolf becomes embarrassed when he realizes others are watching his posing, and the creative endeavours of both are cut short by their approaching curfews. The narrator implies that the early Thomas and his friend wrote about things of which they had no direct experience; while his friend Dan wrote novels about "battles and sieges and kings," the young Dylan wrote poems about lust and death and betrayal. When Dylan recites his latest poem, called "Frivolous is my hate" ("Singed with bestial remorse ... break her dead dark body, break"), to the minister – who should have been shocked – his endeavour is deflated when the minister points out the "obvious" influence of Tennyson.

As with the early stories, fiction or story has the ability to manifest itself in reality. In "Just Like Little Dogs," Tom's deftness at story-telling transports Dylan: "He described her. I saw her clearly ... [she] grew from a few words right out of Tom's story, and I saw her ambling solidly along the sands" (178). Dylan becomes not only a listener but a voyeur, actually within the story itself: "Now the story-telling thing in the arch gave place to the loving night in the dunes ... I lay like a pimp in a bush by Tom's side and squinted through to see him round his hands on Norma's breast" (179). A similar transformation occurs in a metafictional episode in "Old Garbo." At the cinema, Thomas's imagination allows him virtually to become a part of the film that he is watching: "Then I entered an American college and danced with the president's daughter. The hero, called Lincoln, tall and dark with good teeth, I displaced quickly, and the girl spoke my name as she held his shadow" (210–11). This early Thomas consistently prefers fiction to reality.

In "Where Tawe Flows," Thomas is engaged with others in the communal writing of a book about "Provincial Life" – a fictionalized account of a real project Thomas once proposed to fellow Welsh writers.[2] Like the real Thomas, the writer in "Where Tawe

Flows" gets sidetracked from his attempts to write about reality: "He had been writing, that week, the story of a cat who jumped over a woman the moment she died and turned her into a vampire. He had reached the part of the story where the woman was an undead children's governess, but he could not think how to fit it into the novel. ... 'There's no need, is there ... for us to avoid the fantastic altogether?'" (187). The young sensationalist is clearly the eventual author of the Jarvis Valley stories.

In the final story, "One Warm Saturday," Thomas has developed the character to the point where we sense his style is about to change from that characterizing the early stories to that of the tales we are reading in the "Portrait." He still has the tendency to escape reality and leap into the realm of imagination and words. However, it is more story than text into which he ventures, for he becomes involved with conventional literary shapes such as romance archetypes rather than the pre-literary phantasmagoria of the earlier stories. One young woman appears to be more vision than reality: "he saw her as a wise, soft girl whom no hard company could spoil, for her soft self, bare to the heart, broke through every defense of her sensual falsifiers. As he thought this, phrasing her gentleness, faithlessly running to worlds away from the real room and his life in the middle, he woke with a start and saw her lively body six steps from him, no calm heart dressed in a sentence, but a pretty girl, to be got and kept. He must catch hold of her fast" (229). This may be contrasted to "A Prospect of the Sea," where the boy awakes into another dream, and the girl, after a number of transformations, remains fictional. While the character in "One Warm Saturday" still does not see Lou for the "queer tart" that she is, he at least tears himself away from words long enough to act. Lou remains an imaginative creation, but one grounded in reality, and the developing artist sees the potential in real life that far exceeds that of words. In keeping with the tongue-in-cheek rejection of the self-exiled artist inhabiting Thomas's earlier tales, a portrait emerges of an artist gradually searching out a sense of community. In contrast to the early stories, and the younger artist satirized in the *Portrait*, imaginative and artistic creation – specifically stories – become a way to achieve this community.

THE KÜNSTLERROMAN TRADITION

In *Portrait of the Artist as a Young Dog*, Thomas continues his exploration of the nature of art and the creative process begun in the early experimental short stories. In the *Portrait,* he expands his scope, offering investigations into the artist's relationship to the life around him, as well as to his literary inheritance. Thomas returns to a traditional fictional form, writing a "development of the artist" novel in the tradition of Goethe, Rousseau, Dickens, Proust, James, Joyce, and others. Like many novels of the künstlerroman tradition, *Portrait* traces the progression of an imaginative child with precocious powers of observation, through a retreat into the imagination, creating and telling stories, to the eventual emergence of the young adult artist. Thomas explores the central themes common to the artist novel, such as the artistic temperament, the creative process, the artist's relationship to society, and the equation of art with experience.

Like early stories such as "The Orchards," *Portrait* envisions the artist as an easily identifiable type, the "Poet," the "Hero," the "lone wolf," who is ironically undercut by his inability to fulfil these roles as stereotypically imagined. Whether getting lost in his own creations ("The Orchards") or in endless corridors ("One Warm Saturday"), the character usually fails to achieve what he sets out to do. As in Joyce's *Portrait of the Artist as a Young Man,* and indeed in numerous other künstlerromans, Thomas depicts the artist as a divided being with conflicting ideals of detachment, pulled between life as an ordinary man in the world and his consecration as an artist. In the künstlerroman tradition, the artist as hero is often, like Stephen Dedalus, the artist as exile. While Thomas parodies the self-exiled stance of his youth, his "hero," although deciding in favour of community, remains isolated in many stories through fate or the acts of others. The artist is usually left alone at the end of each story. Exile becomes inevitable, although undesirable – and a way out is offered through a sense of community acquired through art, through a shared story-telling.

Such critics as Tindall, Holbrook, and Williams have made the unavoidable comparison to Joyce's *Portrait of the Artist as a*

Young Man, primarily on the basis of the similarity in titles, some concluding that an awareness of indebtedness necessarily makes Thomas's prose "derivative" and "inferior" (adjectives used by both Holbrook and Peach). Thomas himself anticipated just such a comparison, and in his usual style simultaneously denies the influence of Joyce and admits his presence: "I cannot say that I have been 'influenced' by Joyce, whom I enormously admire and whose *Ulysses* and earlier stories I have read a great deal. ... As you know, the name given to innumerable portrait paintings by their artists is, 'Portrait of the Artist as a Young Man' – a perfectly straightforward title. ... I myself made a bit of doggish fun of the *painting*-title, and, of course, intended no possible reference to Joyce. I do not think that Joyce has had any hand at all in my writing; certainly, his *Ulysses* has not. On the other hand, I cannot deny that the shaping of some of my *Portrait* stories might owe something to Joyce's stories in the volume *Dubliners*. But then, *Dubliners* was a pioneering work in the world of the short story, and no good story-writer since can have failed, in some way, however little, to have benefited by it" (551). Thomas's early awareness of Joyce through sources such as *transition*, and his later statement that he wished to write a "Welsh Ulysses" – what would become *Under Milk Wood* – might lead us to take his denial with a grain of salt. While making "doggish fun" of the whole self-portrait tradition, whether in painting or writing, Thomas does make the presence of Joyce undeniable, in a double-edged tribute/parody that is consistent with his "dog among the fairies" attitude to his literary ancestors. Evidence may be adduced to back up Kenneth Sieb's claim that Thomas's change from "man" to "dog" refers not only to the character's being a "young rascal," but also to a position sometimes diametrically opposed to that of Joyce's hero; as Seib suggests, "one even suspects 'dog' of being a Joycean anagram for 'God': thus Thomas's title implies that his fictional Dylan, is, all told, a young god become one more Welsh whelp fallen into dog days. ... The principal character ... like Stephen Dedalus, is more failed than successful artist" (241). Thomas's love of anagrams would lead an experienced reader to notice immediately that "Dog" is "God" reversed, a word play found more than once in the *Collected Letters,* as when Thomas writes to Pamela Hansford Johnson that "in the beginning was a word I can't spell, not a reversed Dog" (CL 137). He advises another friend to dive "into the sea of yourself like a young dog after a pearl," recalling perhaps the fall into the sea of the mythical Icarus. For Thomas, the fall is not an accident resulting from pride but a deliberate plunge into experience; Thomas's sea and his hero are not mythic but human, and the fall represents a conscious participation in life and the sea of experience in order to create art. The nature of art for the two developing artists also differs. For Dedalus, art replaces religion, the powers of the artist serving the function of the priesthood. For Thomas such lofty service is continually undercut, as in his characterization of cousin Gwilym in "The Peaches." Gwilym is supposedly studying to be a minister, and he is also a poet – he wrote poems to girls and "changed the girls' names to God" (135). One might compare Joyce's "fire and brimstone" sermon to that of Gwilym: preaching on the powers of God and his omniscience, he ends with the observation, " 'O God, mun, you're like a bloody cat' " (128).

Art further replaces religion when Stephen develops his disinterested aesthetic theory, which derives from the epiphany he experiences when he sees the young woman standing midstream, perceived as a moment of stasis in a timeless setting. For Stephen, all true art is static and divorced from kinetic desire. For Thomas, such art represents all that is lifeless. While the early stories often reveal a lyric atemporality, the overall picture suggests that art should be primarily kinetic, not static. Criticizing the earlier self that risked being trapped "in a tower of words," Thomas wrote in 1936 that he feared "an ingrowing, the impulse growing like a toenail into the artifice" (CL 223), and hoped instead for a continued participation in the constant transformations of life. The eventual portrait that develops is of an artist who seems to reject what Dedalus aspires to, not soaring to heights above the mundane world but plunging into the ordinary life around him.

Like Joyce's relation to Stephen, Thomas's relation to his protagonist is a complicated one, being neither solely an endorsement nor a rejection of his earlier self. Dedalus's disinterested theory of aesthetics, in which "the artist, like the God of creation, remains within or behind or above his handiwork, invisible, refined out of existence, indifferent, paring his fingernails" (Joyce *Portrait* 215), proves impossible for Dylan, who finds himself participating wholly with not only his own creations but those of others, entering into the stories that others tell. In the later works the artist cannot be disinterested either toward the world or to his stories. The teller of the stories and his acts of narrating become more dominant fixtures, as does his participation in the stories around him. Hence he eventually comes to realize that his detached stance is merely a pose, and that his natural tendency is toward communion: "I never felt more a part of the remote and overpressing world, or more full of love and arrogance and pity and humility, not for myself alone, but for the living earth I suffered on and for the unfeeling systems in the upper air, Mars and Venus and Brazell and Skully, men in China and St. Thomas, scorning girls and ready girls, soldiers and bullies and policemen and sharp, suspicious buyers of second-hand books" ("Just Like Little Dogs" 177).

Therefore, although the Thomas character and Stephen Dedalus approach art with very different views of the artist's stance, they both foresee a similar function for art, for they both ultimately wish to address the common consciousness of their "race," that is mankind. Both Dedalus and Thomas's character have humanistic motives, but Dedalus is more sure of himself in his artistic calling; the Thomas character shifts versions of what the artist should be more often than Dedalus does, being sometimes aloof and at other times involved with mankind. While Dedalus achieves objectivity through a confident and often arrogant detachment, Thomas strives for it in a different way by focusing on his own being, the "sea" of himself which is intimately connected to the rest of his race. The later Thomas rejects the idea of the poet as a visionary, and opts instead to be the poet as mirror, even then reflecting not mythic universalities but localized, individual portraits of the "*small* world about to fall."

Thomas's hero/artist in *Portrait* explores a number of positions in relation to art. At the end, he has as yet settled into no particular camp, but is wrestling with the call of adventure in real life as opposed to the safety of fiction. His dilemma stems from the fact that he is both an "Artist" and a "Young Man," two roles often seemingly at odds. As a man he is subject to the normal processes of life; as an artist he imagines that he transcends life through creative effort. The man seeks personal fulfilment in experience, while the artist desires freedom from the demands of life.

Often the artist has the ability to step outside the self and recognize the difference between its two aspects. Splits in identity occur in "The "Peaches," when he becomes self-conscious and at first doesn't recognize himself, and in "Old Garbo," when, posing as a journalist, he wishes his father could see him. The difference between the poet and the man becomes evident when, while posing, he senses that he is necessarily an outsider to the events he witnesses and records as a writer, but wishes to participate in as a man: "Oh! to be able to join in the suggestive play or the rocking choir, to shout 'Bread of Heaven,' with my shoulders back and my arms linked with Little Moscow, or to be called 'saucy' and 'a one' as I joked and ogled at the counter, making innocent, dirty love that could come to nothing among the spilt beer and piling glasses" (213). In "Old Garbo" he plays the part of the Universal Artist as impartial observer. In spite of the self-parody – he mentions the "stories [he] would never write" and is accused of "too much platitudinous verbosity" – there are intimations of the impartial observer he might actually become in descriptive passages that are a serious record of the world around him: "I made my way through the crowds: the Valley men, up for football; the country shoppers, the window gazers; the silent, shabby men at the corners of the packed streets, standing in isolation in the rain; the press of mothers and prams; old women in black, brooched dresses carrying frails, smart girls with shining mackintoshes and splashed stockings; little, dandy lascars, bewildered by the weather; business men with wet spats; through a mushroom forest of umbrellas; and all the time I thought of the paragraphs I would never write. I'll put you all in a story by and by" (207–8). The last line of this passage is repeated as the last line of the story, after Thomas, the character, writes the story about the woman called "Old Garbo" – from whom the title of the *Portrait* story derives. The conflation of the

Portrait text with its embedded story illustrates the success of the developing artist in capturing the pathos of desire and loss in the world around him, in spite of the narrator's ironic self-parody. The character shows the story to Mr Farr, who dismisses it as factually inaccurate. Although the young man is perhaps a failure, the artist is not, for he has captured the essence of the woman and her situation, if not the exact details. Further, although the form is autobiographical, the subject of the artist's consideration becomes not himself but others, and he becomes a reflector for the world around him. The separation of the person from the creator is the basis of Jung's theory of the artist, the "collective man who carries and shapes the unconscious psychic life of mankind."[3] This is similar to the idea of the artist that Joyce's Stephen Dedalus proposes, when he vows to "forge in the smithy of my soul the uncreated conscience of my race" (*Portrait* 253). But while the Thomas character quite consciously plays the role of universal poet, and experiments with a number of temporary methods to become the voice of the people, he does not ultimately employ Dedalus's "arms" – "silence, exile, cunning" (247) – to do so. Empathy and participation eventually become the means to serve his people through art.

Before reconciling man and poet, Thomas the character must come to terms with the relation between art, "reality," and experience. The young Dylan experiments with various stances that may be seen as modern versions of the late nineteenth-century aesthetic movement – exalting art above life, he briefly tries to adopt the aloofness of Dedalus, believing that the artist can make use of life only if he stands apart. In "The Fight" and "One Warm Saturday," he begins with a Byronic pose, standing "among them but not of them." The "bohemian" journalist of "Old Garbo" attempts a different tactic, following in the romantic tradition of the artist who must live in order to create. Initially he seems only to succeed in becoming drunk, but the episode becomes a source not only for "this story" (167) but also for as yet unwritten stories, suggested by the other characters mentioned by Mr Farr. He thus supports the tradition of art as the recreation of experience. These two stances, what Maurice Beebe calls the "Ivory Tower" versus the "Sacred Fount" traditions,[4] both offer temptations, and in the end, the Thomas character must effect a balance between the two.

Thomas's attraction toward the "Ivory Tower" of art is clearly seen in the early tales. According to Beebe, in the Ivory Tower tradition art is equated with religion rather than experience. The Thomas in the early poems and stories, which equate the artistic creator with the Creator, is not unlike Stephen Dedalus, who is attracted to art by the same esoteric powers that attracted him to the priesthood. Art becomes a religion, and this new religion of art, as defined by the avant-garde artists in *transition*, owes much to magic and occultism, mysticism, transcendentalism, myth, and the spiritual romanticism of writers and philosophers such as Novalis. The alchemy in "The Lemon," witchcraft in "The School for Witches," inverted Christianity in "The Holy Six," and the magic transformations of "The Map of Love" might be seen as manifestations of the Ivory Tower view of art. For the artists in *transition*, alchemic mysteries are fitting symbols for poetry, as the artist may invoke magic and ritual as a means of penetrating to a secret that will result in his mastery of the universe; this may be seen most obviously in "The School for Witches," and implicitly, in the fear of the madman in "The Mouse and the Woman" and the "answer" in the word spelt by the stars.

Language never loses its magic qualities for Thomas; in his later poems, such as "In Country Sleep," there are numerous references to "spelling" in the sense both of writing and of charms and enchantment. Indeed, the sound patterns in the poems may owe much to the idea of poetry as incantation and ritual. But in the *Portrait* stories the powers of art cease to be used in a purely transcendental way; while language has transformative powers, it does not literally transform the world as it did in "The Map of Love" or "The Mouse and the Woman." It neither provides mastery over the universe nor speaks in the voice of the eternal, but instead is a medium to allow the voices inherent in a smaller world to emerge – in Thomas's case, the voices of the temporal and particular, localized world of Wales. This change may be seen in the way a number of symbols are used in both the early stories and *Portrait*. In "The Enemies," for example, Mrs Owen and her "powers of darkness" use a crystal ball to foresee the coming of their "enemy," the rector Mr Davies, over whom the Owens will have a rather sinister although indefinite control; in *Under Milk Wood*, the two Mrs Dai Breads use a crystal ball not to see others but only themselves, and what they "prophesy" is an act of love. The crystal ball here is merely a reflector of the immediate world around the viewer, like Lily Small's mirror, or the mirror that talks back to Dylan in "One Warm Saturday" – reflectors of the self and the world of which they are a part, not outside or above. The Universal Poet for Thomas is not a god, or the romantic artist-philosopher, prophet, Shelley's "unacknowledged legislator." He is not, as M.H. Abrams characterizes him in *The Mirror and the Lamp*, a "lamp" projecting outward on reality, revealing a superior reality or deeper truth which the expression of his inner self alone provides; instead, he is a "mirror" reflecting the life around him.

The artist must effect a balance between self and a transcendence of self in art. Autobiography is a medium which can effect this because in it the artist's life is subject to artistic shaping; the autobiographical novel stands for the translation of life into art. What might be a form of self-aggrandizement, a privileging of the self, actually uses the emphasis on the particular individual to partially efface the self, the person becoming a reflector for the immediate world around him.

REPRESENTATION OF THE FICTIONALIZING PHENOMENON

Artistic shaping occurs in stories in which the protagonist is a very young child, as in "The Peaches" and "Patricia, Edith and Arnold," as well as in stories in which he is a young man with the self-conscious awareness of an artistic vocation. *Portrait* offers a reflection of the world of which Thomas is an inseparable part, by making his character both an omniscient narrator and a subject with limited vision within the text. "The Peaches," the opening story of the volume, makes apparent the contrast between the innocent child and the ironic, experienced adult narrator, but the child is the focalizer of the story, through whose perception we see the farm and its inhabitants. While the adult describes the farm, it is with the child's vision: "There was nowhere like that farm-yard in all the slapdash country, nowhere so poor and grand and dirty as that square of mud and rubbish and bad wood and falling stone" (127). While the joining of opposites, "poor" and "grand," may be a rhetorical strategy on the part of the narrator to direct our sympathies toward the farm and Annie, it is also an act of perception on the part of the focalizer/character – and what the child sees, or doesn't see, is central to the story.

It is in this opening story that the character is established as a potential artist with keen powers of observation and a high degree of imagination. Looking through the window of a pub, the child watches the secret, inaccessible, puzzling world of the adults, and his limited vision is made apparent by "a stained blind ... drawn half over [the window]. I could see into half of a smoky, secret room" (122). This fragmentary scene then suggests an imaginative continuation, an attempt to complete a story: "The passage grew dark too suddenly, the walls crowded in, and the roofs crouched down to me, staring timidly there in the dark passage in a strange town, the swarthy man appeared like a giant in a cage surrounded by clouds, and the black old man withered into a black hump with a white top; two white hands darted out of the corner with invisible cards. A man with spring-heeled boots and a two-edged knife might be bouncing towards me from Union Street" (122). The boy's fear and imagination get the better of him, and he slips into the nightmare world characteristic of the early stories: "I began to whistle through my teeth, but when I stopped I thought the sound went hissing on behind me. I climbed from the shaft and stepped close to the half-blind window; a hand clawed up the pane to the tassel of the blind; in the little, packed space between me on the cobbles and the card-players at the table, I could not tell which side of the glass was the hand that dragged the blind down slowly" (123).

Autobiography, which replays the self as narrative, is a fitting medium for an artist who, as a child, has a natural tendency to place himself within stories. The "giant in a cage" and the man "with spring-heeled boots" are archetypes from fairy-tales. Beginning with the familiar scenarios of folk-tales, the boy extends this fictional world into the real world around him, creating his own horror story from the image of the hand that he perceives "clawing" and "dragging." These words are hints as to the mentality of the child/focalizer, but the reader ceases to see this as a created, artificial event. Combined with the suspenseful rhythms of the sentences, as imposed by the external adult narrator, this seems to be the beginnings of an ominous tale, the secondary story now taking the place of the first in the perceptions of the reader, who is directed by the focalization of the boy. From this nightmarish reality the boy climbs onto yet another level of story-making, when the situation recalls, via association, another narrative: "A story I had made up in the warm, safe island of my bed, with sleepy midnight Swansea flowing and rolling round outside the house, came blowing down to me then with a noise on the cobbles. I remembered the demon in the story, with his wings and hooks, who clung like a bat to my hair as I battled up and down Wales after a tall, wise, golden, royal girl from Swansea convent" (123). From a partial glimpse of a rather ordinary pub the boy slips through levels of fiction, much the way Marlais does in "The Orchards." The stories within stories blur the distinction between fiction and reality. However, there is a difference between these two stories, for "The Orchards" takes place wholly on the secondary and tertiary fictive levels, whereas "The Peaches" treats those as an imaginative excursion, always grounded in reality.

    The Jarvis Valley stories contain a number of elements that echo Welsh folk-tales, such as abducted preachers ("The Enemies") or disappearing faeries ("A Prospect of the Sea"). When brought together and amplified by the spirit of the valley, they take on an added degree of relevance, for they place the character in a larger, mythic world. Making himself the "hero" of the embedded narrative, the boy in "The Peaches" tells himself a story which is similar to such tales as "The Orchards" and "A Prospect of the Sea," with a fabular Wales peopled by demons and archetypal, inaccessible girls. Yet the stories differ in significant respects, for while the Jarvis Valley stories are predominantly mythical throughout, the stories made up by the boy in

"The Peaches" as a whole are grounded in folk-tale rather than in myth. The fictions of folk-tale become a way for the child to understand reality, setting him up for dealing with real-life experiences, such as fear and loss. The origination of the story that the boy tells himself as consolation, "made in the warm safe island of my bed," functions as a context in which he can safely explore his fears, the knowledge gained from which he can then extend to the larger world. As Bruno Bettelheim suggests, fairy-tales "offer figures onto which the child can externalize what goes on in his mind" (65) in controllable ways, so that he feels less engulfed by unmanagable chaos. The formal structures of narrative consistent within fairy-tale are a controlling device: although fairy-tales have dreamlike features within them, they have a dependable structure with a definite beginning, and a plot that moves toward an equally definite but satisfying solution. Unlike dream, the process of the story does not get lost, and there is always a return to reality. Rather than exploring the mental processes of writing as Thomas does in such stories as "The Orchards" and "The Mouse and the Woman," "The Peaches" uses narrative to explore the interior of the child's mind as he uses the structure of stories to manage reality. In the typical fairy-tale structure, the child is led through the fictional forest but is always returned to reality at the end, strengthened, as Bettelheim suggests, by the excursion into fantasy. Consequently the boy in "The Peaches" moves through levels of fantasy (a possible reality, a mystery story, a blatant fiction, and the controlled anarchy of the fairy-tale world) and is brought back to reality when the "warm lamplight from the bar dazzled me and burned my story up."

Yet the phenomenal world of the *Portrait* stories is never uncoloured by imagination. The boy's ride home contains the seeds of other potential stories, such as the ghost story that might develop from the hangman's house, long abandoned, with the light shining from the window. When he arrives at Gorsehill, he is not merely inside the house, but is also within a created fictional world, having transformed the corridors: "I might have been walking into the hollow night and the wind, passing through a tall vertical shell on an inland sea-shore" (124). We see the first glimpses of the self-consciously alienated artist stance: "I thought that I had been walking long, damp passages all my life, and climbing stairs in the dark, alone" (126). In a safer context, no longer isolated, his vision changes from dark to bright; again he slips from a partially imaginary scene into a full-fledged fairy-tale scenario, surrounded by his own stories and those of a communal folk tradition: "One minute I was small and cold, skulking dead scared down a passage in my stiff, best suit, with my hollow belly thumping and my heart like a time bomb, clutching my grammar school cap, unfamiliar to myself, a snub-nosed story-teller lost in his own adventures and longing to be home; the next I was a royal nephew in smart town clothes, embraced and welcomed, standing in the snug centre of my stories and listening to the clock announcing me" (125). While he primarily identifies himself as a "story-teller," a "poet" rather than a mere boy, he is both the teller of stories and subject of the tales, both within "The Peaches" and the embedded fairy-tale, in which he is the "royal nephew." He separates his identities as narrator and character, especially when uncomfortable with the scenarios he has created – watching himself "lost in his own adventures," he is "unfamiliar to [him]self" (125); not wholly in control of his stories, his character-self and creator-self become disjointed. Yet the scenario in which he finds himself has all the transformative powers of the typical fairy-tale, and as the clock strikes he is transformed into the royal nephew/hero both the centre of attention in the room and, "in the snug center" (125) of his stories, no longer an outsider. This shift of attention is similar to the way the reader, engaged in the embedded text, ceases to notice the narrator; completely enmeshed in story, Dylan the "snub-nosed story-teller" (125) vanishes in the face of the story told, and his existence as character predominates.

The Cinderella story functions as an integrating device for the young boy, for within the character's fictional projection of himself, his multiple identities appear less as separate beings than as layers of personality. "Like a prince taking off his disguise," he reveals his identities according to the various costumes that he wears; he can easily slip from being a "snub-nosed story-teller" in a school cap, a royal nephew, a city boy, or a country boy without estrangement, by wearing the costume appropriate to the role. "I wanted to wear my old suit, to look like a proper farm boy and have manure in my shoes and hear it squelch as I walked to see a cow have calves and a bull on top of a cow, to run down in the dingle and wet my stockings, to go out and shout, 'come on, you b–', and pelt the hens and talk in a proper voice. But I went upstairs to put my striped suit on" (130). Dylan's old suit – the costume of the Welsh country boy – is described as "proper," a word that we may attribute to the focalizer rather than the narrator here, for it is used in the sense of being real, genuine, natural, or suitable, not in the rhetorical sense of "decent" or "respectable" that the experienced adult narrator, or for that matter Mrs Williams in the story, might use it. What the boy deems "proper" is precisely the opposite of Mrs Williams's definition of the word.

The difference between the city and country is also revealed in the clothing of the two women. In contrast to Mrs Williams – who, with her pretentious city airs, her perfume, powder, and rings, is "fitted out like a mayoress or a ship" and sways on her "ankles swollen over her pointed shoes" – Annie, "who had forgotten to change her gymshoes," wears the incongruous although more practical footwear, "which were caked with mud and all holes," but which were themselves characteristic of the farm. Annie's mode of dress is "proper" in the same sense that Dylan's old suit is, being suitable to the environment; Mrs Williams's sense of propriety in attire is ironically out of place. The natural world of the farm, with all its decay, is associated with procreation and teeming with life; it is the place of play and of the imagination. Annie's poor attempts to hide her country origins and to aspire to Mrs Williams's urban sophistication result in unnatural or even deathlike images: her "black shining dress that smelt of mothballs" (130), the ever-dusty best room with its "shrouded harmonium" (130), and even the long-preserved tin of peaches. The deathliness of these false attempts at sophistication may be contrasted to the natural decay of the farm.

Just as the decay inherent in life can't be kept from the farm, the two boys, after a day of play, begin physically to resemble the wild natural world as if in sympathetic identification with it:

"our jackets were torn and our stockings were wet and our shoes were sticky; we had green moss and brown bark on our hands and faces" (133). Pan-like, they seem to grow naturally out of their environment. The difference between the life and death of the farm and the deathlike existence of the urban world, like the difference between Dylan's two suits, is made evident again by the emphasis on the clothing of Dylan's friend Jack, who, after their rift, joins his mother in more ways than one, driving off "still and stiff" in his best suit.

Like the country in "In Country Sleep," the setting of "The Peaches" is a place of imagination, a playground of both possibility and identity: "On my haunches, eager and alone, casting an ebony shadow, with the Gorsehill jungle swarming, the violent, impossible birds and fishes leaping, hidden under four-stemmed flowers the height of horses, in the early evening in a dingle near Carmarthen, my friend Jack Williams invisibly near me, I felt all my young body like an excited animal surrounding me ... the memory around and within flying, jumping, swimming, waiting to pounce. There, playing Indians in the evening, I was aware of me myself in the exact middle of a living story, and my body was my adventure and my name" (132). The boy's previous estrangement from himself is here mended, as it was in the Cinderella scenario, with his awareness of his identity. His strong sense of his physical being, and the equation of his physicality with his name, hints at an edenic world where there is no disjunction between being and meaning: like the names earned in naïve romance, his name is his essence, because his name is equated with his physicality (body = name) and his being is determined by action. Partly through the innocence inherent in the child's world, and partly through the creativity of play, gestures may be made toward a return to the edenic state. When greeted by Annie he found himself in "the snug center of his stories," and here he is "in the exact middle of a living story." As autobiographical subject of the stories he creates, he is both removed from the world and acting out the world in a self-enclosed playground of fiction. Thomas illustrates a variety of relationships between tellers and their stories. Sometimes there is a rift between a narrator/character and his stories, such as in "One

Warm Saturday," with its ironic distances. In other stories, such as "The Peaches," there is an identification not only between teller and story, but also between these and the world. The boy Dylan is the story he tells when the narrator says "my body was my adventure and my name."[5] Surrounded by his "young body," the "jungle of the farm," and his "adventures" – identified in "The Peaches" and in the early short stories as the stories themselves – he is identified with the world, and the world is his creation. Autobiography, the telling of the self, is the medium not only of *Portrait* but of all the embedded narratives within it. Going beyond his self-concerns in the embedded stories, Thomas extends the edenic identification between name, physical being, and action to the larger world that we see in *Portrait*. In what ultimately might be characterized as "metafictional autobiography," *Portrait* tells stories about a character telling stories about himself.

This edenic world, allowing an identity between being, essence, and story, is possible through recreation in story, partially reconstructed through memory. Here it is the external narrator who observes in the boy "memory waiting to pounce" – past, present, and future are rolled into one in the timeless world of the child. The stories recreated, through memory, by the adult in the fallen world, are a gesture toward this once-possible state. The boy himself, living his story, is in a perpetual present with no awareness of temporal divisions. It is also significant that the child views the country identity as having a "proper voice," for this too is characteristic of a gesture toward the edenic world; we may see this as a precursor to *Under Milk Wood*, where the voices of the Welsh villagers may be the voice of the town itself.

Important to this sense of identity for the boy is the nature of play and the communal nature of its imaginative creation. The "fall" may be seen to occur with the rift between the boys, a separation caused by Jack's unwillingness to fully enter the world of his friend. Reality intrudes when Jack overhears Uncle Jim and Annie criticizing his mother, and Jack then refuses to enjoy the world in which he previously played. Suddenly he rejects the imagination of Dylan and Gwilym, telling his distorted, stripped down (but from his perspective literal) version of events to his mother: "'And he called you a bloody cow, and he said he'd whip the hell out of me, and Gwilym took me to the barn in the dark and let the mice run over me, and Dylan's a thief, and that old woman's spoilt my jacket'" (136–7). Before Jack leaves, the boys play alone, each going his own way. Dylan climbs a tree and watches Jack below him, determined to recreate their game of Indians "all alone, scalping through the bushes, surprising himself round a tree, hiding from himself in the grass. I called to him once, but he pretended not to hear. He played alone, silently and savagely" (136). Dylan's attempt to recreate their sense of communal play is futile: "My bough lurched, the heads of the dingle bushes spun towards me like green tops, 'I'm falling!' I cried, my trousers saved me, I swung and grasped, this was one minute of wild adventure, but Jack did not look up and the minute was lost" (136). Through the punctuation and the rhythm of this sentence, Thomas as narrator recreates the sense of the near fall, regenerating in retrospect the story, the "one minute of wild adventure." But to the boy within the text, the moment is "lost" because Jack does not respond to the invitation, and without response, the dialogic play is irreclaimable. There is something absurd about Jack playing alone at a game that clearly requires at least two players; Dylan likewise finds his potential "adventure" futile, and "climbed, without dignity, to the ground." It is perhaps significant that Dylan's final, aborted adventure with Jack involves a literal fall, emblematic of the linguistic fall that occurs with the acquisition of meaning. It is Jack who has already fallen. Dylan, still a part of the edenic world of the farm is "saved," but is, however, "falling," suspended in a world "bound to fall," as later stories in the volume attest. The loss of his friend and their communal play is only the first of numerous losses which characterize the fallen world.

"Fern Hill" enacts a similar movement from identity to isolation. Recalling his childhood summers spent on Ann Jones's farm in Carmarthenshire, Thomas describes his young self as "prince of the apple towns," an identity similar to that of the child in "The Peaches," a "royal nephew" from a fairy-tale. The adult speaker of the poem is at an ironic distance from his youthful self-perception, aware that, as a character within a story, he is out of time, and yet, being mortal, subject to it, in a story that begins "once below a time." Here too the child is identified with the natural world through such descriptions as "green and golden." The "holy," "blessed" "simple" world is an edenic one: "it was all shining, it was Adam and maiden ... so it must have been after the birth of the simple light / In the first, spinning place." But time, personified, soon causes the inevitable fall, and "the children, green and golden / Follow him out of grace." With the fall occurs a separation apparent in the split self: the adult narrator, looking back on his self as a child, watches the child begin to retreat from his vision as "time" takes him "by the shadow of [his] hand." Because the child and the farm exist in a symbiotic relationship before the fall, when the child leaves, the farm, in its edenic identity, also ceases to exist for the adult, who wakes "to the farm forever fled from the childless land." However, the poet uses recreation in memory to restore the timelessness of the story he was once a part of, and returns to a state of suspension, both "about to fall" and not-yet-fallen, in the last lines of the poem: "Time held me green and dying / Though I sang in my chains like the sea."

In "The Peaches," the temporality of the fallen world, in contrast to the eternal present of the edenic one, is evident in the decay of the farm: "The ramshackle outhouses had tumbling, rotten roofs, jagged holes in their sides, broken shutters, and peeling whitewash; rusty screws ripped out from the dangling, crooked boards, the lean cat of the night before sat snugly between the splintered jaws of bottles, cleaning its face, on the tip of the rubbish pile that rose triangular and smelling sweet and strong to the level of the riddled cart-house roof" (127). The narrator seems to have captured the farm in the process of transformation, which, in spite of the decay, is more appealing than the frozen, lifeless image of Jack and his mother driving stiffly and pristinely back to the city. The plurals in the sentence also give a feeling of multiplicity which adds to the richness of the farm. The mingling of the past with the present tense – the boards "tumbling" and "dangling," the cat "cleaning its face," the rubbish "smelling sweet and strong" – recreates both the edenic, eternal present of the boy and the process inherent in the temporal fallen world of which the farm is a part. As later tales will make apparent, the recreation through narrative retelling is a way of partially forestalling the completion of the fall, by creating representations of this lost condition.

"The Peaches" offers examples of the poet who is sometimes already fallen, sometimes not yet fallen, and sometimes living in an overlapping region common to both states. At the point of play where the boy's "body" is his "name" and his "adventure," there is an identity with self that precedes the separation that occurs with the subject's entry into the symbolic order. But earlier in the story we are already witness to moments where the boy has entered into the symbolic register, those moments when, as a character within the stories he creates, he is "unfamiliar to [him]self." The split between his selves, external story-teller and character within the story told, or between what Genette calls the "speaking subject" and the "subject of utterance" (*Narrative Discourse* 41), reflects the gap separating being from signification. As the focalizer he attains subjectivity through his signification in the symbolic order, and undergoes a gradual movement away from being; as the subject of the utterance he is excluded from the real by the language which creates the symbolic order. The subject within the story is thus defined by a linguistic structure that does not address his being, but which determines his cultural existence. No longer is the boy's body his name; instead, he is defined by such linguistic/cultural determinants as "Prince," "Hero," or "Poet," taking meaning from, as well as determining the meanings of, other signifiers in the symbolic order. As the subject, he becomes subordinate to the symbolic order which then determines his identity and desires.

One consolation for the separation from being is that, for the potential artist, there is more than one symbolism, or mode of symbolism, within the symbolic order. There is, on one level, the adult world of meaning which the child only partially understands – a limitation which explains his ability to move back and forth between states, occupying a border country between the pre-fallen and the fallen worlds. The rift with Jack occurs with Jack's intimations of this world through the conversation he hears, plunging him into the fallen world of adult meaning. For

Dylan, the potential artist, other examples of the symbolic order are linguistically created worlds, characterized by the stories he creates or imitates, such as the fairy-tales which inform his flights of fancy. The embedded story early in the tale, with the demon and the royal girl, illustrates the separations that occur with the subject's entry into the symbolic order. The boy's object of desire here, as in many of Thomas's early stories, is an unattainable female whose identity is derived from fairy-tales, and is hence a linguistic being who is part of the "other" – language, the symbolic order – forever beyond the reach of the subject. While his fears and desires might originate in the real world, the object of his fears and desires (the fairy-tale princess), originates in fiction, and the subject continuously arrives at an impasse. As in the early tales, "The Orchards," for example, or the embedded tale of the royal girl from Swansea convent, the hero can never close the gap between himself as subject, as a signifier in the symbolic order, and the object of desire, who is also a signifier in the same linguistic structure. They acquire meaning through their relation to each other, but only in terms of their difference, and hence they can never come together as a unified whole. The very presence of an object of desire is evidence of the subject's entry into the symbolic order, the fallen linguistic world. But she is clearly less real than he is, derived from tales culturally acknowledged as fictional, and he is only partially fallen into the symbolic order, still having one foot in the real, widening the gap between them even further. Yet ironically this gap between the subject and the object of his desire becomes the impetus for moving forward, and such movement becomes the informing operation of narrative. Hence Dylan, as future artist within the *Portrait*, creates narratives to fill in the gaps between things that he sees but does not fully comprehend; likewise Thomas as narrator external to the stories within the text employs the same strategy by turning memories of his own past into narrative structures. But these memories are momentary glimpses which are also necessarily incomplete because of the lack of omniscience characteristic of his internal position.

There is an inevitable failure of correspondence between the actual, the source of the drives, and the symbolic order in which the narratives are created, as the young Dylan in "The Peaches" begins to sense with the loss of his friend. The older Dylan at the end of the volume not only gains a conscious awareness of the difference between the imaginary and the real, but also must effect a compromise between them, after being forced to choose between the two. Betrayed by his fantasies at the end of "One Warm Saturday," he loses the real-life Lou. However, there are suggestions that, without having to deny either life or art, the emerging artist will devise ways to allow life and art to modify each other. The real-life, "hardly known and never-to-be forgotten people" of the last paragraph, imprinted on his memory and amplified by his imagination, will be the stuff of future stories. In turn, such stories, like the scenarios conjured up for Ray in "Who Do You Wish Was With Us," become consolations to make the "real" world more bearable.

"The Peaches" sets up many themes that are further explored and developed in the other stories in *Portrait*. While it traces the growth of the poet, *Portrait* is not strictly chronological, but is loosely structured to reflect the fluid, lyrical qualities of memory, each story roughly equivalent to insights marked as points in time. The third story in the volume, "Patricia, Edith and Arnold," for example, reveals the boy at his youngest, under the care of a housemaid; he has neither the fledgling independence of the boy in "The Peaches" nor his self-conscious sense of identity as a story-teller. As such, his imaginative play is more fully "real" to him, and he does not tell the story so much as live it: "The small boy in his invisible engine, the Cwmdonkin Special, backed the Flying Welshman from the washhouse to the open door of the coal-hole and pulled hard on the brake that was a hammer in his pocket: assistants in uniform ran out with fuel; he spoke to a saluting fireman, and the engine shuffled off, round the barbed walls of China that kept the cats away, by the frozen rivers in the sink, in and out of the coal-hole tunnel" (144). With the first-person narratives there is a split between the two selves, the one an external story-teller, the other within the story; here the subject has not yet objectified himself. Creating some distance with his third-person narrator, and eradicating the ironic tone present in the first-person stories, Thomas does not tell us that the boy imagined these things – he tells us that the boy *did* them. For the slightly older boy in "The Peaches" a retreat into story is used partly to override the distress caused by a failure of correspondence between his drives and the symbolic order, while for the younger child in "Patricia, Edith and Arnold" fiction is a natural domain from which he is called away by intrusions of reality. Only later is he forced to deal with discrepancies between the two worlds. In his pre-fallen state, there is no split between fiction and reality: "He knew that this was an afternoon on which anything might happen; it might snow enough for sliding on a tray; uncles from America, where he had no uncles, might arrive with revolvers and St. Bernards; Ferguson's shop might catch on fire and all the piece-packets fall on the pavements" (145). His is a world in which the wish-fulfilment of fairy-tale is a possibility.

Even more than the boy in "The Peaches," he is an outsider to the world of the adults. He lacks knowledge of the sexual games that Arnold is playing with Patricia and Edith, and he seems oblivious to their pain: "they were old and cuckoo, sitting in the empty shelter sobbing over nothing." Outside of loss, he is in a state of pre-lapsarian innocence. Solipsistically concerned only for his own being, he tunes them out periodically for his play. Yet he is not completely unaware of the goings-on around him; "he notices everything" (147), as Patricia points out, but there is a gap between what he sees and what he understands. While his repetition by rote is often embarrassing to others – such as when he conflates two stories to announce that his mother has "gone on a randy with Mr Robert. Randy, sandy, bandy" (144) – it is more significant for the truth he unwittingly reveals. For example, the boy does not understand why Patricia is angry with Arnold, and he "stood bewildered between them" (151), but he instinctively knows that Arnold is lying, and he reveals this through a type of imaginative play: when Arnold tells Patricia that he prefers her to Edith, and says of Edith, "I hate her. Cross my heart!", the boy completes the childish oath in his head ("Cross my heart and hope to die"), and then cries, "Bang! Bang!" ("You're Dead"), thus fulfilling Arnold's "wish." While the three adults around him might consider his cry a non sequitur, his game of cowboys is an apt adaptation of the real situation. The knowledge that he gains through play, like his excursions into fairy-tale, helps him to attain congruence between his perceptions and the exterior world. Yet, to the adults in the story, his response is nonsense. He repeats what he hears without fully understanding it; the words acquire meaning only through repetition and through the original associations he makes in his own mind – in contrast to Arnold's carefully crafted letters, whose words when repeated (exactly, to both Patricia and Edith) are empty of meaning.

Overhearing Patricia and Edith, the child says to himself, "someone has been pulling Edith's toes ... Edith went to market" (148), making associations with a nursery rhyme, the first literature that a child usually encounters, and a natural domain of nonsense. The boy here is not impelled to find meaning in the words he hears, but instead seems happy to acquiesce in the hermeneutic impasse characteristic of the pre-lapsarian condition. The boy himself in this story exists as an undeveloped personality, being rather than signifying. Unlike his older self in "The Peaches," he is not placed within his own story, and his acts of imaginative creation are not consciously created as made-up fiction or story. Because he does not yet see himself as a separate being that functions as a character within his made-up scenarios, he is not yet in the process of self-creation that accompanies the fall into the symbolic order. In his own world, he is not part of a closed system of signification and he does not function as a signifier for anything around him.

"ONE WARM SATURDAY"

The last story in *Portrait of the Artist as a Young Dog*, "One Warm Saturday," is, like "Patricia, Edith and Arnold," narrated in the third person, but it effects a more obvious ironic distance between the external commentator and the main character. There are many parodic allusions to his earlier self, the writer of the early stories and poems, "a man doomed for ever to the company of his maggots" (219). The temporal and cognitive distance created by the third-person narrative estranges his real self even further from the self in the symbolic order, who, appearing as "he," as a separate being, is a fully created character in a story rather than an extension of himself. As in "The Peaches," the focalizer is the character rather than the narrator, for many adjectives are clearly attributable to the self-conscious young Poet who strives to play the stereotypical anguished Artist.

The story begins with the young man drawing a woman in the sand, an act reminiscent of "The Hunchback in the Park." This sand woman is not unlike the traces of ideal innocence and unity expressed in literary terms in earlier stories, the unattainable fairy-tale princesses who, being purely in the realm of art, are eternally desired objects. The young man then draws a man in the sand – perhaps his equally fictitious symbolic self – which is promptly ruined by a child, after which "the young man sat with the shadows of his failure at his side" (219). It is unclear whether it is the character or narrator who sees the young man as a "failure," and by implication, a failed artist. The sand woman is a precursor of Lou, a real woman who later appears in the story. Significantly, the young man loses her too, just as he fails to attain any of the symbolic women he creates. Although Lou is a real woman, the young man fictionalizes her and she becomes yet another impossible object of desire. He apparently becomes a double failure, as both "artist" and "man." But the loss in the real world becomes the source of story, and the narrative impetus, the continuation through signification, ironically becomes the way out of his artistic impasse. As in "Old Garbo," the young Dylan who is the character within the story is a seeming failure, but the older Thomas who emerges, the narrator of the volume as a whole, implicitly has something to offer through his fictional recreation of reality.

The subject of this story is clearly the author of "The Orchards," self-consciously isolated in the world of his poems, trying to remain untouched by the phenomenal world around him. As he watches from a distance, the families on the beach "moved him, he thought dramatically in his isolation, to an old shame and pity; outside all holiday ... beyond the high and ordinary, sweating, sun-awakened power and stupidity of the summer flesh on a day and a world out" (219). He regains an awareness of the body like that in "The Peaches," when his flesh is awakened by the day around him in spite of himself. He compromises his stance of isolated poet, the "man of vision" – in effect, his fictional identity. Observing him being drawn between the life of the "poet" and the life of a young man, we witness a moment of rejection of the earlier self, the Thomas of "The Orchards" who turns away from the real world for the linguistically created world of his poetry: "He thought: Poets live and walk with their poems; a man with visions needs no other company; Saturday is a crude day; I must go home and sit in my bedroom by the boiler. But he was not a poet living and walking, he was a young man in a sea town on a warm bank holiday, with two pounds to spend; he had no visions, only two pounds and a small body with its feet on the littered sand; serenity was for old men; and he moved away, over the railway points, on to the tramlined road" (221). The "bedroom by the boiler" is his "writer's garret," like that of the boy in "The Orchards" who shuts himself in his room. There is another reference to this room in "The Fight," where in his imagination he turns it into a "library" in which he resides as a Poet and man of the world: "I was always waiting for the opportunity to bring someone into my bedroom – 'Come into my den; excuse the untidiness; take a chair. No! Not that one, it's broken!' – and force him to see the poem accidentally. 'I put it there to make me blush.' But nobody ever came in except my mother" (156). Just as the ordinariness of the room is revealed in "The Fight," so too in "One Warm Saturday" the "bedroom by the boiler" is only that. He cannot reject the outer world for more lofty pursuits, because he "had no visions."

Thomas's early stories may easily be called "visionary," emerging from the dark abysses of the demonic and the grotesque; there are few references to everyday life, but many to nocturnal fears, ghostly premonitions, and dark psychic forces. As they are later caricatured, these might be seen as apparent signs of a morbid neurosis. In "One Warm Saturday," the mysteries of the mythic, dark otherworld are at odds with the "sun-awakened" power of the ordinary day. The pull of the artist within him retreats in favour of his identity as a "young man with two pounds to spend" and he is drawn into a game with others, "'the lone wolf playing ball' he said to himself" (220), aware of the incongruity, unlike his earlier self. His sense of distance, from himself and others, proves absurd with this act of self-awareness; like Jack in "The Peaches" stalking himself in a lone game of Indians, he plays a role at odds with its context. Abandoning the "lone wolf" stance, "he felt his happiness return in a boast of the body." The awareness of his physicality, his being in the here and now, momentarily calls to him more strongly than the world of words, yet he continues to maintain a sense of separation as the artist objectifying himself. Leaving the game, he asks out loud, "and what shall a prig do now?" (221). Detached from himself, he watches himself fail to act; as a writer he is not in control of the ineffectual person he creates. His question to himself catches the attention of Lou, and his objective artist self "marked carefully and coldly in one glance, all the unusual details of her appearance" (222). But his apparent act of objective perception is coloured by his ever-present tendency to slip into fiction: "How beautiful she is, he thought, with his mind on words and his eyes on her hair and her red and white skin, how beautifully she waits for me, though she does not know she is waiting and I can never tell her" (222). While he stares with his "mind on words," reality intrudes in the less than dignified form of midges that "flew into his mouth" (222), and he retreats in shame. Again, this fleeting awareness of himself, grounded in reality, proves too much for him, and he seeks advice from his other self regarding his next move. In a literal act of self-reflectiveness, he attempts to gain knowledge from a mirror. His reflection, like the external narrator, has the ironic distance necessary to undercut his own self-conscious poses: "And what shall the terrified prig of a love-mad young man do next? he asked his reflection silently in the distorting mirror of the empty 'Victoria' saloon. His ape-like hanging face, with 'Bass' across the forehead, gave back a cracked sneer ... 'You saw a queer tart in a park, his reflection answered, she was a child of nature, oh my! oh my! did you see the dewdrops in her hair? Stop talking to the mirror like a man in a magazine, I know you too well" (222–3). The "distorting mirror" is an apt metaphor for his tendency to slip into words that alter reality; the "child of nature" is wearing a "Woolworth's rose," a "red paper flower" and "fun-fair jewelry" (222). Yet ironically, the mirror does not seem to be distorting at all, but rather, reflects naturalistically, correcting his romantic vision. "Distortion" is a relative term, for the distorting mirror of art paradoxically can tell the truth. The image that the mirror recalls to Dylan, of a "man in a magazine," further points out the artificiality of its own act of self-reflexivity. Here the act of self-reflection is doubled, and engages the possibility of an infinity of fictional levels, recalling the infinite regress of the early stories. Throughout the story the central character struggles with his tendency to slip away from reality into fiction: "Her voice was as gentle as he had imagined it to be. ... He saw her as a wise, soft girl whom no hard company could spoil ... Phrasing her gentleness, faithlessly running to words away from the real room and his love in the middle, he woke with a start and saw her lively body six steps from him, no calm heart dressed in a sentence, but a pretty girl, to be got and kept" (229). We soon see that her "gentleness" is but a delusion of a writer creating a fictionalized woman rather than viewing the real one in front of him. He extrapolates from the real, idealizing and linguifying her. In so doing, he creates more possibility, but at the expense of her socio-cultural identity. He ultimately awakes to this awareness and the fact that he is being "faithless" to reality when he hides in a purely linguistic world.

However, this is not an easy move away from the safety of his fictions, and he makes numerous false starts. When the "girl he loved" first enters the room as a flesh-and-blood woman rather than an imagined vision, his impulse is to run home and hide under the bedclothes, but "he remembered his age and his poems, and would not move" (226). There is no evidence that he has come any further than the boy in "The Fight," who wrote poems about love and lust although he had no actual experience of them; his poems then become something he must live up to; he must turn his fictions into reality. This of course is no easy task, owing to the excess of his fantasy. As he did in "The Fight," the Thomas character much later in the story borrows Tennyson's voice to express his desires, and once again he is defeated – perhaps precisely because it is not his own voice, nor is it genuinely addressing his own being. Imagining that Lou shares with him the secret language of lovers, he reads Tennyson's "Come into the Garden Maud," hinting broadly that he wishes to be alone with Lou, raising his voice as he recites the lines, "When will the dancers leave her alone? / She is weary of dance and play." Being neither the female subject of the poem nor the "wise, soft girl" he imagines her to be, Lou does not pick up the allusion. His romantic pose is further deflated when Harold, one of the intruding company, says that Tennyson was "a little man with a hump," and the ensuing argument about factual details regarding Tennyson effectively breaks the spell of the poetry.

Later the Thomas character does manage to repeat a fictional scenario in reality, but the results are equally disappointing. He imagines himself slipping away with Lou under the bedclothes: "Who would look for them there, if they were dead still and soundless? The others would shout to them down the dizzy stairs or rummage in the silence about the narrow, obstacled corridors or stumble out into the night to search for them among the cranes and ladders in the desolation of the destroyed houses. He could hear, in the made-up dark, Mr O'Brien's voice cry, 'Lou, where are you? Answer! answer!'" (234). Unfortunately, when this scenario is actualized, it is the young man who gets lost in "obstacled corridors" and he who cries, "'Lou, where are you? ... 'Answer! answer!'" (237) into the real dark. Like Marlais's quest in "The Orchards," the story begins as planned but becomes deflected. Having become the central character in his own story, he loses his visionary woman – precisely because she is visionary and not real. As in a child's excursions into fairytale, he can only emerge from fiction the better for his trials if the fantasy addresses realistic concerns, and if he does not remain caught up in the fantasy for too long. In "One Warm Saturday," the hero has yet to avoid these traps.

However, it may be implied that the older Thomas who is the author of the volume as a whole has outgrown these tendencies, and has effected a balance between the factual world and his need to create stories. As in such stories as "The Peaches," "Old Garbo," and "Who Do You Wish Was With Us," loss in the real world is partially compensated for when the lost potential is recreated in story or memory; we see this for example in the ending of "One Warm Saturday," where "the light of the one weak lamp in a rusty circle fell across the brick-heaps and the broken wood and dust that had been houses once, where the small and hardly known and never-to-be-forgotten people of the dirty town had lived and loved and died, and, always, lost" (238). The Thomas character in "One Warm Saturday" and "Old Garbo" may be seen in some ways as being the same literary type as Marlais and Childe Roland, an untested adventurer setting out for something that eludes him, yet something he must continue to quest for. He is an artist who paradoxically reaches his goal in spite of his apparent inability to do so. The losses of the ordinary people, the writer included, become the stuff of stories, a recreation which turns an absence into a presence. Being "hardly known," the people are fragments which yield a partially invented fiction; but, unlike the mythic people of the Jarvis Valley, these fictionalized characters have some basis in reality. Where Marlais comes to rest upon fictionality, Thomas here perpetuates "reality." "Never to be forgotten," the people are imprinted on the writer's memory, amplified by his imagination, and passed on through the narrated tales as if a part of local folklore – eternally relevant because, like the characters in fairy-tales, they address the immediate concerns of similar people in the small world on which the stories are focused. The sense of nostalgia that John Ackerman, among others, admires is effective because the stories address personal concerns with which the reader can identify.

Eventual success for Thomas, the external narrator, is planted in "One Warm Saturday" with the character's growing inability to ignore the world around him. The "distorting" mirror, like an oracle, and like fiction itself, speaks the truth, however superficially altered: "Older and wiser and no better, he would have looked in the mirror to see if his discovery and loss had marked themselves upon his face in shadows under the eyes or lines about the mouth, were it not for the answer he knew he would receive from the distorted reflection" (223). It is not really necessary for his speaking reflection to reveal the truth to him, for, in spite of his fantasies, he is aware of a difference between fiction and reality, even as he seems to live within those fictions. The stories he creates, like the distorting mirror, become a way for him to face the truth of himself. With each fiction he is ironically led back to his being, and with it, to the phenomenal world:

> He shook off the truthless, secret tragedy with a sneer and a blush, straightened his melancholy hat into a hard-brimmed trilby, dismissed the affected stranger. In the safe centre of his own identity, the familiar world about him like another flesh, he sat sad and content in the plain room of the undistinguished hotel at the sea-end of the shabby, spreading town where everything was happening. He had no need of the dark, interior world when Tawe pressed in upon him and the eccentric, ordinary people came bursting and crawling, with noise and colours, out of their houses, out of the graceless buildings, the factories and avenues, the shining shops and blaspheming chapels, the terminuses and the meeting halls, the falling alleys and brick lanes, from the arches and shelters and holes behind the hoardings, out of the common, wild intelligence of the town. (225)

Unlike the boy in "The Peaches," whose estrangement from himself is a necessary result of his childhood initiation into self-consciousness, the older character in this story has had time to examine his various self-images and to test them against reality. Hence he rejects the melodramatic mourner as "affected" and "truthless," and reconciles his own inner being with the phenomenal world. "In the safe centre of his own identity," he returns to the security that the awareness of his body brings to him while playing in childhood, when his being grounds him and provides a secure home base from which to venture. His excursions may be made safely because the world into which he ventures is a part of him, "familiar," and "like another flesh." In "The Peaches" it was "in the snug centre" of his stories that the boy found the comfort to deal with the world, but here the more mature Dylan is centred in reality. In a reversal of the fairy-tale pattern, he moves from reality into a harmless and familiar world of fiction by transposing the world around him into story, as he proposes in "Old Garbo" and again in the last lines of the story and volume. Here he writes of the "small and hardly known and never-to-be-forgotten people." His rejection of the "dark interior world" for the world of "eccentric, ordinary" people marks his transition from being the writer of the mythical, surreal Jarvis Valley stories to being that of the more "realistic" *Portrait of the Artist as a Young Dog*. Significantly, one of the catalysts for this change is Tawe "pressing upon him" with the insistence of reality. Tawe, first mentioned in the story "Where Tawe Flows," refers to both the town and the river ("Abertawe" is the Welsh name for Swansea, meaning "at the mouth of the river Tawe"). The river stands for the community of the eccentric Welsh town, which, represented by the group of writers, becomes the true focus of the tale – rather than the hero, "young Mr Thomas," whose stories of vampires and cat-women represent the immature, and soon to be dismissed, dweller in the "dark, interior world."

"WHERE TAWE FLOWS"

"Where Tawe Flows" may be seen as an "Ivy Day in the Committee Room" turned inside out: the socio-political discussions of a group of men prove merely a cover for clandestine story-telling. This tale presents story-telling as a common and at times pressing human act, into which the participants naturally lapse. Mr Humphries calls story-telling "talking shop," and the tales themselves are described as valuable commodities. In the "chit chat" before their "work" begins, "Mr Thomas" begins to tell his "abattoir anecdote" but is admonished, "you mustn't waste stories" (183). The "work" is a collaborative "Novel of Provincial Life" called, like the *Portrait* story which describes its writing, "Where Tawe Flows," and its subject is "everyday man." The collaborators create stories that are to varying degrees about themselves. Mr Humphries, for example, who "was a schoolteacher, a tall, fair man with a stammer, who had written an unsuccessful novel" (181), writes a story featuring a character who "was a sensitive schoolmaster of advanced opinions, who was misjudged and badly treated"(186). Although Mr Thomas lapses into the fantastic with his story of a vampire, he acquiesces in favour of Mr Evans's story of Mary Morgan, a "real" and ordinary woman. All of the writers of the "Novel" are in fact representatives of "everyday man," for none has such an artistic vocation as might have been envisioned by the author of the less mature stories. "Young Mr Thomas," rather than being the self-professed "Poet" of earlier days, is an unemployed soon-to-be journalist, and his fellow writers are by profession a teacher, an insurance collector, and a rubber-products salesman. There seems to be reference here to Marxist ideas of collectivity and working-class fiction, perhaps a nod to Thomas's friend Bert Trick, who was, as Paul Ferris notes, "passionately concerned with both literature and left-wing politics" (*CL* 23n). Yet although Mr Humphries advises that they "get their realism straight" following Mr Thomas's fantastic offer, their novel of everyday life is not a naturalistic slice of life. Their stories are artistically shaped versions of reality, as is evident when they make a point of leaving out a description of the slums. We might even guess at the future failure of Mr Thomas as a journalist, for, like his friends, he is not dispassionately objective. They all are, instead, compassionate, benevolent "translators of man's manuscript" ("Prologue" 107) who in some ways prefigure *Under Milk Wood*'s Eli Jenkins, the chronicler of his own town in his "White Book of Llareggub." Although Eli "tells only the truth in his Lifework" (*UMW* 81), it is through benevolent and innocent eyes that he sees what he will set down in verse. The writers in "Where Tawe Flows" foreshadow Eli Jenkins's appeal to the audience in his "Sunset Poem" to "see [their] best side, not [their] worst" (*UMW* 87).

Eli's "White Book," as a portrait of Llareggub, may be a version of *Under Milk Wood*, the work that contains it, which is itself a portrait of Llareggub. Likewise, the fictitious "Where Tawe Flows" (the "Novel") is a version of the *Portrait* story by the same name, within which it is contained. As in the earlier stories such as "The Orchards," Thomas indulges in self-reflection, but here it is as much communal as solipsistic. Artists, and Thomas himself, are still much in evidence. In both cases, where the story and the story-within-the-story mirror each other, the reader moves from one fictive level to another, yet without losing her/his sense of what level of fictiveness is in operation. This is partly accomplished through the extensive use of dialogue, and a foregrounding of the narrative voices drawing us back to the act of story-telling, perhaps as important as the story itself.

Just as Eli is one of many voices in *Under Milk Wood*, "young Mr Thomas" in "Where Tawe Flows" is only one of a number of story-tellers, and is in fact relegated to a secondary position, for the bulk of the tale, the story-within-the-story of Mary Morgan and her suitors, belongs to Mr Evans. The spread of voices, and the decentring of the Thomas character, may be seen as yet other steps toward the "play for voices." In another way, the Thomas character functions not only as an Eli Jenkins, but also as a Captain Cat, for, being less of a teller, he begins to function as a listener, who, like the actual reader, enters into the tale. The narrative of "Where Tawe Flows" is similar to that of "Just Like Little Dogs," where the Thomas character is a listener to the internal story told by Tom, able imaginatively to enter into Tom's story as he "lay like a pimp in a bush by Tom's side" (179). Imaginative participation on the part of the listener/reader in both *Portrait* stories looks forward to the collaborative role of the reader in *Under Milk Wood*. Tellers and listeners alike are participants in the stories, and thus in the towns depicted, for the stories the characters tell of their town are portraits of themselves. Like Llareggub, the river Tawe and the village near it stand symbolically for the people; similarly the world around the Thomas character serves as a "second flesh," or as the "voice" of the country in "The Peaches," prefiguring *Under Milk Wood*, revealing the intimate connection between self and world.

Artistic shaping of reality occurs also in "One Warm Saturday," whose final vision is one that, like "Where Tawe Flows," is at the same time a personal and a communal reflection. In "One Warm Saturday" there is a building up of images similar to the poems and not unlike the descriptions of the farm in "The Peaches," giving a sense of teeming life, in spite of many examples of decay. Combined with the constant movement of the townspeople, the description reflects the creative-decreative forces at work in the world. Much of the richness derives from the incongruities of the town, which is at once "shabby" and "shining," "undistinguished" but with a "wild intelligence." The oppositions inherent in the "blaspheming chapels" reflect a real, compromising world far from the ideal, mythic structures of the Jarvis Valley tales, where religion appears only in the extreme (and usually in the negative). The "graceless" buildings further suggest a fallen world, as much as the images of decay do; but they prefigure the paradoxes of Llareggub in *Under Milk Wood*, which is both a fallen world and a "Heaven on earth." The narrator of "One Warm Saturday" writes in the future tense of the "wide town and the small world that would be bound to fall" (235), but thus far is not yet completely fallen.

Among the "hardly known," to some extent fictionalized people is included the artist himself, who makes himself a character in a partially invented autobiography that is both based on reality and artistically shaped. This transformation into fiction in some ways effects an erasure of being as the artist enters the symbolic order; but Thomas takes this fading of the artist's being even further, for his self, as subject, becomes marginalized in favour of the "eccentric, ordinary people" around him, thus turning the usual focus of autobiography inside out: the artist's task, through self-representation, becomes ultimately to write of the world, not himself. Thomas's autobiographical fiction differs then in some ways from the narrative development of the average künstlerroman. According to Maurice Beebe, the typical artist novel requires that "the hero test and reject the claims of love and life, of God, home, and country, until nothing is left but his true self and his consecration as an artist" (5). The young Thomas, in his self-exile and his pose of the Poet as godlike Creator, resembles Joyce's Stephen Dedalus, who argues for just such an alienation; Stephen believes that the artist must withdraw from life, using it in his art but isolating himself from its interests. Stephen's consecration as an artist and his elevation of his craft to religious dimensions lead him to a theory of aesthetics that is perhaps like that of the early Thomas, but which differs significantly from that of the later one. The Thomas character of the early stories initially ignores the world so completely that he becomes lost in his art. But there are paradoxes in his aesthetic which, like Stephen Dedalus's, lead him, as a transcendent artist, to return to that which he hopes to transcend. The Thomas character eventually realizes, in *Portrait,* that his "true self" is inseparable from the world around him; his task is not to serve art, but to use art to serve life.

ADVENTURES IN THE SKIN TRADE

The unfinished novel *Adventures in the Skin Trade* was conceived as a sequel to *Portrait*, although in a very different form. The first three chapters were written between May and June, 1941. The idea for the book periodically was resurrected, and Thomas was still stating his intention to finish it in 1953 (CL 913), but it remained unfinished. The three existing chapters were published separately: "A Fine Beginning" appeared in *Folios of New Writing*, Autumn 1941 (CS xii); "Plenty of Furniture" and "Four Lost Souls" appeared in *New World Writing*, in November 1952 and May 1953. They were first published together posthumously in 1955.[6] Like Joyce's *Ulysses,* following *Portrait of the Artist as a Young Man,* it traces what happens when the character of the earlier work is about to launch his career. While Stephen Dedalus returns to Dublin from abroad, "Dylan Thomas," a.k.a. Samuel Bennet, goes to London, a new and very different environment, seen by the character not only as a new field of possibility but also as representing a more literal rejection of his roots. More fantastic in scope than *Portrait,* it takes a number of themes introduced in *Portrait* to greater, at times absurd, lengths. In the first of the three existing chapters, entitled "A Fine Beginning," the hero Samuel Bennet literally attempts to erase his past self before embarking on a new life by systematically destroying the contents of his parents' front parlour, defacing photographs and other memorabilia. His actions represent the radical rejection of history and tradition he believes necessary for the fulfilment of his destiny.[7] Fully embracing Thomas's antipathy to restrictive structures, Samuel is no longer motivated by a sense of good and evil, and he sets out, a "moral and emotional empty vessel," to experience the "real life" of "real people." He plans to make his true present the point of origin for a new departure. Yet for Samuel, the phrase "a fine beginning" is ironic, for his adventures are anything but what he planned. With each successive disappointment Samuel repeats the phrase to himself, reflecting the fact that he is stuck in his new beginning, and getting nowhere. By rejecting the earlier notion of moving "in the direction of the beginning," he calls into being the problems of attempting to live without a past, by its absence thus reinforcing its necessity.

Samuel is initially driven by an antipathy toward what will become a salient feature in Thomas's works: nostalgia. He self-consciously attempts to cut himself off from his roots: "Come and look at Samuel Bennet destroying his parents' house in Mortimer Street ... he will never be allowed to come back" (242). Before he leaves, he destroys his father's history papers because "history is lies" (241). He claims that he doesn't want to go back, but he soon discovers that he can't get away from his past. In the London train station, the first person he meets is Ronald Bishop, a person from his home town: "Samuel said silently into his glass: A fine beginning. If I go out of the station and turn round the corner I'll be back in 42" (249). The more he protests that he cannot go home, the more he is reminded of it: "Mortimer Street has tracked me down ... there was no escape" (252). When he meets the eccentric Allingham, he imagines that his London adventure is finally beginning, but this too is not what he hoped for. He is led to Allingham's home on Sewell street, which "look[ed] just like the streets at home" (257). Inside are rooms piled to the ceiling with furniture – unusual, but again a reminder of the effects of domesticity that Samuel tried to leave behind: "It gets to you, sometimes you know ... all this furniture" said Mr Allingham, "you get to feel kind of trapped" (258). Like Ronald Bishop, the people Samuel encounters are also a reminder of the home that he can't seem to leave behind him. Expecting the wild, exotic women that he had read about and seen in films, Samuel is confused by the ordinary women who inhabit London's pubs and nightclubs, women "dull as sisters, red-eyed and thick in the head with colds" (285). In the "Gayspot," Samuel thinks, "This was all wrong. They spoke like the women who wore men's caps and carried fishfrails full of empties in the Jug and Bottle of the Compasses at home ... these women with the shabby faces ... might have lurched in from Llanelly on a football night, on the arms of short men with leeks" (285).

Adventures in the Skin Trade is a comic comment both on Thomas's early life as a writer and on the content of his work at that period. His early poems are both directly and indirectly linked to Swansea, and often contain reactions to his respectable, Anglo-Welsh Nonconformist background. Poems such as "I have longed to move away" illustrate the wish to recoil from the society that bred him. Many of the stories involving imaginative journeys and rites of passage are about young men attempting to expand beyond their restrictive milieux. Playing the part of the "The Poet," Thomas himself "escaped" to London in 1933, the year in which *Adventures* is set. Curiously, neither Dylan Thomas nor Samuel Bennet succeeded in writing anything while in London. By 1938 Thomas had had enough of London, the "city of the restless dead" (*CL* 343), saying to Vernon Watkins that "it really is an insane city, & filled me with terror ... there's no difference between good and bad" (*CL* 343). *Adventures in the Skin Trade,* written in 1941 after his return to Wales, is anything but an endorsement of the kind of aimless adventure Samuel Bennet considers to be real life.

Bennet is a parodic version of the young Thomas, a self-conscious writer striving to be a poet. When the narrator advises us in the first paragraph to "call him Samuel Bennet" (239), there is an echo of Melville's *Moby Dick* and all that is implied by "call me Ishmael": the suggestion that we are about to read an adventure of epic heroism – a possibility that is soon disposed of, and the suggestion that the name we are given is not the true identity of the character. Bennet undergoes a curious series of transformations while attempting to fulfil the role of poet, necessitating first of all a stripping of his previous identity, that of an ordinary middle-class Welsh boy. He considers the destruction of his parents' front parlour "destroying the evidence" (242) of his soon-to-be past life, and, starting with a clean slate – or rather *as* a clean slate – he decides to let himself be shaped by events. Mr Allingham, however, soon deflates Samuel's philosophy by rationalizing, "You're not going anywhere. You're not doing anything. You don't exist" (255). The bizarre adventures on which he allows himself to be led result in a confusion of identity much like that inflicted upon Lewis Carroll's Alice; of little use is

Allingham's advice that "there's no need to complicate things if you keep your head and know who you are" (255). Samuel eventually finds himself in a dance club where "they never play waltzes ... it's just self-expression" (286). However, having lost his previous self, he has no new one to express, and he is swept into the gender-bending atmosphere of the club, where he ends up dancing with George Ring.

Samuel's sense of reality is curiously caught up in a complicated relationship with fiction. His position in existence is made difficult by his desire to fit the conditions of being to fictional equivalents. In spite of the fact that he says he is not planning anything ("I came up really to see what would happen to me. I don't want to make anything happen myself" [255]), he does self-consciously plan his life, as if he were writing a story: "First of all, when I reach there, I'll have a Bass and a stale sandwich, he decided. I'll take them to a table in a corner, brush off the cake crumbs with my hat, and prop my book against the cruet. I must have all the details right at the beginning. The rest must come by accident" (247). The details of his arrival are duplicated exactly as planned, including unexpected accidents (such as getting his finger stuck in the bottle of Bass, which remains with him for the duration of his adventures). His initial actions in the train station are posed: "the image was false and the book was chosen for strangers. He did not like or understand it" (253). His conscious planning, and his placing himself in already imagined scenes, contradicts his claim that he wants to be passively shaped. However, more than he realizes, Samuel is merely a character acting out a role over which he truly has little control, in spite of the fact that he initiated it. Samuel's expectations of London derive from what he has read in books or seen in films. We know what he hoped would happen to him by what he claims he did not expect to happen to him, such as "that the nightclub women under the pavement should sing and twang like sirens or lure off his buttons with their dangerous, fringed violet eyes. London is not under the bedclothes where all the company is grand and vile by a flick of the cinema eye" (285). Samuel always anticipates what will or will not happen to him, based on already played out scenarios from books: "I do not expect any old cobwebbed Fagan, reeking of character and stories, to shuffle out of a corner and lead me away into his grand, loud, filthy house; there will not be any Nancy to tickle my fancy in a kitchen full of handkerchiefs and beckoning, unmade beds. I did not think a choir of loose women immediately would sing and dance around the little tables, in plush clothes and advertized brassieres, as I walked into London for the first time, rattling my fortune, fresh as Copperfield" (253). Ironically, Samuel's adventures do turn out to be a modified version of this Dickensian scenario, with Allingham leading him away like Fagan to his flat full of furniture, Polly "tickling his fancy" in a bathroom, and an assortment of androgynous characters singing and dancing around little tables in the clubs. Usually when Samuel measures reality against his fabular expectations it does not fit; it is only when he dismisses possibilities as fiction that they materialize.

Samuel's initial pose in the train station is a sign of things to come, for the world in which he finds himself is equally fictional. As Allingham tells him, "don't you believe everything you see, especially after it's dark. This is all pretending" (284). He has unwittingly walked into a living work of art. When Samuel meets Polly Dacy, he discovers that fictions can be dangerous. At first it is Samuel who is caught up in imaginative creations. Like the characters in "The Mouse and the Woman" and "A Prospect of the Sea," Samuel creates a composite vision of Polly, based on stereotyped images from stories he has read or made up: "In the second she took to push the door open and come in, he made her a hundred faces; he made her talk and walk in all the disguises of his loves at night; he gave her golden hair, black hair, he knew that she would be gypsy-skinned and white as milk. Polly come and put the kettle on with your white, slender, brown, broad hands, and see me waiting like a grenadier or a caliph in the mousy cubicle" (266). Of course, the reality of Polly has nothing to do with his imagined version, for she is "a girl with a long, pale face and glasses. Her hair was not any of Samuel's colours, but only dark and dull" (266). Polly only partially fulfils the requirements of his fantasies, and the incomplete identification confounds him. He tries desperately to make his reality conform to his previous fictions: "He could not think of anything to say.

Here was the locked door he had often made up in stories and in his head, in bed in Mortimer Street, and the warm, hidden key, and the girl who was willing for anything. The bathroom should be a bedroom and she should not be wearing glasses. ... He did not feel any emotion at all. O God, he thought, make me feel something, make me feel as I ought to, here is something happening and I'm cool and dull as a man in a bus. Make me remember all the stories. I caught her in my arms, my heart beat against hers, her body was trembling, her mouth opened like a flower" (268–9).

Samuel deals with the real by attempting to reactivate its fictional equivalent. However, he learns that his words cannot live up to the actual mystery of things. Even more, he learns that it is dangerous to become too involved with the unreal world of words, for when he meets Polly, he meets his match: someone who has an equal capacity for imagining. She has what may be a pathological ability to pretend that the cold, greasy bathwater is a pool on a midsummer night, and that eau-de-cologne is brandy that she offers to her "darling Sam," her dead lover. Turning the tables on Samuel, she fictionalizes him: "She would be in her locked bedroom now, crying for Sam gone, at her window staring out on to the colourless, slowly disappearing street and the tall houses down at heel; or depicting, in the kitchen, the agony of a woman in childbirth, writhing and howling round the crowded sink; or being glad at a damp corner of the landing" (275). Samuel's near poisoning by Polly is an illustration that fiction can come perilously close to turning into reality. Later, in the club, Samuel fears that the borders between fiction and reality will again be crossed, when he feels threatened by a man with a scar, and he thinks, "I don't want a cut on my face. Don't cut my lips open. They only use razors in stories. Don't let him have read any stories" (288). Samuel's dilemma may be characterized by the paradox that things that are supposed to happen only in stories do happen in real life. Because he initially attempted to model his new life on fictions, he is literally the author of his own fate.

According to a letter to Peter Baker, a prospective editor, Thomas's original plans for the novel called for Samuel Bennet's gradually being stripped of the "skins" of his identity, eventually to be left naked as a new-born on a train platform, ready for another new departure:

... as the story progresses so he loses more and more clothes, bit by bit ... Eventually, ... he winds up without any clothes at all, and finds himself outside Paddington station a moment before dawn. Standing there naked, having had every garment fall from him simultaneously with the acquisition of every new experience, he wonders: "Now I am here, outside Paddington station, just [steps] from where I began my pilgrimage, as naked as the day I was born. What'll happen to me? Will a very rich woman in a Rolls-Royce and a fur coat pass me by in the almost dawn, stop her chauffeur, and befriend me and lard me with charity and nymphomania? Or will a policeman pick me up for indecent exposure, my having shed all the skins of my semi-proletarian, bourgeois, provincial upbringing? Or will a romantic tart clutch me to her used bosom, in the Catholic tradition of Francis Thompson? Or will, when dawn breaks, I see everyone walking about the streets, going to work, conducting traffic, going about their daily dullness, as naked, as utterly naked as I?" (CL 512)

Sharing the fate of many of Thomas's plans, the novel never materialized. In the three chapters that were finished, events dissolve into an anarchy so complete that no linear plot could be resurrected from it. These existing chapters, however, are worthy of consideration in spite of, or even because of, their lack of completion. It may be argued that the disorder that characterizes the three chapters mirrors the city that is as central to the story as Samuel. His publishers dismissed *Adventures* as, according to Thomas, "just a fragment of comic romantic taradiddle without a real structure & purpose" (CL 664); Dent objected that Thomas's writing is "more coprolitic than ever, and seems to be quite without intellectual control ... [he is] slipping into a state of literary irresponsibility" (CL 488). Thomas, however, insisted that the "whole conception of the book is made to a most formal pattern" (CL 512); the letter to Baker not only shows an intended plan, but also reveals a great deal about the three existing chapters.

The letter partially explains the title, with its commercial implications, for "trade" refers to something gained in exchange for the identities, or "skins," that Samuel loses in the course of his adventures; it also hints of prostitution and slavery. As in "The Peaches," clothes ("skins") symbolize the roles that the characters play. Mrs Dacy, for example, "dressed in black almost down to the ankles," is described as a "mourner" as well as a "corpse," and is representative of the "restless dead." Samuel sets out for London "dressed in a brand-new brown tweed overcoat, a brown town-suit, a white starched shirt with a woollen tie and a tie pin, and black, shining shoes" (246), the proper uniform for a budding poet/journalist in a big city. However, the adventures he undergoes do not match his attire. The loss of his overcoat is the first shedding of his "skins." Others before him might have undergone the same transformation, hinted at in the description of the third club, the "Cheerio," which is compared to a "cupboard full of cast-off clothes moving in a wind from nowhere" (289). When Samuel sheds his clothes "with the acquisition of every new experience," he is also described frequently as a "baby"; it may be argued that, as for the boy in "The Peaches," his body – all that he is left with – becomes his identity, his "adventure" and his "name." Ultimately, if the story had been finished, he might have found his true self in such an identity. This transition is apparent in the questions that Samuel asks himself in the planned ending. On the brink of another beginning, he imagines a number of possibilities, some of which, characteristically, come from already read or envisioned fictions. However, the last possibility offers a vision of ordinary life, and along with it, the recognition that Samuel is no different from the common man on the street. Ultimately, then, Samuel reflects Thomas's move away from fantastic, solipsistic linguistic creations to compassionate depictions of humanity.

However, this proposed end is never realized. Samuel's grotesquely comic, as well as irrational, adventures deteriorate into a surreal vision in which people become fish and animals. Thomas's anti-hero – whose name, Samuel Bennet, is uncannily similar to "Samuel Beckett" – in letting himself be shaped by circumstance, plays out the absurd moves of the "end-game" of civilization. London, the "city of the restless dead," resembles that "city of destruction" in "Prologue to an Adventure"; indeed, *Adventures in the Skin Trade* may be seen as a comic version of that early story. Distanced in time, Thomas can allow himself a liberating degree of self-parody. The third story of *Adventures*, "Four Lost Souls," describes a scene similar to that in "Prologue to an Adventure." Samuel is led by Mr Allingham, George Ring, and Mrs Dacy through the streets of the "wilderness" of London, in the rain, to several bars. The narrator of "Prologue" is jostled in the "wilderness" of the city, in the rain, and comments, "this is a strange city, gentlemen on your own, gentlemen arm-in-arm making a rehearsed salute, gentlemen with ladies, ladies this is a strange city" (104). Foreshadowing Samuel's fate, he calls himself "the nakedest and baldest nothing" (104). Entering two pubs with Daniel Dom, the "Seven Sins" and the "Deadly Virtue," he encounters "sexless, golden singers and the sulphurous hermaphrodites" (107) that echo the patrons that Samuel encounters, such as "a crimped boy [that] danced like a girl, and the two girls serving [who] were as harsh as men" (284). The most striking comparison is between the ends of the stories, both of which involve long, richly descriptive paragraphs. "Prologue to an Adventure" ends with a vision of a flood engulfing the city of destruction, issuing in the adventure proper, to which the given story is merely an overture: "We saw a wave jumping and the last bright eyes go under ... the sea of destruction lapped around our feet ... and the waves grew down into the pavements" (108). From the time of Samuel's disaster in the bath, there are numerous references to drowning. After awakening from his drunken state, "he sank into the ragged green water for the second time, and, rising naked with seaweed and a woman under each arm and a mouthful of broken shells, he saw the whole of his dead life standing trembling before him, indestructible and unsinkable, on the brandy-brown waves" (274). Later, in the bar called the "Antelope," "his immediate wisdom weighed so heavily that he clutched at the edge of the counter and raised one arm, like a man trapped in the sea, to signal his sinking" (281). The final extended image in "Four Lost Souls" is not of Samuel overseeing the deluge, as the narrator does in "Prologue," but of Samuel submerged, surrounded by "deep green faces, dipped in a sea dye, with painted cockles for mouths and lichenous hair, sealed on the cheeks; red and purple, slate-grey, tide-marked" (290).

In some respects, the thrust of *Adventures* is like that of *Under Milk Wood*, especially in its projected ending. Indeed, Allingham's conclusion that such strange people are "the salt of the earth" might be read as only half a gesture toward irony, for it reaches toward that humanism that *Under Milk Wood* aspires to. *Adventures* represents where the young Dylan Thomas might have been led astray had he stayed in the world represented by London; but having left the city long before beginning the novel, he was determined to get back into a loving relationship with the Wales that bred him. If *Adventures* had been continued in the spirit in which Thomas's other work was evolving, Samuel Bennet would have gone home again. Rather than *Adventures in the Skin Trade*, it is the "play for voices," *Under Milk Wood*, that becomes the "Welsh Ulysses," the true continuation and extension of *Portrait of the Artist as a Young Dog*.

4 Under Milk Wood

Following the publication of *Adventures in the Skin Trade* in 1941, Thomas devoted most of his time to making a living for his family, and his output of both poetry and prose virtually came to a halt until after the war. His time did not go to waste, however, for the work that he did during the war, in film and radio, helped to propel his writing in new directions. Out of this period came some of the most famous poems, such as "Poem in October," "A Refusal to Mourn," and "Fern Hill." The dramatic and aural possibilities that opened up through radio, combined with a calmer, more sanguine view of the world, resulted in the conception of a creation in an entirely new genre, *Under Milk Wood*. Like the variations in the earlier prose works, the change in style evident in *Under Milk Wood* reflects Thomas's changing conceptions of the artist and his place in the world. In this work Thomas also re-evaluates the conventions of writing. *Under Milk Wood* is a work that defies generic categorization; as a radio play for voices, it is strictly neither poetry nor prose, but a unique hybrid of poetry, prose, drama, and music. It is relevant to this study because it synthesizes the many issues explicit in the prose, and implicit in the poetry.

As early as 1932 Thomas expressed a wish to write a "Welsh Ulysses" (Fitzgibbon 269). After undergoing many transformations over the next twenty years, this idea gradually metamorphosed into the play for voices *Under Milk Wood*. In his book *The Growth of Milk Wood,* Douglas Cleverdon notes that there are eleven distinct versions of the work. Consistent with Thomas's pervading theories of perpetual transformation, *Under Milk Wood* was continually created, decreated, and created anew. Although it was sufficiently unified to be presented before an audience in a trial run in 1953, and although many consider *Under Milk Wood* to be Thomas's last "complete" work, he himself considered it unfinished. Only his death in 1954 precluded further revisions. The last version, on its own and in relation to its predecessors, like the early prose, *Portrait,* and *Adventures,* is valuable as a guide to Thomas's changing conceptions of the artist and his (and his art's) relation to the world. In it we can see many of the concerns of the early work: the cycles of birth and death; the interpenetration of fiction and reality; the possibility of an edenic return and the temporal transcendence partially acquired through lyric structures. Like the earlier works, it is self-referential. Here, however, self-consciousness and self-reflexivity belong not just to the artist, the solipsistic Adam, but also to all of his creations, the characters who inhabit Llareggub, and who likewise create it, being co-creators of their own world.

Like Joyce's *Ulysses, Under Milk Wood* is structured around a period of twenty-four hours; also like Joyce's work, it combines the mythic and the localized, and its heroes are ordinary people. However, Thomas's "Welsh Ulysses" recounts not what happens when the hero of *Portrait* goes to the city (as both *Adventures in the Skin Trade* and Joyce's *Ulysses* do) but what happens when the hero defies his earlier proclamation of self-exile, and returns to his roots. As a Welshman, Thomas returns to Wales, and as a poet, he returns to the roots of poetry: the "play for voices" is an abundantly aural work, combining dialogue, songs, nursery rhymes, chants, and poems.

Eli Jenkins, "poet preacher," is of course an obvious artist figure standing in for Thomas, but there are others as well – in fact, all the inhabitants of Llareggub stand in, in various ways, for the artist. The singular voice of the earlier works is spread out over many voices, and none is privileged. The figure that emerges in this later work is the artist who is the delegate of common humanity. *Under Milk Wood* is representative of a small world communally created by its inhabitants, for all men and women in their own way are creators. Highly lyrical, like the bulk of Thomas's poetry, *Under Milk Wood* emerges as a generic paradox: personal, subjective, and temporally fluid, yet spoken in a voice made of many voices, it constitutes a democratization of the lyric. There is no disjunction between the voices of the people and the voices of the place – the town, the sea, and the surrounding hills. It is no coincidence that Llareggub, this small world, is to its inhabitants a "heaven on earth." *Under Milk Wood*, in contrast to the early prose, is a work in which edenic language is not merely spoken about but spoken.

PREDECESSORS OF *UNDER MILK WOOD*

Thomas's work in radio during and after the war contributed to a broadened opportunity to exploit the potentials of sound, of language, and of dialogue. Radio was a fitting medium for a poet interested in the "sound of shape" and the "shape of sound." Changes in the stories leading up to this time reflect a similar interest. In stories such as "One Warm Saturday" and "Old Garbo," for example, Thomas began to include accurate recordings of other voices in dialogue, such as renderings of Welsh pub life. This trend continues in radio broadcasts that in many ways are prototypes for *Under Milk Wood*.

"Holiday Memory" (CS 304–10) is written in short-story form with a first-person narrator, and resembles the short stories in *Portrait* in theme, tone, and structure, and yet it moves into dramatic presentation in moments of extended dialogue. Fragments of voices from the past mingle in memory, and the listener to the broadcast becomes an eavesdropper within the represented world. Directly addressed, we are told:

And if you could have listened at some of the open doors of some of the houses in the street you might have heard:
"Uncle Owen says he can't find the bottle opener ..."
"Has he looked under the hallstand?"
"Willy's cut his finger ..."

"Got your spade?"
"If somebody doesn't kill that dog ..."
"Uncle Owen says why should the bottle opener be under the hallstand?"
"Never again, never again ..."
"I know I put the pepper somewhere ..."
"Willy's bleeding ..." (305–6).

Other broadcasts, such as the later "Return Journey," abandon the long descriptive passages found in "Holiday Memory" and largely replace them with a predominance of dramatic dialogue.

"Return Journey" (*CS* 316–28) is a radio play for a number of voices. Although there is a narrator who introduces the action and is the focalizer for all that occurs, he is only one of many characters. He is still the central character, but in an ironic way, for his presence is marked by his absence: "Return Journey" recounts Thomas's return to Swansea after the war and his search through the bombed-out streets for his past self, or selves.[1] As in the earlier stories, Thomas manages to split himself into subject and object in a self-conscious reflection; here, however, the rift is so great that he cannot retrieve his own image, for his earlier self, we are told, is "dead." In a move away from both the early solipsistic stories and the künstlerroman *Portrait*, Thomas retreats as both story-teller and central character, allowing other characters – in this case the average and often anonymous people of Swansea – into the foreground.

The dramatic form allows for the predominance of other voices in conversation. In "Return Journey," the voices appear on two levels: that of straight dialogue, in which the narrator interacts with people on the street, shopkeepers, and so on, and that filtered through the narrator's memory, the remembered conversations that are triggered by his reminiscences. Both types of dialogue appear temporally present to the listener, in a lyrical layering of time. Thus, as in "Fern Hill," remembering functions as a mode of retrieval, allowing a partial recovery of the lost world. The return journey is a movement back in time as well as in space, but not in a linear fashion, for past and present mingle. The journey is a search for identity, which the narrator finds not through simple self-reflection but through the reflections of himself in others. The narrator, Thomas, is retracing the steps he took to become the person he is now. All the past, including the remembered voices, has been internalized. As Bakhtin notes, we are the voices that inhabit us, the voices we have heard. Thomas recreates through memory not only the voices but also the experiences themselves, encoded in internalized speech. The recreation is a necessarily shared rather than solipsistic one, for only through talking with others and through their memories of him does he trace the path of his development.

In "Return Journey" Thomas no longer tells stories about himself, but allows dialogue, as a closer approach to real life, to reveal glimpses of his reality. Having created a mask of fiction that includes features of his own face, Thomas is more openly autobiographical, in spite of the decentring of his voice. In this work Thomas catalogues the names of actual places, such as shops that stood before the bombings, on streets that still exist; he lists living people, such as his friends Dan Jones, Fred Janes, and Vernon Watkins, as well as former schoolboys lost in battle. Thomas describes himself in factual terms as "above medium height. Above medium height for Wales, I mean, he's five foot six and a half. Thick blubber lips; snub nose; curly mousebrown hair" (318). There are also references to the Dylan we saw in *Portrait*. He is aware here, as he was in *Portrait*, that he enjoyed self-consciously posing: "He wore a conscious woodbine ... and a perched pork pie hat with a peacock feather and he tried to slouch like a newshawk" (321). In a mingling of fiction and reality, he is searching not simply for his past self in the real Swansea, but also for the fictionalized self that he wrote into such stories as "Old Garbo." Later his search leads him to the seashore where he meets the "Promenade man" with a dog, who refers to the fourteen-year-old Dylan "dawdling" in the arches as the character did in "Just Like Little Dogs." Although they do not recognize him now, these real people of Swansea remember the young boy. As they are also recalling the boy from the *Portrait* stories, fiction and reality cross ambiguously, for such recognition shows that *Portrait* is more factual than we might have first allowed.

While fiction is contaminated by reality, reality bears certain characteristics of fiction. Thomas finds that while the people of

Swansea might indeed be remembering him, they are equally remembering a type that his past selves represented: more than once he is told "Oh yes, I knew him well. I've known him by the thousands." At first such comments merely seem to be humbling. When the barmaid hears his description she says (or, more accurately, Thomas recalls her saying), "What d'you want to find *him* for I wouldn't touch him with a barge pole" (318). Over and over we are told that the "Young Thomas" is not unique. The barmaid points out how common and unmemorable a name Thomas is. The schoolmaster catalogues him as a generic, unremarkable, ordinary boy:

"Oh yes, I remember him well, the boy you are searching for: he looked like most boys, no better, brighter, or more respectful; he cribbed, mitched, spilt ink, rattled his dish and
garbled his lessons with the worst of them;
he could smudge, hedge, smirk, wriggle, wince,
whimper, blarney, badger, blush, deceive, be
devious, stammer, improvise ...
he 'elped to damage the headmaster's rhubarb,
was thirty-third in trigonometry,
and, as might be expected, edited the School Magazine." (324)

In short, his childhood self is no less anonymous and transient than the past and present voices he encounters on his journey. But as an ordinary boy he is recognizable both in fact and in the *Portrait* stories precisely because of his commonness. What the elder Thomas is searching for is not simply an ordinary boy but an archetype, or the archetypal in the ordinary, and it is the archetypal that the Swanseans know well. Further, it is not the archetypal artist who is set apart from the ordinary world because of a special calling, as seen in the self-conscious poets of the early stories. Here, the artist is a common man, as he will be in *Under Milk Wood*. "Return Journey" was written only two years after the end of the war and expresses a great sense of loss, marked especially by the death knell that tolls in the last words: "dead ... dead ... dead ... dead ... dead ... dead ... dead ..." (328).

Although it lacks the joyous, celebratory quality of such later post-war works as "Fern Hill" and *Under Milk Wood*, "Return Journey" does offer signs of Thomas's philosophy that disallows extinction. There are hints of continuation and recovery that will mark the later works, predominantly in examples of prolepsis and analepsis. His journey takes him back in time through the stages "in the progress of the boy [he] was pursuing." His movement forward in time, indicated by the word "progress," is balanced by the return, "in the direction of the beginning," and his search brings him eventually to his earliest years on Cwmdonkin Drive. Through memory he returns to what in Thomasian terms would be an edenic existence, in "the long green days" (324) that echo "Fern Hill" and *Under Milk Wood*.

Like the child in "Fern Hill" and "The Peaches," the boy the elder Thomas seeks is strongly aware of his being, and is not yet self-conscious or indeed conscious of anything connected with the fallen world: still in an elemental state, he is "a boy up to no good but the beat of his blood" (324). He was, the gate-keeper of Cwmdonkin Park tells us, "happy all the time" (328). Uplands, the end of the narrator's journey, is the beginning of the earlier Thomas's journey: "here and around here it was that the journey had begun of the one I was pursuing through his past" (326). The first-person "I" and third-person "his" refer to the same person; the title refers to one journey in two directions, singular and simultaneous. The past is not static but is constantly changing, and is interchangeable with the present. Moments of time intersect as they do in the poems, in what Thomas called the "stream that is flowing all ways." As with "Fern Hill," references to childhood move from the particular to the general,[2] as the gate-keeper refers to the singular and ordinary as well as the archetypal, mythic child: "Oh yes, I knew him well. I think he was happy all the time. I've known him by the thousands" (328). Both the individual and the archetypal are recreated in memory, and both are a part of the search for identity embodied in the search for the poet's past.

The lists of real names of people and places recall those both present and absent, recreated through memory. When he returns to his school, which had been destroyed by bombs, the names of his schoolmates and previous schoolboys killed in World War 1, like the voices he encounters on his return journey, are both gone and still present. Here Thomas most explicitly reveals the possibility of eternal existence, embodied in the adamic identity of being and name: "the names are havoc'd from the Hall and the carved initials burned from the broken wood. But the names remain ... The names of the dead in the living heart remain for ever" (324). Like the dead recalled in *Under Milk Wood*, their continued existence is assured through the memories of the living. Although the lives of those remembering are equally transient, the continuation in spirit is paradoxically "for ever," allowing the immortality of the pre-fallen condition. The retrieval of lost names and voices, the temporal crossings, and the retrieval of an edenic state of identification will be more fully realized in *Under Milk Wood*.

The possibilities for retrieval, however, were evident to Thomas very early on in his career. One can see aspects of "Return Journey" in the short story "Brember" (*CS* 347–8) that Thomas wrote in 1931, at the age of sixteen. In "Brember" (aurally suggestive of "remember"), the narrator (unnamed until the end of the story) returns to an old house that he knew as a child, in a "journey" that functions as a recovery; his return is "to throw apart the veil of years, to bring back to him all that old house had meant" (348). In the music room, the heart of the house, "the longing always at the back of his mind was realized, the lost thing found, and the forgotten thing remembered. This was the end of the journey" (348). The narrator picks up a book called "The House of Brember" that chronicles the family represented by the physical house to which he returns. This book functions like the list of names of the dead in "Return Journey." Although "Brember" is a ghost story with a melodramatic ending (juvenilia, after all), we might see in it the seeds of future stories, in the character's search for his name and his identity: "Each page was familiar to him, the family, generation by generation, men of thought rather than action, all visionaries who saw the world from the cloud of their own dreaming. He turned over the pages, until he came to the last: George Henry Brember, last of the line, died. ... He looked down on his name, and then closed the book" (348). Like Peter the poet in the "The Visitor," George Henry Brember is ambiguously dead and alive at the same time – or perhaps he is a ghost who does not know he is dead until he reads it in the book. Either way, George and Peter share a similar self-consciousness and doubleness. The book called "The House of Brember" within the story "Brember" functions as a metafictional self-reflective device that mirrors, if it does not recreate, George's life. He continues to exist on the page in the written chronicles, and also outside of it, as he reads it.

This story bears similarities to "The Mouse and the Woman"; the madman's action of writing "the woman died" and the accompanying ambiguous fate of the woman resemble the action of George reading of his death on the page. In both works, the setting down of the words on the page might signify the end of any further acts of transformation, and thus signify the end of life both literally and figuratively. The end of George's journey is an act of self-recognition that, like the end of "Return Journey," results in death. Like the narrator of "Return Journey," searching for his lost self, George Brember also searches, then "closes the book." But, as in "Return Journey," there is in "Brember" a consciousness that is still present to recount the tale. The search for lost origins may culminate in their retrieval in a book, a work of art, or in memory, which serves a function similar to that of art. George's gesture of examining his life in a book reflects the solipsism of the early stories and that parodied in *Portrait*. In the later "Return Journey," the people the narrator encounters in memory function the way the book does, as the older Thomas sees himself recreated by others. When Eli Jenkins in *Under Milk Wood* sets down the lives of Llareggub's inhabitants in his "White Book of Llareggub," Thomas combines the functions of the written documents (the madman's writings and "The House of Brember") with the remembered voices of "Return Journey," and in part resolves the problems of existence of the earlier ambiguous acts. Eli's acts of setting down lives in writing function as modes of retrieval and continuation, rather than termination. Although there are many differences between the early and later works, perhaps the greatest is an abandonment of solipsistic concerns about the central characters' existence, a change to a more humanistic concern for the continued existence of others.

More commonly cited as an early model for *Under Milk Wood*, "Quite Early One Morning" (CS 291–5), a talk for the BBC, clearly foreshadows the play for voices in both theme and structure. It has a simple time sequence, beginning with the awakening of the town. There is a retired sea Captain, Tiny Evans, who is a model for captain Cat; there are Dreams; Mrs Ogmore Pritchard appears, with her commands for immaculate order. As it is in *Under Milk Wood*, the natural world is imbued with an almost human identity, and the "bilingual sea" is allowed a voice equal in presence to the voices of the town's human inhabitants. The sea's "bilingual" nature is itself a foreshadowing of the peculiar Welshness that grounds Llareggub in the particular. Near the end of the broadcast the "voices of the town" blow up over the "slow-speaking sea," not in the free-flowing fragments of *Under Milk Wood*, but as more or less rhymed and metred stanzas:

> I am Captain Tiny Evans, my ship was the Kidwelly,
> And Mrs Tiny Evans has been dead for many a year
> "Poor Captain Tiny all alone," the neighbours whisper
> But I like it all alone and I hated her ...
> Open the curtains, light the fire, what are servants for?
> I am Mrs Ogmore Pritchard, and I want another snooze.
> Dust the china, feed the canary, sweep the drawing-room floor;
> And before you let the sun in, mind he wipes his shoes. (294)

These voices, however, lack the sense of love and acceptance found in those of *Under Milk Wood*, as does the work as a whole, which presents the town as somewhat oppressive. Captain Tiny Evans embodies a consciousness closer to Caradoc Evans than to Captain Cat.[3] This work is filtered through a first-person narrator who is like "a stranger" (292, 293). He watches the town wake, but never with the sense of joy and life that is apparent in *Under Milk Wood*. It is winter rather than spring, and images are predominantly deathlike, such as the by now familiar "stuffed pheasants, ferns in pots, fading photographs of the bearded and censorious dead, autograph albums with a lock of limp and colourless beribboned hair lolling out between the thick black boards" (292), variations of which have already been seen in "The Peaches" and "After the Funeral." In "Quite Early" birds sing, "not for love or joy, but to keep other birds away" (292). The narrator himself expresses no wish to participate. Things are very different in *Under Milk Wood*, where the guiding voices lead us into the town, showing it to us from within; the narrator of "Quite Early One Morning" remains outside, literally and figuratively looking down on the town.

Although the inhabitants dream colourful dreams, the narrator is suspicious of them and remains distant: he "could not believe" Miss Hughes's eastern dreams, and "could not imagine" Cadwallader Davies's western ones. The generosity of Llareggub's Eli Jenkins may be contrasted to

Parchidig Thomas Evans making morning tea,
Very weak tea, too, you mustn't waste a leaf.
Every morning making tea in my house by the sea,
I am troubled by one thing only, and that, belief. (294)

It is no Eli Jenkins who lovingly watches over the town, but the oppressive Welsh chapel, which "stood grim and grey, telling the day there was to be no nonsense. The chapel was not asleep, it never cat-napped or nodded nor closed its long cold eye. I left it telling the morning off and the sea-gull hung rebuked above it" (293).

The only reference to artists or artist figures is a critical one, and again may be contrasted to Milk Wood's Eli Jenkins, poet-preacher, who lovingly tries to capture the spirit of his town in his poems and in his "White Book." In "Quite Early," the only artists are invading, non-native painters of touristy picturesque villages who falsify reality, "man-dressed women with shooting sticks and sketch-books and voices like macaws [painting] the reluctant heads of critical and sturdy natives who posed by the pint against the chapel-dark sea which would be made more blue than the bay of Naples – though shallower" (293).

Rather than being the recorder or container of the voices of others as he was in "Return Journey," the narrator of "Quite Early" remains a stranger, and the work ends with a hint of futility as the voices retreat: "Thus some of the voices of a cliff-perched town at the far end of Wales moved out of sleep and darkness into the new-born, ancient, and ageless morning, moved out and were lost" (295). In spite of the pervasively negative tone, the loss at the end is balanced by a positive-sounding timelessness, in the "new-born, ancient and ageless morning." It is perhaps this sense of timelessness above all that is carried over from "Quite Early One Morning" into *Under Milk Wood*.

Other aspects of the play may have their sources in a variety of lesser-known broadcasts. For example, "The Londoners," part of a series called "This Is London" (1946), has the same framework as *Under Milk Wood*. It begins with the narration: "It's nearly half past six on a summer morning. Montrose Street is awake. ... But most of the houses are still sleeping. In Number 49, all is quiet. Lily Jackson is dreaming." It ends with the narration: "It's a summer night in Montrose Street. And the street is sleeping. In Number 49 all is quiet. The Jacksons are dreaming" (CL 597n). Mog Edwards and Myfanwy Price may have their sources in another play called "Two Streets," which is about two people, a boy and a girl, whose lives are parallel but who never meet.[4]

Another, more openly acknowledged, prototype for *Under Milk Wood* is a project that Thomas called "The Town that was Mad." In a letter to Richard Hughes,[5] Thomas outlines his proposed plot, in which he envisions a town brought to trial to defend its eccentricity, to avoid being classified as an "insane zone." The play was meant to contrast Llareggub and the surrounding world – the individuality and freedom of the eccentrics versus the sanity of the conformists. After hearing the prosecution's descriptions of normality, the people of the town beg to be cordoned off. One might compare this to Thomas's initial portraits of the artist as a madman, as in "The Mouse and the Woman." In an early letter to Trevor Hughes, Thomas says that "artists, as far as I can gather, have set out, however unconsciously, to prove one of two things: either that they are mad in a sane world, or sane in a mad world. It has been given to few to make a perfect fusion of madness and sanity" (*CL* 90). In "The Town that was Mad" Thomas moves toward a more playful madness; this will be accorded the people of Llareggub, who themselves prove to be artists.

Douglas Cleverdon notes that one-third of the work was already written before any signs of the plot appeared, and that the form imposed itself on Thomas because of the play's beginning, growing organically from that. In 1950–51 Thomas discarded the proposed plot altogether. Fortunately the work was being written as a BBC "Feature," which is distinguished from a "play" in that it had "no rules determining what can or cannot be done" (Cleverdon 17); a feature may be dramatic in form but has no need of proper dramatic plot. Therefore Thomas could allow the fluidity of the opening sequence full rein, and the shape of the work could determine itself rather than be artificially imposed. In 1951 he abandoned "The Town that was Mad," but out of it came the provisionally titled "Llareggub," which would fully blossom into *Under Milk Wood*.

In a letter to Princess Caetani, who published the incomplete script in the quarterly *Botteghe Oscure*, Thomas offers a brief explanation of "The Town that was mad" and describes the spirit of the new work:

I told you, as you may remember, that I was working on a play, mostly in verse. This I have reluctantly, and I hope, temporarily, abandoned ... but out of my working, however vainly, on it, came the idea of "Llareggub" ... out of it came the idea that I write a piece, a play, an impression for voices, an entertainment out of the darkness, of the town I live in, and to write it simply and warmly and comically with lots of movement and varieties of moods, so that, at many levels, through sight and speech, description and dialogue, evocation and parody, you come to know the town as an inhabitant of it. That is an awkward and high-falutin way of speaking: I only wanted to make the town alive through a raw medium. ... [The town is] seen from a number of eyes, heard from a number of voices – through the long lazy lyrical afternoon, through the multifariously busy little town evening of meals and drinks and loves and quarrels and dreams and wishes, into the night and the slowing-down lull again and the repetition of the first word: Silence. (CL 813–4)

The "raw medium" of radio provided numerous possibilities for the aural imagination, allowing Thomas to explore the potential of the voices and sounds of Welsh village life. The ultimate result, unlike earlier attempts, is a warm and comic creation seen, perhaps most importantly, from an insider's perspective, and which draws the reader into the work.

ARTIST FIGURES IN *UNDER MILK WOOD*

Captain Tiny Evans of "Quite Early One Morning" is replaced in *Under Milk Wood* by "blind Captain Cat." In contrast to the misanthropic Tiny Evans, Captain Cat is a loving familiar of the town. He loves the dead Rosie Probert, and dreams of the many drowned whom he addresses as "my dead dears" (6). Captain Cat participates in the innocence of the town, joining the children as they sing the nonsense song "Johnny Crack and Flossie Snail" (56–7). Captain Cat was originally meant to be the narrator and central character. In "The Town That Was Mad," he is the spokesperson for the townspeople and insists on a trial to defend their "innocence." In later versions he is not the sole focalizer, but shares a central position with the anonymous First and Second Voices. The First Voice, whom Thomas calls in his letter to Caetani the "exhibitor and chronicler," primarily describes externals such as the layout of the town and events as they occur. As a historical "chronicler" he narrates events in time, and speaks primarily in the present tense. The Second Voice is a narrator of a different sort: omniscient, he details the internal rather than the external world, describing the dreams and thoughts of the characters:

FIRST VOICE ... From where you are, you can hear their dreams.
    Captain Cat, the retired blind seacaptain, asleep in his bunk in the seashelled, ship-in-bottled shipshape best cabin of Schooner House dreams of

SECOND VOICE never such seas as any that swamped the decks of his S.S. Kidwelly bellying over the bedclothes and jellyfish slippery sucking him down salt deep into the Davy dark where the fish come biting out and nibble him down to his wishbone, and the long dead nuzzle up to him. (3)

Captain Cat himself also functions as a type of narrator, directing what, and how, we see and hear. He provides a link between the First and Second Voices and the audience, for he both describes the town for us, like the First Voice, and reveals the workings of his own mind and those of others, as the Second Voice does. He is a character within the work as well as a narrator, and is the vehicle through which the reader is drawn into an intimate encounter with the town.

As Daniel Jones notes in the preface to *Under Milk Wood*, a blind man provides a "natural bridge between eye and ear for the radio listener" (viii). Captain Cat has an intrinsic knowledge of the town through its sounds. We hear Llareggub as he does, and we recreate it in our imaginations through the sounds that he relates to us: "All the women are out this morning, in the sun. You can tell it's Spring. There goes Mrs Cherry, you can tell her by her trotters, off she trots new as a daisy. Who's that talking by the pump? Mrs Floyd and Boyo, talking flatfish. What can you talk about flatfish? That's Mrs Dai Bread One, waltzing up the street like a jelly, every time she shakes it's slap slap slap. Who's that? Mrs Butcher Beynon with her pet black cat, it follows her everywhere, miaow and all ... Can't hear what the women are gabbing round the pump. Same as ever. Who's having a baby, who blacked whose eye, seen Polly Garter giving her belly an airing, there should be a law, seen Mrs Beynon's new mauve jumper, it's her old grey jumper dyed, who's dead, who's dying, there's a lovely day, oh the cost of soapflakes!" (47). In relaying the voices of the gossips, Captain Cat almost becomes them. Such slippage is characteristic of the work as a whole, in which voices, both past and present, merge into one another. Sound and voice become more fluid transmitters of information than sight. From Captain Cat's description of the people around the pump, as he hears them from a distance, we imperceptibly move closer to the pump until we are virtually standing among the gossips.

Although he is blind, Captain Cat is described as being "like a cat" because he "sees in the dark" (92). But his "sight" is made possible through sound. The play begins in darkness, on a "bible-black" moonless night. When it was first performed on stage in 1953 the play began by literally emerging out of the darkness. As John Malcolm Brinnin describes it, "The stage was dim until a soft breath of light showed Dylan's face: 'To begin at the beginning. ...' One by one the faces of the other actors came into view as the morning light of Milk Wood broadened and Dylan's voice, removed and god-like in tone yet pathetically human in the details upon which it dwelt, made a story, a mosaic, and an aubade of the beginning movements of a village day" (*Dylan Thomas in America* 174). Events emerge both out of darkness and out of "silence" – the word appearing as a stage direction at the beginning of the script. The First Voice's opening words, "To begin at the beginning," suggest the world coming into being in Genesis; as with earlier works by Thomas, the world is created by "the Word," here spoken by a voice that emerges out of the silence, as Brinnin notes, "god-like." The sense of hope suggested by Thomas's description of the play as an "entertainment out of the darkness" is reflected in the characterization of Milk Wood as a new world. The separations evident in the fallen world are often absent in the edenic Milk Wood, and sight and sound are one. The importance of sound is made evident by the many imperatives to the audience to "listen," as well as by the descriptions which often relate to sound, as in the "lulled and dumbfound town" (1).

Silence itself is a sound: "you can hear the dew falling and the hushed town breathing" (2). While we seemingly begin as watchers observing the town – "only your eyes are unclosed" – we soon are made aware of our importance as listeners, as the primary perceptions shift to aurality. Sight merges with sound in an inescapably synaesthetic world, in which we "can hear the invisible starfall" (2). Because of Captain Cat's perceived position as spokesperson for the town, the identification is further made when the silent town is described as "blind as Captain Cat." As silence is to blindness, so sound is to sight, and in Milk Wood, sight and sound are interchangeable. Because of Captain Cat's hearing he can "see in the dark," as he sits at his window and "hears all the morning of the town"; and because of what he hears, we as audience can also see. The richness of everyday sounds, both human and natural, are catalogued throughout the work, primarily by Captain Cat and the First Voice, in long descriptive passages rich in imitative, lyrical movements, alliteration, and onomatopoeia: "There's the clip clop of horses on the sunhoneyed cobbles of the humming streets, hammering of horse-shoes, gobblequack and cackle, tomtit twitter from the bird-ounced boughs, braying on Donkey Down ... tills ring, sheep cough, dogs shout, saws sing. Oh, the Spring whinny and morning moo from the clog-dancing farms, the gulls' gab and rabble on the boat-bobbing river and sea and the cockles bubbling in the sand, scamper of sanderlings, curlew cry, crow caw, pigeon coo, clock strike, bull bellow, and the ragged gabble of the beargarden school" (49). *Under Milk Wood* addresses the audience's aural imagination, and is structured musically, more like a fugue than a narrative. The above passage, like many in the work, recall Thomas's comments in "Notes on the Art of Poetry," in which he describes his earliest attraction to words for their sound properties. "What the words stood for, symbolized, or meant, was of secondary importance. What mattered was the *sound* of them. ... And these words were, to me, as the notes of bells, the sounds of musical instruments, the noises of wind, sea and rain, the rattle of milkcarts, the clopping of hooves on cobbles, the fingering of branches on a window pane, might be to someone, deaf from birth, who has miraculously found his hearing. ... I cared for the shapes of sound that their names, and the words describing their actions, made in my ears; I cared for the colours the words cast on my eyes" (547–8). The sound of these words, "fresh with Eden's dew," recalls the elemental descriptions of sounds in Llareggub. As a world spoken into being out of silence, like the sounds made known to someone "deaf from birth," it bears traces of a language in which the sound of the word is identified with its being. Such rudimentary sounds are natural for a work reflecting an edenic world of childlike innocence.

While Captain Cat shares a narrative function with the First and Second Voices, Eli Jenkins shares other aspects with them that reflect Thomas's conception of the artist. In his letter to Princess Caetani, Thomas says that both "the First voice, and the poet preacher, never judge nor condemn but explain and make strangely simple and simply strange" (CL 814). Described in Thomas's plan as being one of two prominent voices (the other being Captain Cat), Eli Jenkins perhaps represents that part of Thomas that David Perkins and others see as a reconnection to his romantic roots, for Jenkins is a "sensitive observer and recorder of man in nature." Like the First Voice, he proposes to chronicle the outward "facts" of the town: he "tells only the truth in his Lifework ... the Population, Main Industry, Shipping, History, Topography, Flora and Fauna of the town he worships in – the White Book of Llareggub." However, his chronicles are not unbiased, for the town is not only the place in which Jenkins worships, it is also *what* he worships. He sets down not precisely "facts," but loving portraits of everyone in the town. Bessie Bighead, for example, "alone until she dies," is esteemed anyway, "her history laid out in pages there with as much love and care as the lock of hair of a first lost love" (83). "The Reverend Eli Jenkins, Poet, Preacher," is a versifier first and a minister only secondarily; for him, poetry and the beauty of nature – inseparable for his romantic inclinations – are far superior to abstract philosophy and the rigidity of the Welsh chapel culture. He worships in nature rather than in a church, in the "ceremonial dusk" and the "dark under the chapel in the skies."

David Perkins calls Dylan Thomas a "major poet" of the "neo-romantic" style because of what he sees as predominant mystical intuitions, emotional intensity, natural imagery, and personal utterance (171).[6] His argument is based on Thomas's quite early pronouncement that he was "in the path of Blake." Indeed, as a reflection of this side of Thomas's artistry, Eli is a type of romantic poet, a solitary mind seeking relation with the cosmos. The world is both the inspiration for his poetry and the audience to which it is addressed: "looking out at the day and up at the eternal hill, and hearing the sea break and the gab of birds, [he] remembers his own verses and tells them softly to empty Coronation Street that is rising and raising its blinds" (27). His poem, which is his "morning service," is addressed to the town in general rather than to its inhabitants, and his Sunset Poem is recited to Llareggub Hill. Milk Wood itself is "to the Reverend Eli Jenkins, a greenleaved sermon on the innocence of men" (94–5). "Reverend" refers more to Eli's stature than to his profession; his religion, with poetry at its core, in fact borders on the pagan. He dreams of the "Eisteddfodau," the Welsh regional and national poetry/arts festivals that have faux-druidic associations, and in his dreams he "intricately rhymes, to the music of crwth and pibcorn, all night long in his druid's seedy nightie in a beer-tent black with parches" (23). With his "bard's white hair" (27) he truly sees himself as a spokesperson for the people and an intermediary between the world of man and that of, not precisely God, but the multiple Welsh gods manifest in the natural world. Jenkins's beliefs predate Christianity, and he sees Llareggub as a living continuation of the mythic world recorded in the *Mabinogion,* worshipping, for example, "Llareggub hill, that mystic tumulus, the memorial of peoples that dwelt in the region of Llareggub before the Celts left the land of Summer and where the old wizards made themselves a wife out of flowers"(91).[7] With Eli Jenkins, Thomas ironically returns to the priestly function of the artist earlier rejected in *Portrait;* here, the artist is not a godlike figure, as he was in the earliest stories, but an intercessor between the temporal world of man and the timeless world of myth. Eli is aware that his articulations are not the "first Word," for he consciously puts himself into relation with the utterances of previous creators recorded in Welsh mythology. Indeed, when Eli calls his chronicle the "White Book of Llareggub," he places himself in an exhalted context by intentionally echoing such real ancient Welsh manuscripts as the "Black Book of Carmarthen," the "White Book of Rhydderch" (1300–25), and the "Red Book of Hergest" (1375–1425), among others. And, because writing is a conscious gesture one makes toward society, Eli makes his contribution to the mythological dialogue with a sense of responsibility to the people for whom he speaks.

The "White Book of Llareggub" is Eli's "Life Work" in more than one sense: as a continuing chronicle, it temporally exists with his own physical existence, as well as being his consuming passion. But perhaps more important, it is a work about life itself. As the people *are* the town, so the book containing descriptions of both is equally about the town, as he contends, and about life in general. The First Voice tells us that the "White Book" is a "real" book that we can consult; on a purely metaphorical level this is so, for the White Book *is* life. More literally, perhaps, the White Book, as a portrait of Llareggub, parallels or is the same thing as *Under Milk Wood,* which we are "consulting" as we read or hear it. Like the book in "Where Tawe Flows" that is a type for the containing story by the same name, the fictional text is recreated in the real world, if in a more romanticized form than the social-realist novel-in-progress.

Significantly, Eli's morning poem-prayer is immediately followed by Lily Smalls looking in her mirror and criticizing herself, albeit with a sense of humour, ending with a declaration that she is loved; like Lily Smalls's mirror, Eli's poems and his White Book (and consequently Thomas's poems and *Under Milk Wood*) offer loving portraits, "warts and all." In contrast to the voice of the guidebook, whose condescension reflects an outsider's contempt for a world still in touch with its past, the White Book is a self-reflection, equally biased but more accepting. The somewhat sinister-sounding "Black Book of Llareggub" in "The Orchards" is transformed into a white book, suggestive of purity and innocence, and offers a different interpretation of the timelessness hinted at by the distorting mirror that is the voice of the guidebook. The White Book is a more useful guide to locating the self in place. The metaphoric possibilities of geography recall the early story "The Map of Love," in which people are intimately grounded in place – not only in the present, but also in a mythic past. Eli's book is a means of reconciling the separations of the fallen world. It is a way of joining the people and place to myth. Giving local meaning to universal stories, Thomas mends the tragic separation of the local and temporal from the universal and timeless that was witnessed in the early story "The Tree." Eli's book is also a way of reconciling the inner and outer worlds, what Thomas saw as the physical world and the imaginative one, for Eli's writing both subjectifies the world and objectifies the self. His "life" work is a reflection or map of himself and his people, their place in the temporal world and in the timeless structures of myth.

Eli Jenkins is a serio-comic character, who may be a self-parody of Thomas the "romantic" poet. However, when Thomas performed this part himself in the original New York reading, he allowed Eli's simple poems the same dignity with which he read his own poems and those of other poets whom he admired. Having proclaimed himself "Ann's bard on a raised hearth" in "After the Funeral," he only half mocks Eli's claim to bardhood. When Eli recites his sunset poem "to Llareggub Hill," it is a prayer containing sentiments common to Thomas's poems, such as the continuity of existence in spite of the fact that everything is "born to die." Eli is not concerned with whether or not the townspeople heed his words; yet at the same time he addresses not the townspeople as potential listeners, but us, the invited listeners brought into the town. His petition to the "Lord" turns into an appeal to the audience somewhat reminiscent of a Shakespearian epilogue, when Eli, for the first time, like the First and Second voices, seems to address us directly:

> We are not wholly bad or good
> Who live our lives under Milk Wood,
> And Thou, I know wilt be the first
> To see our best side, not our worst. (87)

Eli then makes a Festean exit with a conclusion to his prayer that emphasizes the cyclical nature of life and its continuity, and hopes for another new beginning tomorrow, mirroring the actual structure of *Under Milk Wood*:

> O let us see another day!
> Bless us this night, I pray,
> And to the sun we all will bow,
> And say good-bye – but just for now! (87)

In the later poem "Over Sir John's Hill," Thomas refers to himself as "young Aesop fabling to the near night," and it is as just such a fabler that Eli appears in his recitation to Llareggub hill, and in his "mythic" White Book. As an artist Eli takes great pleasure in form, as his regular, although simply formed, poems illustrate. As fabler as well as chronicler, Eli embodies a notion of the artist as an organizer and shaper of the raw material of life.[8]

THE LYRICAL IMPULSE

In "Notes on the Art of Poetry," Thomas reiterates his attraction to the sounds of words and says, "what I like to do is to treat words as a craftsman does his wood or stone or what-have-you, to hew, carve, mold, coil, polish, and plane them into patterns, sequences, sculptures, fugues of sound expressing some lyrical impulse, some spiritual doubt or conviction, some dimly-realized truth I must try to reach and realize" (549). While often cited in relation to Thomas's poetry, this passage is equally applicable to *Under Milk Wood*. The polyphonic play indeed has the texture of a fugue, and often slips from sense into sound with the imitative harmony common to the lyric. *Under Milk Wood* emphasizes sound and pictorial imagery rather than narrative or dramatic movement. Its rhythms revolve around an implied centre instead of thrusting forward in a narrative linear motion, and we can, as in most lyrics, "hear the end in the beginning" (Frye et al., 269). *Under Milk Wood*'s connections to the lyric are perhaps seen most clearly in its musical qualities. As well as featuring the more obvious musicality produced by the numerous songs, nursery rhymes, and poems, the play contains localized passages shaped by musical principles. The work emerges as a shaping of sounds according to a rhythmical drive, growing out of the darkness and silence, the associations of words grouped by elements of rhyme, assonance, alliteration, and punning. These lyrical cadences are as evident in the prose passages as in those written in verse – for example, in the imitative metre that emerges in the opening: "To begin at the beginning: It is spring, moonless night in the small town, starless and bible-black, the cobblestreets silent and the hunched, courters'-and-rabbits' wood limping invisible down to the sloeblack, slow, black, crow-black, fishingboat-bobbing sea. The houses are blind as moles (though moles see fine tonight in the snouting, velvet dingles) or blind as Captain Cat there in the muffled middle by the pump and the town clock, the shops in mourning, the Welfare Hall in widow's weeds. And all the people of the lulled and dumbfound town are sleeping now" (1). The rhythmical variations imitate the rocking motion of the waves heard in the heavily stressed "sloeblack, slow, black, crowblack, fishingboat-bobbing sea," in the lingering rhythm of the "processional salt slow musical wind," or in the ticking of the clock echoed in the words, "Time passes. Listen. Time Passes."

The prose passages are musically poetic, being strongly accented and highly alliterated. But while arguably less sophisticated in terms of technique, the parts in verse are no less musical. Songs and nursery rhymes are based on the folk rhymes and simple metres common to orally transmitted works. Eli Jenkins's morning song and sunset poem, for example, are written in variations on the ballad stanza form:

Dear Gwalia! I know there are
Towns lovelier than ours,
And fairer hills and loftier far,
And groves more full of flowers,

And boskier woods more blithe with spring
And bright with birds adorning,
And sweeter bards than I to sing
Their praise this beauteous morning. (27)

With its simple *abab* rhyme, and its regular quatrains of alternating iambic tetrameter and trimeter lines, Eli's simple songs seem almost trite. Indeed, the high degree of variation from the standard ballad stanza indicates that Eli is an artist not completely in control of his medium. Yet Thomas perhaps values Eli's poems precisely for their simplicity, which is a reflection of the immediate, spontaneous nature of the ballad, orally transmitted. And as folk art, they embody a common, shared experience. However, underneath the simplicity is a sophistication that belies the poems' naïveté. Like nursery rhymes, nonsense, and game songs, Eli's ballads, as much as the mimicking rhythms of the prose passages, reflect Thomas's consciousness of language as it exists at the level of sound. Thomas once said that "a poem on a page is only half a poem"(QEOM 126). Eli's poems aid Thomas in retrieving the lyric's roots in music and the musical qualities of language.

Music is explicit as well as implicit in *Under Milk Wood*, occurring in both natural and man-made forms. The wind in the above example is described as processional music moving down Coronation Street; beyond the town, "the music of the spheres is heard distinctly over Milk Wood. It is 'The Rustle of Spring' "(57), perhaps suggestive of Stravinsky's "The Rite of Spring," but in a far more harmonious form than Stravinsky's work.[9] Nature is personified and given a human voice: "the morning is all singing" (59). Complementary to this, since rhythm is a common and natural phenomenon for both humankind and its environment, music is a reflection of natural rhythms.

Organ Morgan, the organist, dreams of everyday sounds mingling with and turning into music, an interesting correspondence to the transformations that *Under Milk Wood* itself effects. Ironically, Organ Morgan is overwhelmed by the celebration, crying "Help ... there is perturbation and music in Coronation Street! All the spouses are honking like geese and the babies singing opera. P.C. Attila Rees has got his truncheon out and is playing cadenzas by the pump, the cows from Sunday Meadow ring like reindeer" (18–19). And Eli Jenkins, who also hears music in his dreams as he "intricately rhymes, to the music of crwth and pibcorn," illustrates that the natural rhythms taken up by the people of Llareggub are merely instinctively Welsh. Rather than being shocked by the contents of Polly Garter's song, he is impressed by its form, and he effectively puts off any criticism with the exclamation, "praise the Lord! We are a musical nation" (60). Rhyme and rhythm are seen as natural impulses, and music has an intrinsic innocence, as Polly's song mingles with the songs of the children, who "tumble and rhyme on the cobbles" (63). The harmony inherent in the music of Milk Wood reflects a state of edenic innocence preceding the dissonance of a fallen world. Llareggub's eccentric and at times archaic Welshness is merely a closer identification with the rhythms of the unfallen world, and reflects a mysterious connection with aspects of reality not available to the less harmonious and less lyrical outside world.

Many modern poets and critics – Ezra Pound, William Carlos Williams, Paul Valéry, and Northrop Frye among them – see the lyric as being at the deepest roots of poetic language, what Valéry called "music forcing itself into articulate speech" (Welsh 133). When Thomas exploits the controlling rhythms that he derives from the associative possibilities of sounds, he returns not merely to the roots of lyric, but to the roots of *all* language. What many view as Thomas's "romanticism" is based largely on his early proclamation that he is "in the path of Blake" (CL 25); later in his career he goes back to, or beyond, the romantics to retrieve the communal rhythms of the folk tradition that predated written literature. He leaves behind the individual psyche responsible for romantic proclamations. Thomas's new rhythms are shared not only among the people of Llareggub but also with the audience.

Thomas's early poems are heavily patterned, formal structures conceptualized on the page; his artist figures in the early prose are likewise dependent on the physical constraints of writing, such as those seen in the literal image of the pencil on the paper in "The Orchards," or the woman who exists on the page in "The Mouse and the Woman" – all creators and their creations are at the mercy of the relative fixity of the visual principles of writing. The later works, both poetry and prose, stress the visual to a much lesser extent, emphasizing instead the musical principles of verbal organization through the rhythm and sounds of words and the shaping, temporal movements associated with the ear. Whereas in the early works visual principles "killed" life when things were locked into timeless forms, in his later work Thomas resolves this problematic result of art by appealing more to the aural imagination. A listener's perception of sounds moving successively in time can never be frozen and rendered lifeless, for the continued movement and transformation implied by the sounds' completely temporal nature precludes this. A sound image, being fluid and ephemeral, disappears as soon as it is uttered, and thus does not have to undergo the deliberate decreation inflicted on the earlier, "visual" creations. Most truly existing in time, such vocalized creations may thus be seen as within the fallen world. Yet, because of the synchronic nature of lyricism, the same work can be paradoxically also out of time, and therefore an embodiment of the not-yet-fallen. The natural rhythms of time and human experience provide the context for the utterance of a mythic timelessness, embodied by the participation of past voices, the harmonies of music and the incantations of a holistic world – this simultaneously fallen and not-yet-fallen world is the "Heaven-on-earth" that Eli Jenkins and Marianne Sailors believe they are a part of.

Described as the "genre of arrested movement" (Cameron 5), the lyric is a most appropriate form with which to communicate the timelessness of Llareggub that paradoxically is expressed in its temporality. As the voice of the guidebook disparagingly says, Llareggub is from another era: "Though there is little to attract the hillclimber, the healthseeker, the sportsman, or the weekending motorist, the contemplative may, if sufficiently attracted to spare it some leisurely hours, find, in its cobbled streets and its little fishing harbour, in its several curious customs, and in the conversation of its local 'characters', some of the picturesque sense of the past so frequently lacking in towns and villages which have kept more abreast of the times" (26). The slow pace of the town dismissed by this outsider's voice is more kindly referred to by Thomas, in such phrases as "the long lazy lyrical afternoon." Lyric structure and texture are suggested in the self-containment of this world, withdrawn from that of the ordinary, external environment. The voices of Llareggub's inhabitants which make up the voice of Llareggub itself need no external context. In both structure and theme, *Under Milk Wood* embodies lyrical unity and harmony in its multiplicity, rather than the conflicts and tensions characteristic of narrative.

It is one of the tendencies of the lyric to be concerned with temporality in both its formal arrangement and its subject matter. This is often illustrated in the thematic concerns of death and immortality, frequently explored in Thomas's poetry, but no less so in *Under Milk Wood*. The dramatic temporality of *Under Milk Wood* is cyclic rather than linear, reflecting mythic rather than historical time. From the First Voice's opening monologue in which he tells us "Time passes. Listen. Time passes" (also repeated later in the work), our attention is drawn to temporality and to Llareggub's own consciousness of it. As a timeless place that is simultaneously subject to time, Milk Wood is to Marianne Sailors "the garden of Eden" in which she counts the days. Lord Cut-Glass, "in his kitchen full of time," attempts to hold at bay the temporality that may be associated with the external world by confusing his "enemy," which may be mortality or Time itself, for he owns sixty-six clocks all set at different hours. Lord Cut-Glass thwarts time by multiplication rather than reduction, a strategy analogous to Thomas's polysemy. More public timekeepers, like Lord Cut-Glass's clocks, are also freely manipulable to the rearrangement of temporal laws, such as the clock in the Sailor's Arms that "says half past eleven. Half past eleven is opening time. The hands of the clock have stayed still at half past eleven for fifty years. It is always opening time in the Sailor's Arms" (40). The town itself even outwits a natural marker of time, for it is up and moving ahead of the cock's crow, which is "Too late … too late," as Captain Cat notes. Llareggub is a town that, through outright temporal defiance, embraces eternity in any form it can. Images of spring and birth are intertwined with images of death: "Noah's Ark" clocks and grim-reaper clocks, babies and old men, the voices of the living and the dead, all coexist. Marianne Sailors's Eden is Lord Cut-Glass's Armageddon, yet even he, with all his clocks, cannot keep out the opposing impulse that accompanies the rebirth of spring: "The lust and lilt and lather and emerald breeze and crackle of the bird-praise and body of Spring with its breasts full of rivering May-milk, means, to that lordly fish-head nibbler, nothing but another nearness to the tribes and navies of the Last Black Day who'll sear and pillage down Armageddon Hill to his double-locked rusty-shuttered tick-tock dust-scrabbled shack at the bottom of the town that has fallen head over bells in love" (22–3).

Lord Cut-Glass's fear of death is ineffectual in this "place of love" because love becomes the ultimate force in defiance of death. Like the "stuffed fox and the stale fern" that come to life as they "cry Love" in "After the funeral," the love that the inhabitants of Llareggub have for the dead keep the dead alive in the imagination, as their voices are raised in memory to join the voices of the living. The timeless continuation made possible by the force of love triumphs over the temporal.

Time, its passing and undoing, is, in many ways, the subject of *Under Milk Wood*, with its circular structure, its emphasis on one day, and its return to where it started, with the "repetition of the first word." In the early prose, the teleological journeys of the artist figures are continually undercut; here, Thomas omits any teleological impulses; there is no story told in *Under Milk Wood*, no "plot" with beginning, middle, and end, no time-bound narrative. Like the later poems such as "In Country Sleep," which stress circularity and a continual present ("this dawn and each first dawn"), the work folds back on itself. While the early stories embody some lyric tendencies, they are framed in narrative and resist to various extents the fuller temporal disembodiment exemplified in *Under Milk Wood*. While the characters in the early stories have problems with definition and with pinning things down in language, their slippery existence is partially balanced by the text as a stabilizing confine. The characters who are artist figures acquire definition by literally writing themselves into it. The text becomes the self-contained world that structures their amorphousness. In *Under Milk Wood*, linguistic slippage becomes less a problem than an accepted condition. Narrative structures recede in favour of mingling voices that fade in and out freely, and lyric fluidity comes to the fore. Early figures such as Marlais are writers rather than speakers. More aural than visual, the world of Llareggub breaks free from the confines of graphic text, revelling in the spontaneity of vocal utterance.

In contrast to the singular, albeit often complex, strain of narrative in the early stories, *Under Milk Wood* has a symphonic texture in which numerous lives are presented simultaneously. Fragments of gossip, for example, fit together as coherently as a more sequential and "logical" conversation; voices from the past mingle equally with those of the present. Likewise, actions in the past are superimposed on those of the present, exemplified by the numerous characters who dream of their childhoods. The disarrangement of temporal order most apparent in the characters' dreams is a reflection of a larger organizing principle that presents time as a subjective experience. Like the clocks, memory functions to wall out temporarily the fallen world which is ultimately inescapable. As in Thomas's recollection of childhood in "Fern Hill," for the duration of the dreams there is no other reality with which the dreamer must contend. As a vision of a communal, subjective dream, Llareggub also need only attend to its own voice; it can banish objective time that accompanies the momentarily locked out social world. A narrative's "plot" is the place of conflict between public and individual reality; the lyric is free from such contention, for while it is conscious of external social forces, it can temporarily hold them at bay. While the fallen world is ultimately unavoidable, the suspension of time empowered by subjectivity makes time bearable. As Sharon Cameron notes, this paradox of the subjective suspension of time and its inescapability is a characteristic of the lyric in general: "The contradiction between social and personal time is the lyric's generating impulse, for the lyric both rejects the limitation of social and objective time, those structures that drive hard lines between past, present and future, and must make use of them" (206). Llareggub is isolated from the outside world through its lyrical subjectivity, but it also manifests the temporal contradictions at the heart of the lyric, for it attempts to slow time even as it is caught up in the temporal advance. It deflects sequential priority in its circularity; like the fusion that occurs in Thomas's title for a later volume of poetry, "Deaths and Entrances," the vision is one in which death is not a moment of closure but a passage or moment of transformation in continual flux. The "beginning" of the poem is not a first moment but a moment of entry; as the play ends "with the first word," there is also no "last word," and everything is left open for further transformation. As in war poems like "A refusal to mourn," death in *Under Milk Wood* is not a finality, but an experience whereby finite identity is transcended and the individual becomes composite; this happens with the voices of the drowned who become as one voice with the living.

Thomas's lyric presents voices not in sequence but in unison. The singular and solipsistic artist of the early stories is replaced by a communal artist figure, embodied by the whole town of Llareggub who speaks its subjective perceptions into existence. Neither an Adam nor an Aesop, Thomas's final artist figure is, like its precursor Abertawe in "Where Tawe Flows," all the town. *Under Milk Wood* is the fictional Llareggub's creation as much as it is Thomas's.

THE DEMOCRATIZATION OF THE LYRIC

Having mastered the lyric genre in his poetry, Thomas could only move into new areas. Lyrical in every way regarding subject matter and structure, *Under Milk Wood* is, however a generic paradox, for it defies the usual definition of the lyric as a solitary voice, and illustrates what might be called the democratization of the lyric.

Through Eli Jenkins and the numerous other voices that create Llareggub, Thomas portrays the artist as specifically not distinct from common man. Portraying himself in the poem "Prologue" as the enabler Noah who builds arks of poetry, he withdraws from his authoritative position, allowing his own ark to give way to "multitudes of arks." The ever-present "I" of the early poems having lost its privilege, the reader as much as the writer becomes the vantage point of *Under Milk Wood*, through the work's many "you-are-here" directions. Thomas's play is dialogic, relying on a discourse with a real or potential audience. Unlike most lyrics, in which the audience seems to be distanced from the poet (in a lyric, it is often thought that the poet is "overheard" rather than heard), the audience here is an obvious and necessary presence. While the artist figures in the early works indulge in writing worlds into creation – isolated and solitary acts needing no audience – the later figures tell worlds into creation. An audience is very much present in the later work: in *Under Milk Wood* and "A Winter's Tale," we are told to "listen" and "look"; we are addressed as "you strangers" to whom "at poor peace I sing" in "Prologue." Even the unaddressed but suggested listeners of "Aesop fabling" suggest a far different stance from that of the solipsistic Adams of the early works. Thomas's emphasis on telling as well as writing, on the act of narration rather than on simple narrative, suggests a communication process at work that functions more productively than the lack of communication at the centre of such early works as "The Tree," "The Orchards," or even *Adventures in the Skin Trade*. Rejecting the earlier narcissism of his artist figures, Thomas creates works of art in which the writer and reader, or teller and listener, are mutually dependent. Repudiating exile as an artistic stance, he circumvents the opposition of self to society that Maurice Beebe traces through both the "sacred fount" and the "ivory tower" traditions of the artist; dissolving any such binary oppositions, Thomas indulges in a sort of carnivalistic participation which acknowledges no artistic authority.

The participatory and polyphonic nature of carnival, as interpreted by Bakhtin in *Rabelais and His World*, is a fitting celebration with which to identify *Under Milk Wood*. Itself a type of anti-genre, the carnival defies the hierarchic distinctions that Thomas came to reject. With carnival, there is no authoritative point of view; everyone participates, and there is no acknowledged distinction between actors and audience, as all are participants. Like Thomas's play for voices, carnivalistic writing has its source in oral tradition: it takes up the spoken discourse of a people and uses it in written literature, thereby invoking transformation rather than simply recording. Like Eli's poem-prayers, the carnivalesque involves a kind of self-creation that goes on orally. Such artistic creation, as Eli sees it, is part of the world's revival and renewal; it embodies a universal spirit in which all participate. "Literature," as it might be loosely defined in the voices of Llareggub, becomes a communal creation of a new world. The atemporal structures of the lyric in part permit the possibilities of the carnivalesque, for as Bakhtin notes, "the ultimate word of the world and about the world has not yet been spoken, the world is open and free, everything is still in the future and will always be in the future" (*The Problems of Dostoevsky's Poetics* 166).

The earliest artists, characterized by Adam telling stories to himself, soon become challenged by outside voices. The purely solipsistic artists are replaced by the growing "young Thomas" in *Portrait*, who learns to create a self through the selective appropriation of the voices of others, as he does with Tennyson in "The Fight"; later, the artist comes to a more accepting recreation of self through the internalization of these other voices, as in "Return Journey." Ultimately, Thomas's artist figures reach the understanding that the concept of solitude is a fiction. Merging the individual with the collective body, Thomas recreates the lyric as a "unique" voice fragmented as unity in multiplicity. Thomas's lyric replaces the customary first-person speaker with fragmentary multiple voices that both coalesce and retain their individual identities. The distances that remain between the voices are what facilitate the dialogic interplay; such openness, the spaces that invite the bridges of communication, also provide the impetus for future recreations, recalling Thomas's statement in "Notes on the Art of Poetry" that "the best craftsmanship always leaves holes and gaps in the works of the poem so that something that is *not* in the poem can creep, crawl, flash, or thunder in" (554).

Thomas's fragmentation, however, does not reflect the discontinuity that is characteristic of the modern experience. Tempted by momentary glances, Thomas resists the closure of overriding systems by seeing multiple voices as superior to one authoritative voice; he maintains the traditional anonymity of the lyric voice through its fragmentation into many voices, which serves as a departure from the finite constrictions of identity. A total merging, as in a choric voice, would not be possible in a fallen world, however strong the impetus to edenic return; the best that can materialize is the compromise of a heaven *on* earth, having aspects of both the temporal and the timeless. Even though separations and fragments remain, connections are yet possible. As with Mog Edwards and Myfanwy Price, who live their lives at opposite ends of town and never meet, but who communicate through their letters and swear an undying love for one another, an open dialogue, both fragmented and unifying, seems to be the optimum solution. Mog and Myfanwy are perfectly content to live their lives apart.

The pluralistic voices of the democratized lyric, all artist figures and carnival participants, rejoice in their relativity. And it is their temporality and fluidity that involve them with the ever-changing world. In the story "The Peaches," the boy's "fall" occurs with his perceived distinctness from objects and people with which or whom he earlier identified; henceforth he sees himself as cut off, a "lone wolf," and an outsider. With *Under Milk Wood*, Thomas reasserts identification, partly through the communal voice, and partly through a return to place as source, for the voices of the people parallel the voice of Llareggub and the surrounding countryside. As a view of adulthood seen through the eyes of a child, Llareggub is in an infant state with no consciousness of being separate from the world. And the language which defines *Under Milk Wood* is not unlike that in "Fern Hill," which Thomas described as written in words that come from a "never-to-be buried childhood in heaven or Wales" (CL 583).

Full of natural images that undergo linguistic and phenomenal transformations, the play constantly aligns the inhabitants of Llareggub, and indeed the audience as well, with the place. When the First Voice invites the reader to "come now, drift up the dark, come up the drifting sea-dark street now in the dark night see-sawing like the sea" (8), the audience, the street and the natural world become one through the slippage of words: the street and the night are both dark; the sea, the street, and the invited listener all share the word "drift"; together, the audience, the physical town, and the surrounding natural world share in an impressionistic tidal return reflected in both the imagery and the metre of the passage. An embracing humanism marks the difference between this kind of slippage and the metamorphic tendencies in the early stories. While the early works sometimes alarmingly subvert the usual boundaries between self and reality, the later work, performing similar slippage, "comforts" by embracing a wider community. The identification of the audience and Llareggub's inhabitants with the place is effected through the sounds, or the voice, of the location. The rhythmic return of the "seesawing sea" provides what is perhaps the overriding cadence of the work as a whole. The circularity of the play, ending with the "repetition of the first word," combined with the identification of voice and place, offers the possibility of an edenic return.

Because Thomas might, like Eli, "merely believe in heaven on earth" (CL 814), he creates a work in which paradoxes and oxymorons abound: Llareggub is a place with the possibility of the temporal contradictions found in "Fern Hill," where the past is present ("*Now* as I *was* young and easy ...") [my italics]. In this earthly/edenic state, silence is not an obliteration but a fullness of meaning, and what seems an absence allows for presence. Thomas's democratized lyric allows into language possibility and thus the whole world. The lyric genre allows both transcendent moments and temporal markings in time, as Thomas's many occasional poems illustrate. Its rhythms allow Thomas to look back as well as forward, to both the "beginning" and the "for ever and ever" that Mog and Myfanwy, Eli, and Marianne Sailors all anticipate.

Living a lyrical existence, Llareggub is simultaneously temporal and timeless, local and universal. It is the artist who is responsible for such an interplay of seemingly opposing elements, whether conscious of his/her function, like Eli, or oblivious to it, like the ordinary citizens of Llareggub. When Thomas calls himself "young Aesop fabling to the near night," he is not, as might be supposed, advocating a return to a solipsistic expression. Instead, he is moving toward a return to vocal creation, as exemplified by *Under Milk Wood*. Aesop's first appearance in Thomas's work bears this out: the fabler appears in an early manuscript version of "In Country Heaven" as "young Aesop fabling by the coracled Towy" (quoted in CP 260–1). This poem was to be part of a "long poem" by the same name whose central premise was an apocalyptic vision of the destruction of the world. In a note to Princess Caetani, Thomas describes his plan for the work: "The godhead, the author, the first cause, architect, lamplighter, the beginning word ... [is] on top of a hill in Heaven," watching worlds being destroyed. His companions, the "countrymen of heaven," witness the destruction of their various worlds; as the earth is destroyed, the countrymen from earth "tell one another, through the long night ... what they remember ... places, fears, loves, exaltation, misery, animal joy, ignorance and mysteries, all you and I know and do not know. The poem-to-be is made of these tellings."[10] Aesop, as one of these tellers, seems, in this plan, to be sharing the oral recreation of the world with other tellers. Further, this communal telling is not simply recollection but is in fact a re-experiencing and a recreation. The memories of the countrymen of heaven are not in the past tense but in "all tenses," similar to the lyrical time in "Fern Hill" and *Under Milk Wood,* and these memories "can look towards the future, can caution and admonish. The rememberer may live himself back into active participation in the remembered scene, adventure or spiritual condition."[11] Aesop's "audience," like Eli's, are other participants in the communal oral act, telling the world into creation. Thomas's Aesop, like the voice out of the darkness and silence that opens *Under Milk Wood,* is perhaps an allegorist of sorts, being a fabler, but is so only in an unconventional sense, for the text can be made to mean different things, according to the perceiver/participant – meaning is the result of a reciprocal relationship between the text (or world) and the reader. In the exemplary but contradictory existence that is the verbally created Llareggub, the reader or audience is as much an artist, participating in the dialogue that is creation.

Notes

INTRODUCTION

1 While Thomas's work has been called "surreal" (e.g. Treece), Thomas himself denied the label. Like Thomas's early stories, surrealism does exploit the material of dreams, hallucinations, and the state between sleep and waking; Thomas's early stories in particular have the free-flowing appearance of many surrealist works of the period. However, where Thomas differs from the surrealists is in the degree to which he revolts against restraint. The surrealists balked at any control over the artistic process by forethought and intention, sometimes even employing automatic writing. Thomas's insistence on "hewing" and "crafting" his works belies such spontaneity; his poems are formed, not, as he puts it, "turned on like a tap." Further, in a letter to Richard Church (9 December 1935), Thomas corrects the publisher's assertion that he was influenced by surrealism, particularly the fact that, in his understanding, surrealist writing need have no meaning: "I think I do know what some of the main faults of my writing are: immature violence, rhythmic monotony, frequent muddleheadedness, and a very much overweighted imagery that leads too often to incoherence. But every line *is* meant to be understood; the reader *is* meant to understand every poem by thinking and feeling about it, not by sucking it in through his pores, or whatever he is meant to do with surrealist writing" (CL 205).

2 Tindall (1962) defines three distinct "periods" in Thomas's poetry, with which division he claims Thomas himself agreed: the first period, preceding World War II, is characterized by the "womb and tomb" motif; the second phase, including the war poems such as "Ceremony after a fire raid," shows a greater involvement with others; the last phase, characterized by such poems as "Fern Hill" and "Poem on his birthday," shows a more complete acceptance of humanity and the human condition (488). This taxonomy is similar to one that may be applied to Thomas's prose writing.

CHAPTER ONE

1 A similar conflation occurs in the poem "In the beginning" (CP 22) with the word "crosstree."
2 As well as recalling the "force that through the green fuse drives the flower," this passage also resembles the early poem "I fellowed sleep," which Thomas referred to as a "dream poem" (CL 39). In the poem, the speaker and a "ghostly other" "fled the earth" to travel over his "father's globe" and "father's land."
3 The ladder of words is a recurrent image in Dylan Thomas's work, as in "I fellowed sleep":
   Then all the matter of the living air
   Raised up a voice, and, climbing on the words,
   I spelt my vision with a hand and hair ...
   There grows the hours' ladder to the sun ... (CP 24)
   It also appears in a letter to Trevor Hughes, June 1934, in which Thomas says: "in our anatomical creature, we see the creature of the material world as weak and struggling as ourselves. But, day by day, I realize more that, together, we could work out our separate providences, and reach, at least some kind of heaven up a ladder of words" (CL 142).
4 See "Prologue" (CP 3), in which Thomas describes himself as Noah.
5 "I read somewhere of a shepherd who, when asked why he made, from within fairy rings, ritual observances to the moon to protect his flocks, replied, 'I'd be a damn' fool if I didn't!' These poems, with all their crudities, doubts, and confusions, are written for the love of Man and in praise of God, and I'd be a damn' fool if they weren't."
6 The image of scissors appears in a number of Thomas's works, such as the story "The Mouse and the Woman" and the poem "When,

like a running grave" (*CP* 19) ("When, like a running grave, time tracks you down / ... Comes, like a scissors stalking, tailor age"). The recurring image recalls the nineteenth-century didactic moral fable, "The Tale of Little Suck-a-Thumb," about a boy who has his thumb cut off by a scissors-man because he sucks it. Thomas would have encountered a rhyming version of this tale in *Struwelpeter* {mentioned in "Return Journey" (*CS* 327)}.

7 This poem has until recently been referred to as "Author's Prologue," but as Walford Davies and Ralph Maud suggest in their notes to *Collected Poems 1934–1953*, this longer title originated with Thomas's publisher, and was not used by Thomas himself, who simply refered to it as "Prologue" (see also *CL*).

8 More specifically, he refers to himself as the "Drinking Noah of the bay" (*CP* 3): Noah's drinking connects Thomas to the Welsh Prince Seithennin, who was supposed to have caused a flood of Cardiganshire by getting drunk and leaving open the floodgates – thus portraying Thomas once again as both a destroyer and a creator.

9 It is here that Thomas first uses the name "Llareggub," which is "buggerall" spelt backwards. A profane version of Utopia, Llareggub exists nowhere in the known, phenomenal world.

10 I am not aware of any evidence suggesting that Thomas was familiar with Weil's term; however, its seems to be particularly well suited to Thomas's poetic. Wallace Stevens, a poet who is, like Thomas, concerned with the way that imagination operates on reality, also borrows the term from Weil, finding it particularly fitted to his concept of poetry, as well as to the specific imperatives of the twentieth century. In "The Relations between Poetry and Painting" (*The Necessary Angel: Essays on Reality and the Imagination* 1960), Stevens cites Weil, and says that "Modern reality is a reality of decreation, in which our revelations are not the revelations of belief, but the precious portents of our own powers" (175).

11 A fuller treatment of this image is found on pages 40ff.

12 "In the direction of the beginning" is a phrase that recurs in both the poetry and the prose, and is the title of one of the early short stories (*CS* 115).

13 This story possibly is a source for the later poem from *Deaths and Entrances*, "Love in the Asylum" (*CP* 90). Presented in the first person, the poem begins: "A stranger has come / to share my room in

the house not right in the head" and ends with the joining of the speaker and a woman, and the speaker's will to "suffer the first vision that set fire to the stars" – an image reminiscent of the ending of "The Mouse and the Woman."

14 A similar correlation occurs in "If I were tickled by the rub of love" (CP 15), which ends with the line "Man be my metaphor."

15 Thomas's concerns with language parallel those of several contemporary linguistic theorists, some of whom would consider themselves antithetical to one another. While resembling in some ways Julia Kristeva's semiotic language, Thomas's intermediary poetic space may also be likened to what Lacan calls the area of "non-meaning," which overlaps the state of "being" – the pre-linguistic – and that of "meaning." For Lacan, entry into language effects a split with the real (the self, the phenomenal world), confining the subject to the realm of signification. There exists an overlapping region wherein abides a fluid play of signification with as yet no fixed reference point; this area of so-called "non-meaning" is the antithesis of the arrested meaning in the symbolic order. Lacan's area of non-meaning is the natural domain of what he calls the unary signifier, as opposed to the binary signifier which occupies the area of meaning. Unlike the binary signifier, the unary signifier has no other signifier into which it can undeniably be translated or to which it can be referred. The unary signifier is irreducible – it does not "represent" the drives of the pre-linguistic state, nor can it be reduced to them. Many of the more problematic images in Thomas's poems seem to reach back to Lacan's unary signifiers, which occupy the border country between being and meaning.

16 See CL 40, 61, where Thomas gives conflicting dates.

17 In another letter to Johnson he says that "'Uncommon Genesis' is an uncommon story ... and you'll either like it, or dislike it very strongly. I'm hoping you'll like it. It has to be read with an unbiased mind, for it is written in a high and wordily romantic style that could, if the attention was shifted only momentarily off its meaning, be turned to bathos. But if you do really read it carefully & without prejudice, I don't think you will laugh" (CL 61).

18 J.H. Martin, letter to the editor of the *Times Literary Supplement*, 19 March 1964, 235, and Keidrych Rhys, *TLS*, 26 March 1964, 255.

19 Defined in "Revolution of the Word Dictionary," *transition* no. 21, (March 1932), 323-4.

20 The madman resembles "the hunchback in the park" (*CP* 93) who makes "a woman figure without fault" in the "unmade park." These creations also have a parallel in Welsh myth: In "Math, son of Mathonwy" in the *Mabinogion*, a wizard magically creates a woman named Blodeuedd as a wife for the hero (Gwyn and Thomas Jones 68).
21 Another allusion to the *Struwelpeter* story (see note 6 ch. 1 re: "A Prospect of the Sea").
22 This may be a reference to Thomas's early poem "After the Performance of Sophocles' Electra in a Garden" (7 July 1933) (*Notebook Poems* 208), published in *Herald of Wales*, 15 July 1933, as "Greek Play in a Garden" and mentioned in "Return Journey" (*CS* 318), or to the event that inspired the poem, a performance of "Electra" in a garden at Sketty.

CHAPTER TWO

1 The "second waking" idea appears in other contexts, e.g. "I dreamed my genesis" (*CP* 25), in which the speaker "dies" twice in a dream, each time resurrected:
   And power was contagious in my birth, second
   Rise of the skeleton and
   Rerobing of the naked ghost ...
   I dreamed my genesis in sweat of death, fallen
   Twice in the feeding sea, grown
   Stale of Adam's brine ...
Regarding his "dream poem" "I fellowed sleep," Thomas spoke of the equality between the worlds of sleep and wakefulness: "I want to sleep and wake, and look upon my sleeping as only another waking" (25 December 1933, *CL* 82).
2 A similar image occurs in the "Altarwise by Owl-light" sonnet v (*CP* 60), where biblical images merge with those from a Western:
   And from the windy West came two-gunned Gabriel,
   From Jesu's sleeve trumped up the king of spots,
   The sheath-decked jacks, queen with a shuffled heart;
   Said the fake gentleman in suit of spades,
   Black-tongued and tipsy from salvation's bottle.
3 The use of towers as symbols of art is not unique to Thomas. W.B. Yeats, for example, employed the motif in *The Tower* (1928) and *The Winding Stair* (1933); however, the two poets' approaches are

quite different. In "In my craft or sullen art," in fact, there are suggestions of the poet in "The Tower"; Thomas seems to be using Yeats as his anti-type:

> Not for the proud man apart
> From the raging moon I write
> On these spindrift pages
> Nor for the towering dead
> With their nightingales and psalms
> But for the lovers ... (CP 106).

4 In a letter to Henry Treece (23 March 1938), Thomas writes: "Out of the inevitable conflict of images – inevitable, because of the creative, recreative, destructive, and contradictory nature of the motivating centre, the womb of war – I try to make that momentary peace which is a poem. I do not want a poem of mine to be, nor can it be, a circular piece of experience placed neatly outside the living stream of time from which it came; a poem of mine is, or should be, a watertight section of the stream that is flowing all ways" (CL 282).

5 Browning's title is derived from Edgar's song in *King Lear* (III. iv. 171–3):

> Childe Roland to the Dark Tower Came,
> His word was still – Fie, foh, and fum,
> I smell the blood of a British man.

As Edgar is feigning madness in this scene, his song is meant to be meaningless, yet it is ominous. Browning's use of the first line is equally disturbing in its opacity. For Thomas, Childe Roland's end echoes the ambiguity of Marlais's goal. Edgar's song is also easily recognizable as the oath repeated by the giant in the folk-tale "Jack and the Beanstalk," alluded to in "The Orchards." In an early version of "Jack and the Beanstalk" called "Jack the Giant-Killer" (Lang), the hero defeats the giant by blowing on a magic golden trumpet, another possible source for the trumpet in "The Orchards." Without explicitly alluding to all of these tales, Thomas complexly interweaves them, creating a palimpsest of fable in which Marlais takes part.

6 "Essay on Shelley," 1852, in *Victorian Poetry and Poetics* 336.

7 In some letters to Trevor Hughes and others, Thomas seems to present himself and his cronies in this mock-heroic light, especially regarding drinking bouts: "Our words – 'give me a half-pint, a Ho-

vis, a book by Paul de Kock, and thou, thou old lavatory chain' – are spells to drag up the personified Domdaniel pleasure. Everything we do drags up a devil. Last night, Dan and I, none too brightly, for the womb of the Mermaid [Tavern] was empty, and the radio-gram blaring, discovered we had too little feeling" (CL 161).

8 In a letter to Bert Trick, Thomas described this story, initially called "Daniel Dom," as "based on the Pilgrim's Progress, but tells of the adventures of Anti-Christian in his travels from the City of Zion to the City of Destruction" (summer 1935, CL 193). While an inversion of Dom Daniel, "Daniel" is also an anagram of "denial." Elsewhere, Thomas uses "deniers" and "doom" (echoing "Dom") together for the anarchist/artists, such as in "I see the boys of summer" ("we are the dark deniers") and in sonnet VII of the "Altarwise" sequence ("Doom on deniers at the wind-turned statement").

9 The word "cipher" is ambiguous in a typically Thomasian fashion, for it may be used to denote both presence and absence. The OED defines it variously: as a noun, it may be a symbolic character such an arabic numeral, letter, hieroglyph or astrological sign, or combination of symbolic signs; as a verb, "cipher" means "to express (as thoughts or words) by written or graven characters; make plain by visible evidence." It refers not only to the expression of meaning but also to the concealment of it, in the transformation of a text through the use of such devices as codes and anagrams. A cipher is also cited as a mediator "between the existent and the transcendent." But another meaning of "cipher" negates any secret hidden meaning, being "the symbol o denoting the absence of all magnitude or quality; ... one that has no weight, worth or influence." All of the above definitions may apply simultaneously in Thomas's examples.

CHAPTER THREE

1 See, for example: Pratt 149; Korg (1948) 184–91; Stanford 155–68; Seib 239–46; T.H. Jones, 23–47; Peach 76, 84.

2 In a letter to Meurig Walters in 1938, Thomas writes: "I have just written to Keidrych Rhys suggesting that a mass-poem – though that's an ugly name – should be written by all the contributors to 'Wales'. That is, that each person should write a verse report of his own particular town, village, or district, and that all the reports,

gathered together, should be made, not by alteration but by arrangement, into one long poem. The poem would be called Wales, & wd take a whole number of the paper. The poem would be written by *all* the writers concerned, & not by individuals" (CL 286).

3 C.G. Jung, "Psychology and Poetry," an essay which Thomas might have been familiar with through its publication in *transition* 1:2 (spring 1930), 23–45.

4 *Ivory Towers and Sacred Founts: The Artist as Hero in Fiction from Goethe to Joyce* (1964).

5 In *Poets of Reality*, J. Hillis Miller cites this passage in "The Peaches" as an example of a trend in all of Thomas's work to transcend the Cartesian dualism of subject and object:
"There is no need to achieve by expansive stratagems of sensation or imagination an identification with all things. That identification is given with existence itself and can never be withdrawn. There is no initial separation between subject and object. The self is not set apart from things or people which are other than itself. ... He is the center of an adventure which is the total cosmic adventure, and, after the first experience of a birth which is a coming into existence of everything, there is no possibility of adding more to the self. What exists for Thomas as soon as anything exists at all is a single continuous realm which is at once consciousness, body, cosmos and the words which express all three at once" (190–1).

6 *Adventures in the Skin Trade and Other Stories* (New York: New Directions, 1955).

7 A radical break with tradition is, of course, a salient feature of modernism. Bennet's attempt to play out in life what his contemporaries played out in their art is indicative both of his self-consciousness as a "modern artist" and of his ability, or inability, to control the distinctions between the literal and the figurative, between real life and art.

CHAPTER FOUR

1 "Return Journey" shares its premise with the poem "Once below a time" (CP 109), in which "the boy of common thread, / the bright pretender, the ridiculous sea dandy" (Thomas's younger self) moves among images of Swansea life. In a letter to Vernon Watkins (30 January 1940), Thomas refers to the perspective of the poem as a "calling-up-of-memory" (CL 436).

2 While in the early stanzas of "Fern Hill" it is the singular narrator, "I," who is "green and golden," by the sixth stanza it is the "children, green and golden" who follow time "out of grace," indicating that the speaker's situation is a universal one.
3 Captain Tiny Evans may be an actual allusion to the cynical Caradoc Evans, whom Thomas met in the autumn of 1934 (CL 172).
4 MS in the National Library of Wales, Aberystwyth.
5 Referred to in Fitzgibbon (264) and Cleverdon (1).
6 Thomas's writerly concerns that I earlier align with postmodernism are also subjects prefigured by the romantics. Preoccupations such as the art of naming, the world of words, the rift between word and thing, self-consciousness and self-reflexiveness, and the plight of the hyperactive imagination are all traditional romantic themes. Where Thomas's early works move into the postmodern is with their troubled relationship between materiality and referentiality and the fact that, in them, a physical world outside of art may be suspect or absent. It is in his later works that he moves back to a more romantic sensibility, where the ontological status of the physical world is no longer questioned; further, the physical world becomes a source of inspiration for the writer.
7 This is a more explicit allusion to Blodeuedd, the Welsh mythical figure who may be a model for the woman in "The Mouse and the Woman" and the "woman figure without fault" in "The Hunchback in the Park" (see note 20 ch. 1). Blodeuedd (meaning "flowers") was made out of oak, broom, and meadowsweet.
8 In "Over Sir John's Hill," Aesop is paired with a heron, the "elegiac fishbird": "We grieve ... / The heron and I"; "It is the heron and I ... / ... tell-tale the knelled / Guilt." By the end of the poem the bird as artist is privileged, and Aesop is to some extent merely a scribe for the heron, who "makes all the music." Like Eli, Aesop is the recorder of the natural world, the one who hear[s] the tune" and who "grave[s] ... the notes on this time-shaken / Stone for the sake of the souls of the slain birds sailing."
9 In May, 1953, as he was finishing *Under Milk Wood*, Thomas met with Stravinsky to discuss a collaboration for an opera, with Thomas composing the libretto. The planned work was about the "recreation of the world" after global destruction from nuclear warfare; as John Malcolm Brinnin describes the outline that Stravinsky and Thomas tentatively formulated, the only two people alive on

earth would "make a new cosmogony. Confronted with a tree pushing its way upward out of radioactive dust, they would have to name it, and learn its uses, and then proceed to find names and a definition for everything on earth" (*Dylan Thomas in America* 180). The similarity to earlier examples of Adamic naming is clear – although here both an Adam and an Eve seem to be given equal linguistic dominion over the world. The new Eden that they would create sounds much like the one Thomas had already developed in Milk Wood; it is perhaps because of this similarity that Thomas felt the opera "so simple that the libretto [could] be written in the time we're [in Boston]" (CL 889).

10 From a note accompanying the poem "In the white giant's thigh," sent to Princess Caetani, who was to publish the poem in Botteghe Oscure VI (November 1950) along with the note about the "In Country Heaven" plan (quoted in CP 262). The planned longer work was to contain the poems "In Country Sleep," "In the white giant's thigh," and "Over Sir John's Hill" (CL 269n).

11 From Thomas's introduction to the BBC reading of the three "In Country Heaven" poems, 25 September 1950 (quoted in CP 263).

Bibliography

PRIMARY MATERIAL

Thomas, Dylan. *Adventures in the Skin Trade and Other Stories.* New York: New Directions, 1955.
- *Dylan Thomas: The Broadcasts.* Ed. Ralph Maud. London: J.M. Dent and Sons, 1991.
- *A Child's Christmas in Wales and Five Poems.* Read by Dylan Thomas. Caedmon, TC 1002, 1952.
- The Dylan Thomas Collection. National Library of Wales, Aberystwyth, Wales.
- *The Collected Letters of Dylan Thomas.* Ed. Paul Ferris. London: J.M. Dent and Sons, 1985.
- *The Collected Poems of Dylan Thomas 1934-1953.* Ed. Walford Davies and Ralph Maud. London: J.M. Dent, 1993.
- *The Collected Stories.* Ed. Leslie Norris. London: J.M. Dent and Sons, 1983.
- *Dylan Thomas: Early Prose Writings.* Ed. Walford Davies. New York: New Directions, 1972.
- *An Evening with Dylan Thomas.* Selections read by the poet. Caedmon, TC 1157, 1963.
- *The Map of Love.* London: J.M. Dent and Sons, 1939.

- *Dylan Thomas: The Notebook Poems 1930–1934.* Ed. Ralph Maud. London: J.M. Dent and Sons Ltd., 1989.
- Poetry Notebooks: 1930, 1930–32, February 1933, August 1933. Unpublished MSS, property of the Lockwood Memorial Library, State University of New York at Buffalo, Buffalo, New York.
- The Red Prose Notebook. 28 December 1933 – October 1934. Unpublished MS, property of the Lockwood Memorial Library, State University of New York at Buffalo, Buffalo, New York.
- "Notes on the Art of Poetry." *Texas Quarterly* 4 (Winter 1951), 44–53. In Gary Geddes, ed., *Twentieth-Century Poetry and Poetics.* 3rd ed. Toronto: Oxford University Press, 1985, 547–54.
- *Quite Early One Morning.* Broadcasts by Dylan Thomas. Pref. Aneiran Talfan Davies. London: J.M. Dent and Sons, 1954.
- *Quite Early One Morning.* Read by Dylan Thomas. Caedmon, TC 1132, 1960.
- *Selections from the Writings of Dylan Thomas.* vols. 2 and 3. Read by the poet. Caedmon, TC 1018, TC 1043, 1952.
- *Under Milk Wood.* New York: New Directions, 1954.
- *Under Milk Wood.* With the original New York cast, featuring Dylan Thomas. Audiotape. Caedmon, CDL 52005 (2c), 1953.
- *A Visit to America and Selected Poems.* Read by Dylan Thomas. Caedmon, TC 1061, 1952.

SECONDARY MATERIAL

Abrams, Meyer Howard. *The Mirror and the Lamp: Romantic Theory and the Critical Tradition.* New York: Oxford University Press, 1953.
Ackerman, John. *Dylan Thomas, His Life and Work.* New York: Oxford University Press, 1964.
- *Welsh Dylan.* Cardiff: John Jones, 1979.
- "A la Recherche de Temps Galois: Dylan Thomas's Development as a Prose Writer." *Anglo-Welsh Review* no. 83 (1986), 86–95.
Adam International Review. Dylan Thomas Memorial Number, no. 238 (1953).
Amis, Kingsley. "Thomas the Rhymer." *Spectator,* 12 August 1955, 227.

Bakhtin, Mikhail. *The Dialogic Imagination: Four Essays*. Ed. Michael Holquist. Trans. Caryl Emerson and Michael Holquist. Austin: University of Texas Press, 1981.
- *Rabelais and His World*. Trans. Helene Iswolski. Bloomington: Indiana University Press, 1984.
- *Problems of Dostoevsky's Poetics*. Ed. and trans. Caryl Emerson. Minneapolis: University of Minnesota Press, 1984.
- *Speech Genres and Other Late Essays*. Trans. Vern W. McGee. Ed. Caryl Emerson and Michael Holquist. Austin: University of Texas Press, 1986.
Barthes, Roland. *Writing Degree Zero*. Trans. Annette Lavers and Colin Smith. New York: Hill and Wang, 1968.
Beebe, Maurice. *Ivory Towers and Sacred Founts: The Artist as Hero in Fiction from Goethe to Joyce*. New York: New York University Press, 1964.
Bettelheim, Bruno. *The Uses of Enchantment*. 1975. New York: Random House, 1989.
Brinnin, John Malcolm. *A Casebook on Dylan Thomas*. New York: Thomas E. Crowell, Co., 1960.
- *Dylan Thomas in America*. London: J.M. Dent, 1957.
Browning, Robert. "Childe Roland to the Dark Tower Came." In *Victorian Poetry and Poetics*. Ed. Walter E. Houghton and G. Robert Stange. 2nd ed. Boston: Houghton Mifflin Co., 1968.
- "Essay on Shelley" (1852). In *Victorian Poetry and Poetics*. Ed. Houghton and Stange. 2nd ed. Boston: Houghton Mifflin Co., 1968.
Cameron, Sharon. *Lyric Time: Dickinson and the Limits of Genre*. Baltimore: Johns Hopkins University Press, 1979.
Campbell, Joseph. *The Masks of God*. 1959. New York: Viking Press, 1968.
Cleverdon, Douglas. *The Growth of Milk Wood*. London: J.M. Dent and Sons, 1969.
Cox, C.B., ed. *Dylan Thomas*. Englewood Cliffs, NJ: Prentice-Hall, 1966.
Daiches, David. *Two Studies*. Folcroft, Pa.: Folcroft Library, 1970.
Davenport, John. "Dylan Thomas." *Twentieth Century* 50 (10 September 1955), 305–6.

Davies, Aneiran Talfan. *Dylan: Druid of the Broken Body.* London: J.M. Dent and Sons, 1964.

Davies, Edward. *The Mythology and Rites of the British Druids.* London, private printing 1809. Xerox reproduction Ann Arbor, Michigan: University Microfilms, 1974.

Davies, Richard A. "Dylan Thomas' Image of the 'Young Dog' in the Portrait." *Anglo-Welsh Review* 58:26 (Spring 1977), 68–72.

Davies, Walford. "Imitation and Invention: The Use of Borrowed Material in Dylan Thomas's Prose." *Essays in Criticism* (July 1968) 275–95.

– *Dylan Thomas.* Cardiff: University of Wales Press, 1972.

– "Dylan Thomas: The Poet in His Chains." The W.D. Thomas Memorial Lecture, University College of Swansea, 21 January 1986.

– *Dylan Thomas.* Open Guides to Literature. Milton Keynes: Open University Press, 1986.

Davies, Walford, ed. *Dylan Thomas: New Critical Essays.* London: J.M. Dent and Sons, 1972.

Deane, Sheila McColm. *Bardic Style in the Poetry of Gerard Manley Hopkins, W.B. Yeats and Dylan Thomas.* Ann Arbor: University of Michigan Press, 1989.

Deutsch, Babette. "Alchemists of the Word." Chapter 2 in *Poetry in Our Time.* New York: Columbia University Press, 1952. Rev. ed., 1956.

Emery, Clark. *The World of Dylan Thomas.* Miami: University of Florida Press, 1962.

Ferris, Paul. *Dylan Thomas.* Harmondsworth, Penguin, 1979.

Firmage, George, and Oscar Williams, eds. *A Garland for Dylan Thomas.* New York: Clarke and Way, 1963.

Fitzgibbon, Constantine. *Life of Dylan Thomas.* London: J.M. Dent and Sons, 1965.

Fraser, G.S. *Dylan Thomas.* London: British Council, 1957.

Frye, Northrop. *Anatomy of Criticism.* 1957. Princeton, NJ: Princeton University Press, 1971.

Frye, Northrop, Sheridan Baker, and George Perkins. *The Harper Handbook to Literature.* New York: Harper and Row, 1985.

Gaston, Georg, ed. *Critical Essays on Dylan Thomas.* Boston: G.K. Hall and Co., 1989.

Genette, Gerard. *Narrative Discourse.* Trans. Jane Lewin. Pref. Jonathan Culler. Ithaca: Cornell University Press, 1980.

Graves, Robert. "These Be Your Gods, O Israel." *The Crowning Privilege*. The Clark Lectures 1954-55. London: Cassell, 1955.
Hardy, Barbara. *The Advantage of Lyric*. Bloomington: Indiana University Press, 1977.
- "Dylan Thomas's Poetic Language: The Stream That Is Flowing Both Ways." The Annual Gwyn Jones Lecture, University College, Cardiff, 8 May 1987.
Hart, Dominick. "The Experience of Dylan Thomas's Poetry." *Anglo-Welsh Review* 58:26 (Spring 1977), 73-78.
Holbrook, David. *Llareggub Revisited: Dylan Thomas and the State of Modern Poetry*. London: Bowes and Bowes, 1962.
- *Dylan Thomas and Poetic Dissociation*. Carbondale: Southern Illinois University Press, 1964.
- *Dylan Thomas and the Code of Night*. London: Athlone Press, 1972.
Holroyd, Stuart. *Emergence from Chaos*. Boston: Houghton Mifflin, 1957.
Jolas, Eugene, ed. *transition* no. 18 (Fall 1929), no. 19-20 (June 1930), no. 21 (March 1932), no. 22 (February 1933), no. 23 (July 1935), no. 24 (June 1936), no. 26 (November 1937), no. 27 (April-May 1938).
Jones, Gwyn, and Thomas Jones, trans. *The Mabinogion*. 1949. London: Dent, 1986.
Jones, T.H. *Dylan Thomas*. Edinburgh: Oliver and Boyd, 1963.
Joyce, James. *Dubliners*. 1916. London: Penguin, 1981.
- *Portrait of the Artist as a Young Man*. 1916. London: Penguin, 1980.
- *Ulysses*. 1922. London: Penguin, 1968.
Jung, Carl Gustav. "Psychology and Poetry." *transition* no. 19-20 (June 1930), 23-45.
Kenner, Hugh. *The Pound Era*. Berkeley: University of California Press, 1973.
Kershner, R.B. *Dylan Thomas: The Poet and His Critics*. Chicago: American Library Association, 1976.
Kidder, Rushworth M. *Dylan Thomas: The Country of the Spirit*. Princeton, NJ: Princeton University Press, 1973.
Kleinman, H.H. *The Religious Sonnets of Dylan Thomas*. Berkeley: University of California Press, 1963.

Kristeva, Julia. *Desire in Language: A Semiotic Approach to Literature and Art.* Trans. Thomas Gora, Alice Jardine, and Leon S. Rondiez. Ed. Leon Rondiez. New York: Columbia University Press, 1980.

Korg, Jacob. "The Short Stories of Dylan Thomas." *Perspective* 1 (Spring 1948), 184–91.

– *Dylan Thomas* New York: Twayne, 1965.

Lang, Andrew, ed. *The Blue Fairy Book.* New York: Airmont Books, 1969.

Lacan, Jacques. *The Four Fundamental Concepts of Psycho-Analysis.* Trans. Alan Sheridan. Ed. Jacques-Alain Miller. New York: Norton, 1978.

Maud, Ralph. *Entrances to Dylan Thomas's Poetry.* Pittsburgh: University of Pittsburgh Press, 1963.

– *Dylan Thomas in Print.* Pittsburgh: University of Pittsburgh Press, 1970.

Miller, J. Hillis. *Poets of Reality: Six Twentieth-Century Writers.* London: Oxford University Press, 1966.

Moynihan, W.T. *The Craft and Art of Dylan Thomas.* London: Oxford University Press, 1966.

Olson, Elder. *The Poetry of Dylan Thomas.* Chicago: University of Chicago Press, 1954; rev. ed. 1961.

Peach, Linden. *The Prose Writing of Dylan Thomas.* New Jersey: Barnes and Noble, 1988.

Perkins, David. *A History of Modern Poetry.* Cambridge, Mass.: Belknap Press of Harvard University Press, 1976.

Pratt, Annis. *Dylan Thomas' Early Prose: A Study in Creative Mythology.* Pittsburgh: University of Pittsburgh Press, 1970.

Scholes, Robert. *Fabulation and Metafiction.* Urbana: University of Illinois Press, 1979.

Seib, Kenneth. "Portrait of the Artist as a Young Dog: Dylan's *Dubliners.*" *Modern Fiction Studies* 24:2 (Summer 1978), 239–46.

Silet, Charles L.P. *transition: An Author Index.* Troy, NY: Whitson Publishing Co., 1980.

Sinclair, A. *Dylan Thomas: No Man More Magical.* New York: Holt, Rinehart and Winston, 1975.

Stanford, Derek. *Dylan Thomas.* London: Spearman, 1954.

Stevens, Wallace. *The Necessary Angel: Essays on Reality and the Imagination.* 1942. London: Faber and Faber, 1960.

Hoffmann-Donner, Heinrich. *Struwelpeter.* London: Pan Books, 1972.
Tedlock, E.W., ed. *Dylan Thomas: The Legend and the Poet.* London: Heinemann, 1960.
Thomas, Caitlin. *Leftover Life to Kill.* London: Putnam, 1957.
Thomas, Caitlin, and George Tremlett. *Caitlin: A Warring Absence.* London: Pan Books, 1987.
Tindall, William York. *A Reader's Guide to Dylan Thomas.* New York: Noonday Press, 1962.
Treece, Henry. *Dylan Thomas, "Dog among the Fairies."* London: Ernest Benn, 1949.
Tuer, Andrew W. *The History of the Hornbook.* 1897. New York: Benjamin Bloom, 1968.
Weil, Simone. *The Simone Weil Reader.* Ed. George A. Panichas. New York: McKay, 1977.
Welsh, Andrew. *Roots of Lyric.* Princeton, NJ: Princeton University Press, 1978.
West, P. *Doubt and Dylan Thomas.* St John's, Newfoundland: Memorial University, 1969.
Whiting, Lillian. *A Study of Elizabeth Barrett Browning.* 1899. New York: AMS Press, 1973.
Williams, Raymond. "Dylan Thomas's Play for Voices." *Critical Quarterly* 1 (Spring 1959), 18–26.

Index

Abrams, M.H., 100
Ackerman, John, 5, 8, 120
Adam: and essential language, 38; and the fall into language, 40, 53; in "Fern Hill," 109; in "I dreamed my genesis," 175n1; in "I, in my intricate image," 84; and language acquisition, 11; naming, 14, 143, 180n9; pre-linguistic, 16; in "A Prospect of the Sea," 21, 27, 29–30; replaced, 165; solipsistic, 9, 54–5, 88, 137, 166–7; in "Today, this insect," 38
Adam and Eve: in "Ceremony after a fire raid," 37; in "In the beginning," 81; in "The Map of Love," 22; in "The Mouse and the Woman," 33, 35, 46, 52; and multiplicity, 77; in proposed opera, 180n9
Adventures in the Skin Trade, 4, 9, 84, 126–35, 136, 137, 166, 178n6
Aesop, 11, 58, 165, 179n8; fabling, 157, 166, 169–70
"After the Funeral," 6, 146, 156, 163
"After the Performance of Sophocles' Electra in a Garden," 175n22
Alphabet, 33, 37, 40–1, 80–1
"Altarwise by Owl-light," 63, 75, 78, 175n2, 177n8
Ambiguity: in Browning, 68–9; dialectic, 78; in "The Enemies," 24, 25; in "The Holy Six," 24; in "I, in my intricate image," 83; in "In the beginning," 177n9; and interpretation, 7, 17; in "The Mouse and the Woman," 36; in "The Orchards," 60, 176n5; and postmodernism, 15; in "Prologue to an Adventure," 71
Amis, Kingsley, 4
"Anagram," 55, 64. See also "The Orchards"
Anagrams, 17–18, 26, 65, 94, 177n8, 177n9
Anamyth, 44, 57. See also *transition*
Archetypes, 7, 16, 141–2
Artist: *see* God, artist as; madman, artist as; priest, artist as;

reader, artist as; writer, artist as
Auden, W.H., 10, 15, 70
Audience, 11, 150–3, 156, 160, 165, 166, 168, 170
Aurality, 6, 11, 151
Aural imagination, 160
"Author's Prologue," 173n7. *See also* "Prologue"
Autobiography: artistic, 79, 86; disguised, 89; antithetical to dramatic monologue, 70–1; dualism of author and subject, 59–60, 75; effacing self in, 100; in embedded narratives, 107; explicit, 13, 140; fictionalized, 10, 125; in letters, 62; and narrative, 101; in "Old Garbo," 98; in "The Orchards," 31; in *Portrait of the Artist as a Young Dog*, 4; as shaped life, 87; subject of, 106; in "Then was my neophyte," 44

Babel, tower of, 67, 77. *See also* polyphony
Bakhtin, Mikhail, 34, 140, 166
Ball, Hugo, 43
Barth, John, 9
Beckett, Samuel, 15, 43, 61, 133
Beebe, Maurice, 98–9, 125, 166, 178n4
Beginnings: absence of, 28, 31, 83; in *Adventures in the Skin Trade*, 126–7; coterminous with endings, 30, 37, 40, 77, 142, 157; in "I, in my intricate image," 84; indeterminate, 81; of language acquisition, 41; as Logos, 14; as moment of entry, 164; in "The Mouse and the Woman," 47, 51, 52; in "One Warm Saturday," 119; in "The Orchards," 57, 65; in "Prologue to an Adventure," 72; in "A Prospect of the Sea," 21; return to, 37, 57; in "The Tree," 15, 19, 24; in *Under Milk Wood*, 151, 156, 169

Bettelheim, Bruno, 103
Biblical allusions, 30, 32, 35, 39, 67, 79, 81, 84, 175n2. *See also* Adam; Adam and Eve; Babel, tower of; Crucifixion; Eden; Fall, the; Genesis; Logos; Myth: biblical; Noah
Blake, William, 22, 24, 39, 153, 160
Blodeuedd, 175n20, 179n7. *See also* Myth: Welsh
Borges, Jorge Luis, 9, 15
Botteghe Oscure, 148, 180n10
Boyle, Kay, 43
"Brember," 143–4

Brinnen, John Malcolm, 151, 179–80n9
Browning, Robert: "Childe Roland to the Dark Tower Came," 14, 68–71, 75, 120, 176n5
"Burning Baby, The," 65
Byronic hero, 98

Caetani, Princess, 148–9, 153, 180n10
Cain and Abel, 81
Calvino, Italo, 15
Cameron, Sharon, 88, 161, 164
Campbell, Joseph, 16
"Carmarthen, Black Book of," 32, 154
Carroll, Lewis, 48, 128
"Ceremony after a fire raid," 37, 172n2
Chiasmus, 38, 39, 41
"Christ-cross-row," 33, 40, 41. *See also* Cross; Crucifixion
Church, Richard, 171n1
Ciphers, 79, 81, 177n9
Circularity: in "I, in my intricate image," 83; and lyric, 88, 164; in "The Orchards," 55, 57, 58, 60, 87; in *Under Milk Wood*, 156, 163, 168
Cleverdon, Douglas, 137, 148, 179n5
Closure, 164; lack of, 15, 28, 41, 58, 65, 74, 77; resisting, 36, 71, 167
Collected Letters, alluded to, 4, 43, 95, 174n16

Collected Poems 1934–1952, 27
Collected Poems 1934–1953, 30, 173n7
Community, 8, 11, 86–7, 92–3, 122, 168; communal artist, 165; co-creation, 90, 107, 137–8, 166; communal play, 108; communal reflection, 123–4; communal rhythms, 160; communally written poem, 177–8n2; communion, 96
Crane, Hart, 43
Creative destruction: see Destructive creation
Criterion, 55
Criticism, 3; New Criticism, 6–7, 41, 42; of poetry, 62; of prose, 5, 87
Crosses, 15, 41; of tales, 39, 41; "crosstree," 80, 81, 172n1. *See also* Chiasmus; Crucifixion
Crucifixion, images of, 17, 20, 39–40, 67

Davies, Richard A., 8
Davies, Walford, 7, 173n7
Deaths and Entrances, 164, 173n13
Deconstruction, 14
Decreation, 32, 35, 42, 161, 173n10; in poems, 40–1; in stories, 27–8, 36, 49, 73, 77, 124; in *Under Milk Wood*, 137

Dedalus, Stephen, 10, 59, 93–6, 98–9, 125–6. *See also* Joyce, James
Destructive creation, 5, 15, 36, 78, 176n4; in "The Enemies," 24; in "In the beginning," 79–81; in "The Mouse and the Woman," 51, 53; in "The Orchards," 59, 65; in "Prologue to an Adventure," 75; in "Today, this insect," 38. *See also* Decreation
Diachronic, 88
Dialectic, 78
Dialogic, 89, 108, 165, 167
Dialogue: in "Holiday Memory," 138; with Joyce, 10; in *Portrait of the Artist as a Young Dog*, 86, 123; in "Return Journey," 139, 140; in *Under Milk Wood*, 6, 137, 154, 167, 170
Dickens, Charles, 93, 129–30
"Doom on the Sun, A," 17–18. *See also* Jarvis Valley stories
Dramatic form, 148
Dreams, 3, 13, 14, 15; and Browning, 68; and fairy tale, 103; in "I dreamed my genesis," 175n1; in "I fellowed sleep," 172n2; in "The Mouse and the Woman," 35–6,

46, 47–50, 52; in "The Orchards," 31, 55–8, 71; and paramyths, 44–5; in *Portrait of the Artist as a Young Dog*, 90; in "Prologue to an Adventure," 73; in "A Prospect of the Sea," 21–2, 29, 92; in "Quite Early One Morning," 145–6; and surrealism, 171n1; in *Under Milk Wood*, 149, 154, 159, 164

Eden: in "Ceremony after a fire raid," 37; in "The Enemies," 21; in "Fern Hill," 109; in "The Map of Love," 21; in "The Mouse and the Woman," 33, 46, 52; in "Notes on the Art of Poetry," 34, 152; in "The Orchards," 67; in "Patricia, Edith and Arnold," 113–14; in "The Peaches," 106–9; in proposed opera, 180n9; in "A Prospect of the Sea," 20, 21–2, 27, 30; in "Return Journey," 142–3; in "Today, this insect," 38; in "The Tree," 17, 21; in *Under Milk Wood*, 11, 16, 137, 151, 153, 160, 162, 169; in "When once the twilight," 41

Edenic language, 9,
    138, 167. *See also* es-
    sential language
Eighteen Poems, 3, 43
Eisteddfodau, 154
Eliot, T.S., 4, 15, 82
Endings, 20, 27, 69,
    75, 143, 144, 164
"Enemies, The," 18–
    19, 21, 22, 24–5, 27,
    48, 99–100, 102
"Especially when the
    October wind," 65
"Essay on Shelley,"
    176n6
Essential language, 34,
    38, 42, 67. *See also*
    Edenic language
Evans, Caradoc, 8,
    145, 179n3
Exile, 93, 137, 166

*Faber Book of Short
    Stories, The*, 55
Fables, 9, 13, 57–8; in
    "The Holy Six," 25;
    in the Jarvis Valley
    stories, 17; in *The
    Map of Love*, 57–8,
    64; in "The Or-
    chards," 176n5;
    "Struwelpeter,"
    173n6; in "Today,
    this insect," 38–9;
    and *Under Milk
    Wood*, 11
Fabulation, 8, 86
Fairy-tale, 9; in "One
    Warm Saturday,"
    115, 119, 120, 121;
    in "Patricia, Edith
    and Arnold," 113–
    14; in "The Peaches,"
    101, 103–4, 111; in
    "A Prospect of the
    Sea," 28; in "The

Tree," 16
Fall, the: in "Fern
    Hill," 109; in "I
    dreamed my gene-
    sis," 175n1; in "In
    the beginning," 81;
    in "The Map of
    Love," 23; in "The
    Mouse and the
    Woman," 33, 52; in
    "The Orchards,"
    67; in "Patricia,
    Edith and Arnold,"
    114; in "The
    Peaches," 107–9,
    168
Fall into language, 32–
    42, 53
Fallen world: in "From
    love's first fever to
    her plague," 33–4,
    41; and lyric time,
    161, 164; in "One
    Warm Saturday,"
    125; in "The
    Peaches," 110; in
    "Return Journey,"
    142; in *Under Milk
    Wood*, 151, 155,
    160; in "When once
    the twilight," 33–4
Fantastic, the, 57, 87,
    92, 122–3, 126, 133
Fantasy, 3, 9, 15, 29,
    103, 112, 118, 120,
    130
"Fern Hill," 6, 27, 46,
    108–9, 136, 139,
    142, 164, 168–70,
    172n2, 179n2
Ferris, Paul, 123
"Fight, The," 88, 90,
    91, 98, 116, 118,
    167
"Fine Beginning, A,"
    126. *See also Adven-*

*tures in the Skin
    Trade*
Fitzgibbon, Constan-
    tine, 179n5
Floods, 49, 76, 77,
    134, 173n8. *See also*
    Noah; Myths: bibli-
    cal
Focalization, 25, 100–
    1, 102, 105, 110,
    115, 139, 149
*Folios of New Writ-
    ing*, 126
Folklore, 45, 120
Folktale, 15, 29, 68,
    102, 103, 176n5
Folk tradition, 160
Forms, literary, 9–11
"Force that through the
    green fuse drives the
    flower, The," 19, 32,
    34, 172n2. *See also*
    Decreation; Destruc-
    tive creation
"Four Lost Souls," 126,
    134–5. *See also Ad-
    ventures in the Skin
    Trade*
"From love's first fever
    to her plague," 33,
    40–1
Frye, Northrop, 160

Genesis, 13, 37, 38, 39,
    52, 67, 79, 81, 151.
    See also Beginnings;
    Logos
Genette, Gerard, 110
Genre, subversion of,
    10, 25
Gide, André, 43
God, artist as, 13, 14,
    85; in "The Ene-
    mies," 24, 25; in "I,
    in my intricate im-
    age," 82, 84; in "In

the beginning," 79;
in "The Map of
Love," 22; in "The
Mouse and the
Woman," 48;
Stephen Dedalus,
95–6, 99, 125; in
"Today, this insect,"
38–9; in "When once
the twilight," 39

Herald of Wales,
175n22
"Hergest, Red Book of,"
154
Holbrook, David, 7,
10, 93–4
"Holiday Memory,"
138–9
"Holy Six, The," 18,
19–20, 22, 24–7, 65,
99
Hughes, Richard, 147
Hughes, Trevor, 46, 50,
62, 147–8, 172n3,
176n7
"Hunchback in the
Park, The," 46, 115,
175n20, 179n7

"I dreamed my genesis,"
63, 175n1
"I fellowed sleep,"
172n2, 172n3,
175n1
"I have longed to move
away," 128
"I, in my intricate im-
age," 55, 82–4
"I see the boys of sum-
mer," 177n8
"If I were tickled by the
rub of love," 174n14
"In the beginning"
(poem), 37, 39, 40,
55, 63, 79–83,

172n1; as phrase, 9,
16, 17, 32, 95
"In Country Heaven,"
169, 180n10,
180n11
"In Country Sleep," 99,
106, 163, 180n10
"In the Direction of the
Beginning," 34, 53;
as phrase, 142,
173n12
"In my craft or sullen
art," 176n3
"In the white giant's
thigh," 180n10,
180n11
Indeterminacy, 58, 78,
Influence, literary, 7
Intertextuality, 54

"Jack the Giant-Killer,"
68, 176n5
Janes, Fred, 140
Jarvis Valley, 66, 67,
80, 83, 120
Jarvis Valley stories,
17–32, 46, 92, 102,
122, 125
Jenkins, Eli, 11, 123–4,
137, 144, 146, 161;
as artist figure, 8,
153–6, 158–9, 165
Johnson, Pamela Hans-
ford, 17, 42, 62, 63,
95, 174n17
Jolas, Eugene, 44–5,
48, 51, 57. See also
transition
Jones, Dan, 140, 150,
177n6
Jones, Gwyn, 175n20
Jones, Thomas,
175n20
Jones, T.H., 177n1
Joyce, James, 15;
Dubliners, 94, 122;

*Portrait of the Artist
as a Young Man*, 10,
59, 93–6, 98–9,
125–6; and *transi-
tion*, 43; *Ulysses*,
94, 126, 137
Jung, Carl Gustav, 43,
98, 178n3
"Just Like Little Dogs,"
89, 91, 96, 124, 140

Kafka, Franz, 43
King Lear, 176n5
Korg, Jacob, 7, 177n1
Kristeva, Julia, 42, 45,
174n15
Künstlerroman, 90, 93,
125, 139

Lacan, Jacques,
174n15
Language, 8, 10; acqui-
sition of, 38, 40–1;
relation to world, 11;
structures created
by, 6. See also Edenic
language; Essential
language; Semiotic
language
Lehmann, John, 3
"Lemon, The," 99
Letters, Thomas's, 4,
58, 61–3, 78, 131–3.
See also *Collected
Letters*
Listeners, 160, 124
Literacy. See Readers:
characters as, mis-
reading, problems of
interpretation
Llareggub, 11, 65,
173n9, 124, 125,
148. See also *Under
Milk Wood*
"Llareggub, Black Book
of," 31–2, 56, 155

Index

"Llareggub, White Book of," 123, 144, 146, 153, 154, 155
Logos, 14, 37, 49, 53, 63, 77, 79
"Londoners, The," 147
"Love in the Asylum," 173–4n13
Lyric, 88–9, 112, 137, 139, 148, 152; democratization of, 11, 138, 165–70; lyric time, 95, 170; *Under Milk Wood* as, 157–65

Mabinogion, 31, 154, 175n20. See also Myth: Welsh
Madman, artist as, 13, 84; in "The Mouse and the Woman," 8, 32–3, 35–6, 46, 52, 99, 144, 175n20
Madmen, 31, 39, 56, 88
Madness, 20, 51, 63, 90, 147–8
Magic, 45, 99, 175n20
Maps, 3, 15, 22, 28, 156
"Map of Love, The," 14, 18–24, 27–8, 44, 48, 99, 155
Map of Love, The, 4, 5, 18, 55, 57
Martin, J.H., 174n18
"Math, son of Mathonwy," 175n20. See also *Mabinogion*
Maud, Ralph, 173n7
Melville, Herman, 128
Metafiction, 3, 5, 13; in "Brember," 144; in "The Mouse and the Woman," 35; in

"Old Garbo," 91; in "The Orchards," 61; in *Portrait of the Artist as a Young Dog*, 8, 87, 107; and postmodernism, 9, 15; in "A Prospect of the Sea," 28
Miller, J. Hillis, 178n5
Mirrors, 29, 44–5, 73–5, 96, 100, 117–18, 120–1,155. See also Self-reflexivity
Modernism, 10, 11, 55, 70–1, 80, 173n10, 178n7
Modernists, 15, 57–9, 98, 160. See also Joyce, James
Monologic, 88–90
"Mouse and the Woman, The," 46–53, 55, 89, 130, 147, 160, 179n7; autobiographical, 8; compared to "Brember," 144; compared to "Love in the Asylum," 174n13; dream, 90; the fall into language, 32–3, 35–7, 40; and Logos, 63; metafictional, 103; "Struwelpeter," 172n6; and *transition*, 42–3, 45, 99
Multiplicity, 33, 52, 77, 109, 161, 167; of fictions, 58; of interpretations, 33, 42
Music, 35, 45, 136, 154, 179n8; of creation, 50; instruments, 152; musical principles of language, 157–61, 63;

song, 11, 149, 158. See also Lyric
Myth, 13, 29, 75, 103, 161; biblical, 16, 31, 81, 84; and Browning, 70; in early stories, 86, 88, 96; Jarvis Hills as mythic, 18, 27, 102, 120; Logos, 79; in "The Mouse and the Woman," 33, 35, 46; in "One Warm Saturday," 116; in "The Orchards," 55–6, 66–8; in "The Peaches," 95; in "Prologue to an Adventure," 72; in "Return Journey,"142; rewriting 28, 30–1; in "Then was my neophyte," 44; in "Today, this insect," 38; and *transition*, 44–6, 51; in *Under Milk Wood*, 11, 155, 162; Welsh, 7, 31–2, 56, 154, 173n8, 175n20, 179n7. See also Adam; Adam and Eve; Babel, tower of; Eden; Floods; Logos; *Mabinogion*
Mythologizing of the creative process, 4, 85

National Library of Wales, 32, 179n4
Names, importance of, 27, 106–7, 110, 122, 128, 133, 143
Naming, 14, 27, 179n6. See also Adam: naming

Narrative, 5, 101, 103, 112, 114, 166; contrasted to lyric, 11, 161, 163, 164; embedded narratives, 102, 107, 111, 124; in everyday experience, 6, 63, 87, 115; fable, 57; poems, 11; in *Portrait of the Artist as a Young Dog*, 87–9; in "Prologue to an Adventure," 77; in *Under Milk Wood*, 153, 157. *See also* Stories-within-stories
Neuberg, Victor, 62
New World Writing, 126
New York Times Book Review, 5
Noah, 22, 30, 162, 165, 172n4, 173n8. *See also* Floods; Myth: biblical
Nostalgia, 6, 8, 86, 120, 127
Notebooks, 39. *See also* Red Prose Notebook
Notebook Poems, 175n22
"Notes on the Art of Poetry," 34, 152, 157, 167
Nursery rhyme, 114, 137, 157–9

Objectification of self, 117, 156
Objectivity, 70, 88, 96, 97, 123
"Old Garbo," 91, 119, 121, 138; similarity to early stories, 85,

97–8, 120; Thomas as character in, 89, 115, 140
Olson, Elder, 5
"On no work of words," 61
"Once below a time," 178n1
"Once it was the colour of saying," 6
"One Warm Saturday," 114–22; community in, 91, 138; the fall in, 125; fiction and reality in, 100, 106–7, 112, 124; relation to early stories, 85, 92, 93, 98
Oracles, 50, 100
"Orchards, The," 55–61, 65–71, 76, 79, 83, 90, 111, 176n5; Marlais as Thomas, 8, 13; Marlais contrasted to later figures, 84; and myth, 31–2; relation to *Portrait of the Artist as a Young Dog*, 86–7, 89, 91, 93, 102–3, 115–16, 119–20; and "Prologue to an Adventure," 72; and reading, 64; symbolic landscape in, 74, 82; contrasted to *Under Milk Wood*, 123, 155, 166; and writing, 33, 54, 160
"Over Sir John's Hill," 157, 179n8, 180n10

Paradox: in criticism of Thomas, 5; characteristic of Thomas,

78; of edenic existence, 143; and quests, 30, 68, 120; the truths of fiction, 118, 131; of language acquisition, 14, 33, 40, 61; Llareggub as, 125, 161, 164, 169
Paramyth, 45–6, 51
Parody, 61–3, 73, 94, 97–8, 114, 116, 128, 134, 144
"Patricia, Edith and Arnold," 89, 100, 112–14
Peach, Linden, 7, 8, 10, 54, 94, 177n1
"Peaches, The," 89, 100–14, 115, 133; and "After the Funeral," 146; compared to Joyce, 95; edenic identification in, 124, 178n5; the fall in, 119, 168; and "Fern Hill," 6; relation to early stories, 90; self-consciousness in, 97, 116, 117, 121, 142
Perception, 46, 73, 101, 117; altering reality, 23, 27; and language, 26
Perkins, David, 153
Pilgrim's Progress, 177n8
"Plenty of Furniture," 126. *See also Adventures in the Skin Trade*
Plurality, 42
"Poem in October," 136
"Poem on his birthday," 172n2

Poems, collected, 28, 77. See also *Collected Poetry*
Poetic forms, 5, 7
Poets, Romantic. See Romantic poets
Polyphony, 6, 11, 41, 157, 166. See also Babel, tower of
Portrait of the Artist as a Young Dog, 4–5, 8–10, 85–126, 144, 167; relation to *Adventures in the Skin Trade*, 126; relation to early stories, 6, 84, 85–92; relation to "Holiday Memory," 138; relation to "Return Journey," 139–41; relation to *Under Milk Wood*, 135, 137
Postmodernism, 8, 11, 15, 42, 58–9, 61, 71, 179n6
Pound, Ezra, 15, 160
Pratt, Annis, 5, 7, 54, 177n1
Pre-linguistic state, 14, 27, 174n15. See also Adam; Eden
Priest, poet as, 8, 14, 95, 99, 153–4
"Prologue," 30, 77, 165, 166, 172n4, 173n7
"Prologue to an Adventure," 30, 54, 71–2; beginnings in, 81, 88; relation to *Adventures in the Skin Trade*, 134–5
Prose-poetry, 5
"Prospect of the Sea, A," 27–31, 52; decreation in, 49; dream in, 21–2, 90, 92; the Jarvis Valley, 18, 20; myth in, 44, 102; "Struwelpeter" in, 175n21; woman as fictional creation in, 130

Questors, 14, 55–8, 64, 65, 77. See also Quests
Quests, 44, 51, 58, 68–71, 83; Grail, 51, 84. See also Questors
"Quite Early One Morning," 145–7, 149, 159

Radio broadcasts, 11, 138–9
Readers, 58, 68, 73, 89, 104, 170; characters as, 14, 26, 36–7, 49, 144; as co-creator, 60, 124; directly addressed, 69, 83; misreading, 16, 22, 23–4, 64; problems of interpretation, 15, 16, 33, 39, 41–2, 64; in *Under Milk Wood*, 149, 150, 155, 165–6; and writing, 17, 51, 74, 81
Realism, 5, 7, 9, 87, 123; anti-, 43, 45, 57, 85
Red Prose Notebook, 18, 43, 55, 64. See also Notebooks
"Refusal to Mourn, A," 61, 136, 164
Repetition, 29, 68, 73–4, 114; of beginnings, 65–6, 81, 126, 163

"Return Journey," 139–43, 144, 147, 167, 173n6, 175n22, 178n1
"Rhydderch, White Book of," 154
Rhys, Keidrych, 174n18, 177n2
Riding, Laura, 43
Rilke, Rainer Maria, 4, 43
Romance, 29, 88, 92, 106
Romantic poet, 11, 14, 64, 179n6; Thomas as, 156. See also Romanticism
Romanticism, 98, 118, 153, 155, 160, 174n17. See also Romantic poet

Saussure, Ferdinand de, 34, 75
Scholes, Robert, 9
"School for Witches, The," 99
Seib, Kenneth, 94, 177n1
Seithennin, Prince, 173n8. See also Myth: Welsh
Self-consciousness, 3, 11, 97, 144, 178n7, 179n6
Self-portraits, 94
Self-referentiality, 3, 33, 42, 137
Self-reflectiveness, 28, 54, 73, 117–18, 123, 144, 155. See also Mirrors
Self-reflexivity, 5, 8, 9, 29, 33, 36, 87, 137, 179n6

Semiotic language, 42, 174n15
Shelley, Percy Bysshe, 14. *See also* Romantic poets
Silence, 151–2, 157, 169
Sitwell, Edith, 62
Solipsism, 5, 113, 144; literal images of, 29, 44; movement away from, 11, 84, 123, 133, 139–40, 165, 169
Sound, 160, 161
Spectator, The, 4
Spelling, 49–50, 99, 172n3; spells, 177n6
Spender, Stephen, 15
Split self, 109, 139
Stanford, Derek, 4, 6, 177n1
Stein, Gertrude, 43
Stevens, Wallace, 173n10
Stories, 15; -within-stories, 3, 87, 102, 111, 123–4
Story-tellers, 6, 8, 15–16, 61, 76, 91, 104, 106, 122; contrasted to solipsism, 86, 89–90, 96, 110, 112, 167; multiple, 124; objectifying self, 28, 52, 58
Story-telling, 11, 48, 165–6; shared, 93, 170. *See also* Story-tellers
Stravinsky, Igor, 159; proposed collaboration with, 179–80n9
Struwelpeter, 46, 172–3n6, 175n21

Subjectivity, 71, 88, 110, 138; and experience, 87, 156, 164; and perception, 85, 165
Surrealism, 5, 7, 43, 68–9, 87–8, 90, 122, 171n1; and visions, 76, 133
Synaesthesia, 75, 151
Synchrony, 30, 67–8, 76, 84, 88, 139, 161

Teleology, 88, 163
Tennyson, Alfred Lord, 91, 118–19, 167
"Then was my neophyte," 42, 44–6, 51
"This Is London," 147
Thomas, Dylan, as character, 8, 13, 27, 31, 33, 55, 90, 126, 139. *See also* "Old Garbo"; "Orchards, The"; *Portrait of the Artist as a Young Dog*
Thomas, R.S., 8
Time, 11, 44, 110, 155, 161, 168; atemporality, 95, 166; as character, 51; disarrangement of, 114, 134, 164, 169; and fairy-tale, 16; images of, 72, 75; lyric, 69, 88–9, 95, 142, 162–4, 170; real, 87, 145, 149, 158; "stream of," 176n4; temporal world, 45, 74; transcended, 137; timelessness, 10, 28, 95, 147, 154–6, 167

Times Literary Supplement, 174n18
Tindall, William York, 7, 93, 172n2
"Today, this insect," 38–9, 41
Towers, 23, 55, 65–6, 68, 72–3, 76, 83, 88, 175–6n3; of words, 86, 95. *See also* Babel, tower of; Yeats, W.B.
"Town that was Mad, The," 147, 148. *See also Under Milk Wood*
transition, 42–6, 57, 94, 99, 174n19, 178n3
Translation: reading and decoding, 36, 50, 63, 74, 77, 123, 174n15; as transformation, 14, 55, 80–1; writing as, 37, 47
"Tree, The," 14–24, 27, 32, 44, 155, 166
Treece, Henry, 6, 7, 78, 171n1, 176n4
Trick, Bert, 123, 177n8
Twenty-Five Poems, 3
"Two Streets," 147

Ulysses (character), 64. *See also* Joyce, James: *Ulysses*
"Uncommon Genesis," 35, 43, 174n17. *See also* "The Mouse and the Woman"
Under Milk Wood, 136–70; artist figures in, 8; communal creation in, 90; Edenic existence in, 6, 11, 16–17, 107,

125; Llareggub, 65; predecessors of, 138–49; and proposed opera, 179–80n9; reader in, 124; and realism, 9, 86; relation to prose, 4, 10; self-reflection in, 100, 123–4; as "Welsh Ulysses," 94, 135. *See also* Jenkins, Eli; Llareggub

Valéry, Paul, 160
Vertigral poetry, 44–5. See also *transition*
"Vest, The," 89
"Visit to Grandpa's, A," 88–90
"Visitor, The," 18, 20–1, 89, 144
Voices: communal, 98, 99, 168; disembodied, 48, 83; in dialogue, 138; echoes, 74; First and Second, 149–50, 153; god-like, 151; of Guidebook, 155; and identity, 105, 107, 118, 140; and landscape, 11, 19, 20, 25, 64, 145, 159, 172n3; lost, 76, 147; mingling, 150, 161–5; multiple, 6, 30, 67, 86, 90, 124, 137, 168; "play for voices," 148–9 (see also *Under Milk Wood*)

Wales, 99, 135, 137, 168; Carmarthen, 18, 32; Fern Hill, 8, 108; fictionalized, 16, 17; Laugharne, 8; Llanstephan, 63; South, 66; Swansea, 8, 56, 86, 128, 140, 178n1
"Wales"(Journal), 177n2; as title of poem, 178n2
Walters, Meurig, 177n2
Watkins, Vernon, 36, 61, 65, 128, 140, 178n1
Weil, Simone, 32, 49, 173n10
Welsh language, 67
Welsh myth. *See* Myth: Welsh
Welsh Short Stories, 55
"Welsh Ulysses," 94, 135–7
Welsh writers, 91. *See also* Evans, Caradoc; Thomas, R.S.
"When all my five and country senses," 75
"When, like a running grave," 172–3n6
"When once the twilight locks no longer," 33, 39–40, 41
"Where Tawe Flows," 89, 91, 122–5, 155, 165
"Who Do You Wish Was With Us," 90, 112, 119

Williams, Raymond, 93
Williams, William Carlos, 43, 160
"Winter's Tale, A," 9, 165
Women as artistic creations: in *Adventures in the Skin Trade*, 130; Blodeuedd, 179n7; in "The Hunchback in the Park," 175n20; in "The Map of Love," 22, 32, 35, 47, 48, 52, 160; in "The Orchards," 55; in *Portrait of the Artist as a Young Dog*, 111, 115, 118; in "A Prospect of the Sea," 28
Words, 5, 6, 9, 34, 44, 151. *See also* Jolas, Eugene; Logos
World I Breath, The, 4, 18,
Writers, characters as, 46, 49, 55–8, 74, 79
Writing, 32–3, 35–7, 48, 144, 154, 160, 163; rewriting, 28, 30; self-reflexive, 59–60. *See also* Reading; Self-reflexivity
Written worlds, 13–14, 54, 85, 86; Jarvis Valley as, 16, 32; in "The Mouse and the Woman," 37, 51; in poems, 79, 82

Yeats, W.B., 175–6n3